DIGGING FOR GOD
AND COUNTRY

Neil Asher Silberman

DIGGING FOR GOD AND COUNTRY

Exploration, Archeology, and the Secret Struggle for the Holy Land 1799–1917

❖

ALFRED A. KNOPF

NEW YORK 1982

Copyright © 1982 by Neil Asher Silberman
Maps Copyright © 1982 by David Lindroth
All rights reserved under International and Pan-American Copyright Conventions.
Published in the United States by Alfred A. Knopf, Inc., New York, and simultaneously
in Canada by Random House of Canada Limited, Toronto. Distributed by
Random House, Inc., New York.

A letter from M. W. Shapira to Dr. Ginsburg dated August 23, 1883, as published in
The Shapira Affair by John M. Allegro, is reprinted with
the permission of The British Library.

LIBRARY OF CONGRESS CATALOGING IN PUBLICATION DATA
Silberman, Neil Asher,
Digging for God and country.
Bibliography: p.
Includes index.
1. Archaeology—Palestine—History.
2. Palestine—History—1799–1917. I. Title.
CC101.I75S57 1982   956.94'03   81–48104
ISBN 0-394-51139-5   AACR2

Manufactured in the United States of America
First Edition

In memory of

HARRY KIMBALL

a man of strength

Contents

Maps of Palestine and of the city of Jerusalem
will be found following page xv.

Illustrations

Americans on the Jordan. From Lynch, *Narrative,* opp. p. 234.

Entrance to the Tombs of the Kings. From J. T. Barclay, *City of the Great King* (Philadelphia: 1858), opp. p. 179.

The Dome of the Rock. From W. H. Bartlett, *Jerusalem Revisited* (London: 1855), opp. p. 122.

George Grove. From Charles L. Graves, *The Life and Letters of Sir George Grove* (London: 1903), opp. p. 86.

Platform of the Haram ash-Sharif. From W. H. Bartlett, *Walks*, opp. p. 143.

Charles Wilson. From Charles M. Watson, *The Life of Major General Charles William Wilson* (London: 1909), opp. p. 22.

Wilson's Arch. From *Illustrated London News*, April 24, 1869.

Ashkenazi Jews. From Charles Warren, *Underground Jerusalem* (London: 1875), opp. p. 359.

Charles Warren in an underground shaft. From *Illustrated London News*, April 24, 1869.

The Moabite Stone. From Héron de Villefosse, *Notice des Monuments provenants de la Palestine et conservés au Musée de Louvre (Salle Judaïque)* (Paris: 1879), opp. p. 1.

Claude Conder at Jericho. From H. H. Kitchener, *Book of Photographs of Biblical Sites* (London: 1876), No. 5.

Official emblem of the Great Survey. From Claude Conder, *Tent Work in Palestine* (New York: 1878), frontispiece.

Shapira cartoon. From *Punch*, September 8, 1883.

Following page 138:

Cross-section of Tell el-Hesy. From F. J. Bliss, *A Mound of Many Cities* (New York: 1894), Plate II.

Diplomatic procession in Jerusalem. From the Matson Collection, Library of Congress, Washington, D.C.

Kaiser Wilhelm at the Tombs of the Kings. From the Matson Collection, Library of Congress, Washington, D.C.

View of Samaria excavations. From the Matson Collection, Library of Congress, Washington, D.C.

The German camp at Megiddo. From G. Schumacher, *Tell el-Mutasellim* (Leipzig: 1908), p. 4. Reproduced with the permission of Deutscher Verein zur Erforschung Palästinas.

G. A. Reisner at the Samaria excavations. From the Matson Collection, Library of Congress, Washington, D.C.

News story of the Parker expedition. From the *New York Times*, May 7, 1911.

The Ottoman governor of Nazareth. From the Matson Collection, Library of Congress, Washington, D.C.

Montague Parker. From the archives of the École Biblique et Archéologique Française, Jerusalem.

The surrender of Jerusalem. From the Matson Collection, Library of Congress, Washington, D.C.

British forces enter Jerusalem. From the Matson Collection, Library of Congress, Washington, D.C.

Preface

This book, unlike many other works written in recent years about the archeology of Israel, is only indirectly concerned with buried artifacts and ancient cultures. The focus of this book is much closer to our own times. Its object is to turn the techniques of modern archeology upon a branch of modern archeology itself; to trace the historical background and delineate the cultural environment of the western exploration of the Land of the Bible from the beginning of the nineteenth century to the end of World War I.

Biblical archeology is a unique cultural manifestation of the age in which it was born. For the preceding seventeen hundred years, the Christian world had possessed a stable body of religious tradition about the Holy Land, complete with time-honored legends of miracles and wonder-working shrines. With the advent of the nineteenth-century "scientific" consciousness, however, those traditions suddenly lost their power and the literal accuracy of the Bible had to be defended on new terms. It was through Biblical archeology that the western Christian world began to develop a new understanding of the history of the birthplace of its faith. The course of that development forms the main narrative theme of this book.

It has not been my intention to include a reference to every scholar or explorer who contributed to the advancement of Biblical archeology in the nineteenth century. Although the scientific contributions of such important figures as Titus Tobler, Carl Ritter, Henry Baker Tristram, and George Adam Smith were extremely significant in a scholarly sense, they did not alter the basic course of Palestine exploration. That role was assumed by the various characters of this book, who—by their rank, religious beliefs, or imperial ambitions—manifested especially clearly in their archeological activities the temper of their times, and in so doing perceptibly influenced the subsequent course of Biblical archeology.

.   .   .

Many individuals have helped me with the research for this book and have discussed with me various aspects of the historical periods which it covers. Most prominently I would like to thank Professor Moshe Dothan of Jerusalem. Long before I even contemplated the writing of this book, he was a valuable teacher and friend; more than anyone else, it was he who helped me begin to understand the richness and complexity of the archeology of Israel. Among the other scholars whom I would like to thank for their assistance are Dr. Richard Barnett of London, Mr. Benjamin Yaffe of Jerusalem, and Dr. David Patterson of the Centre for Postgraduate Hebrew Studies at Oxford, who extended much-appreciated courtesy to me during my stay there. My historical understanding benefited greatly from their knowledge, though I alone bear responsibility for my conclusions.

My research was also made possible by the assistance rendered by the staffs of various institutions. These include the Sterling Memorial Library and the Beinecke Rare Book and Manuscript Library of Yale University; the Olin Memorial Library of Wesleyan University; the Prints and Photographs Division of the Library of Congress and the National Archives in Washington, D.C.; the Ashmolean and Bodleian libraries at Oxford; and the Manuscript Department of the British Library and the archives of the Palestine Exploration Fund in London. Each of these institutions possesses a treasure trove of material relating to nineteenth-century Palestine, which, someday, might be considered as archeologically valuable as any assemblage of Bronze Age pottery or Hellenistic coins.

Mr. Stephen Elliott of Sachem Publishing Associates in Guilford, Connecticut, has been a tireless and invaluable supporter of this book since its very inception. Dr. Kelvin James of New York City has been of vital help in shaping the narrative and refining its style. My editor, Charles Elliott, has freely offered his wisdom and experience at every stage of the work. Thanks to him, it is a far better book than it would have been otherwise.

I would not have been able to complete what at times seemed to be an endless task of research and writing without the constant support of family and friends. My wife, Ellen, above all, lived at close range to the sound of my typewriter, and this book is as much a product of her patience and understanding as of any other single element. I hope that the result of my efforts will justify her confidence in me.

N.A.S.

Branford, Connecticut
July 2, 1981

Author's Note

For the sake of convenience, I have used the geographical terms "Palestine" and "the Holy Land" interchangeably throughout this book to refer to the territory now encompassed by the modern nations of Israel and Jordan, as well as the Sinai peninsula. During the Ottoman period, the era with which this book deals, the area was administratively divided and incorporated into the larger province of Syria, and had no single official designation.

As regards the spelling of Hebrew, Arabic, and Turkish words, I have tried to maintain a consistent pattern of transliteration. In the case of specific *tells*, however, I have adopted the spelling used by the excavator. In the instances where certain places or names are well known in their English forms, I have retained the most common spellings.

All Biblical quotations are taken from the Revised Standard Version.

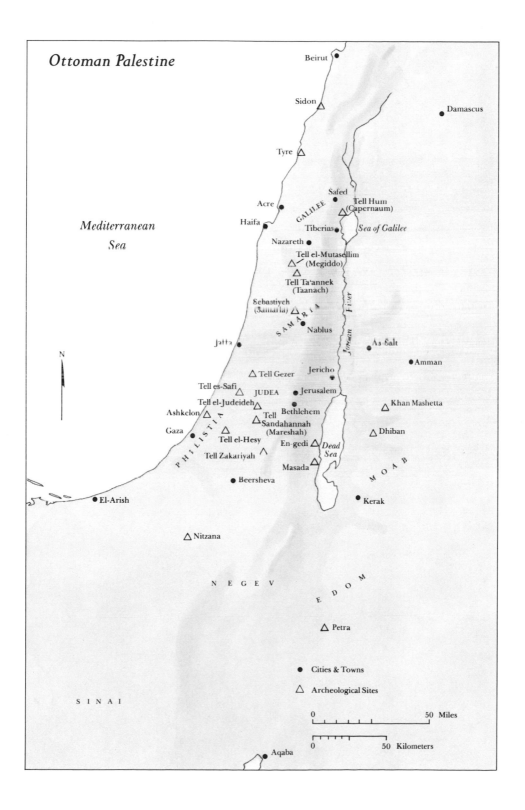

Ottoman Palestine

Beirut

Sidon

Damascus

Tyre

Mediterranean Sea

Safed

Acre   Tell Hum (Capernaum)

Haifa   Tiberias   *Sea of Galilee*

GALILEE

Nazareth

Tell el-Mutasellim (Megiddo)

Tell Ta'annek (Taanach)

Sebastiyeh (Samaria)

SAMARIA

Nablus   As-Salt

Jaffa   Amman

N

Tell Gezer   Jericho

Jerusalem

Tell es-Safi   JUDEA

Tell el-Judeideh   Bethlehem   Khan Mashetta

Ashkelon   Tell Sandahannah (Mareshah)

Gaza   Dhiban

Tell el-Hesy   En-gedi   *Dead Sea*

Tell Zakariyah   Masada

Beersheva   MOAB

El-Arish   Kerak

Jordan River

PHILISTIA

EDOM

Nitzana

N E G E V

SINAI

Petra

● Cities & Towns

△ Archeological Sites

0   50 Miles

0   50 Kilometers

Aqaba

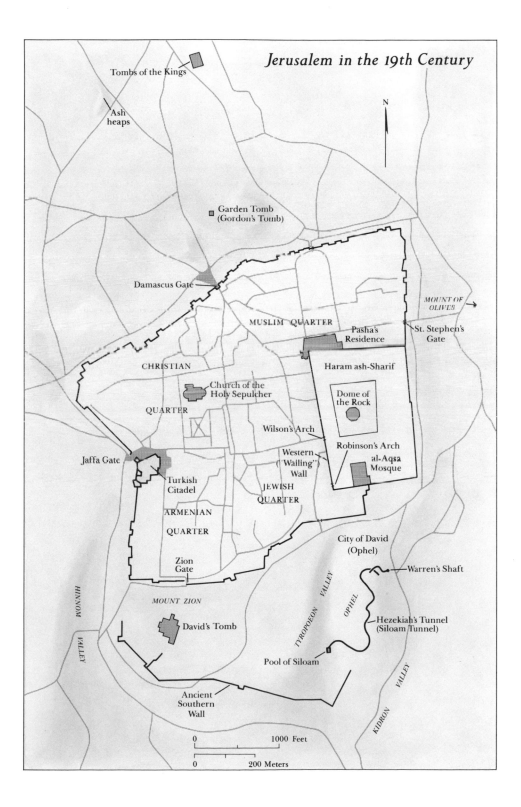

Jerusalem in the 19th Century

Tombs of the Kings

Ash heaps

N

Garden Tomb
(Gordon's Tomb)

Damascus Gate

MOUNT OF
OLIVES

MUSLIM QUARTER

Pasha's
Residence

St. Stephen's
Gate

CHRISTIAN

Haram ash-Sharif

Church of the
Holy Sepulcher

Dome of
the Rock

QUARTER

Wilson's Arch

Robinson's Arch

Jaffa Gate

Western
("Walling")
Wall

al-Aqsa
Mosque

Turkish
Citadel

JEWISH

ARMENIAN

QUARTER

QUARTER

City of David
(Ophel)

Zion
Gate

Warren's Shaft

MOUNT ZION

David's Tomb

Hezekiah's Tunnel
(Siloam Tunnel)

Pool of Siloam

Ancient
Southern
Wall

HINNOM

VALLEY

TYROPOEON VALLEY

OPHEL

KIDRON

VALLEY

0   1000 Feet

0   200 Meters

✤ I ✤

A LAND OF MYTHS

❖ I ❖

The Lure of the Holy Land

PALESTINE AND THE
RELIGIOUS IMAGINATION
OF THE WEST

"Palestine is no more of this work-day world," quipped Mark Twain at the conclusion of his own journey through the Holy Land in 1867. "It is sacred to poetry and tradition   it is dream-land."

Mark Twain had come, like a modern pilgrim, to visit a land wreathed in veneration and myth, to see for himself the birthplace of his own Christian faith. What he found contrasted harshly with his preconceptions, yet despite the barrenness of the landscape, the discomforts of the Middle Eastern climate, and the unreliable banter of the local guides, he apparently fell prey to his "dream-land." Following a bone-jarring itinerary southward from Beirut to Jerusalem on horseback, he faithfully described the sites of the Old and New Testaments in a series of colorful newspaper dispatches later published in *The Innocents Abroad.* The contemporary state of the country and its inhabitants served him only as comic relief; his genuine reverence was reserved for Palestine's celebrated past.

Mark Twain was by no means the only western tourist of his time to make such a pilgrimage of the imagination. From the very first year of the nineteenth century to the early decades of the twentieth, those few backward provinces of the Ottoman Empire known variously to the Christian world as "Palestine," "the Holy Land," and "the Land of the Bible" attracted some of the most intriguing personalities of the age. To Napoleon Bonaparte at the head of his revolutionary armies, to Lord Byron in search of poetic motifs, to Herman Melville, P. T. Barnum, Kaiser Wilhelm II, and thousands of other western scholars, clerics, tourists, and adventurers, the lure of "Biblical antiquities" exerted an appeal that was almost hypnotic.

3

At the core of this romantic obsession was a powerful and persistent tradition felt deeply in Christian hearts from the time of the church-building bishops of Byzantium through the two bloody centuries of Crusader conquest and beyond: Palestine was the land on which their Savior had walked, where the awesome events of the Old Testament had burst into history. In its mountain city of Jerusalem the Hebrew kings had built a magnificent Temple to the Lord, and outside its city walls Jesus had been crucified and had risen from the tomb. Christians had long believed that they, not the Jews, were the spiritual inheritors of this land, and for centuries they regarded the discovery, veneration, and protection of its ancient shrines and churches as their own sacred obligation.

Yet the nineteenth-century wave of western travel and exploration was different from the many previous waves of Christian pilgrimage to the Holy Land. The nineteenth century was an age of scientific investigation, and the infant science of archeology offered dramatic new means of uncovering and preserving the Biblical past. The mystique of the Holy Land had been suddenly transformed from pilgrimage to discovery, and the new quest for antiquities brought about a western invasion of Palestine unrivaled since the time of the Crusades. Nearly every square mile of the country was explored by clerics, scholars, and military men. Rival archeological societies and lavishly funded expeditions successively recovered many important Biblical sites from the debris of centuries. Conflicting interpretations and theories about the history of the land were gradually united in a modern, secularized chronology. And in addition to its achievements in the purely scientific sphere, the exploration of Palestine led also to an intense international rivalry with concrete and conflicting national goals.

Around the traditional religious veneration of the Holy Land swirled the hard realities of nineteenth-century political change. The Ottoman Empire was crumbling and the ultimate fate of the Middle East was very much in doubt. The rising imperial powers of Europe vied desperately for influence in that region; and Palestine, situated between Egypt and Mesopotamia, lay at its geographical heart. The search for Biblical antiquities became, therefore, a subtle means of western penetration and competition in one of the most strategic areas of the world—a quiet extension of the "Eastern Question" waged on the battlefield of the past.

In order to understand the scope and depth of emotion expended in the nineteenth-century archeological struggle for Palestine, it is necessary to understand its origins within the history and traditions of the

Christian world. For from the earliest centuries of Christianity to the rise of the great European empires, a fascination with the Holy Land—and the continuing urge to explore it—was never far from the very core of European religious thought.

As early as the second century A.D., the first Christian pilgrims from various parts of the Roman Empire began to arrive in Palestine to retrace the footsteps of Jesus and the Apostles. Traveling through the countryside in small groups, they would pause for prayer and reflection at the places reported by local tradition to be the sites of Jesus' ministry and Passion. As early as the second century, however, Christian pilgrimage began by necessity to take on the character of archeological investigation, for the landscape already bore little resemblance to that of Biblical times.

In A.D. 70, a national revolt of the native Jewish population brought down a brutal suppression by the legions of Vespasian and Titus. Many of the villages of Judea and Galilee, which had been inhabited by Jews almost continuously since the time of the Hebrew kings, were reduced to ruins. The Temple at Jerusalem was destroyed and the city around it put to the torch. The suppression of another Jewish revolt in A.D. 135 completed the desolation of the country, which was thereafter referred to by the Romans as *Palaestina*—a Latinized corruption of the Greek name "Philistia," the land of the Philistines. By imperial edict, Jews were no longer allowed to visit Jerusalem, which was renamed Aelia Capitolina and rebuilt as a Roman garrison town.

Some early Christians saw the exile of the Jews and the destruction of their national independence as divine punishment for their refusal to accept the Gospel of Christ. Yet the vicissitudes of history had their effects on Palestine's Christian legacy as well. Many of the country's major landmarks had been destroyed or profoundly altered by Roman rebuilding. And since it was extremely difficult to be sure of the exact location of many of the holiest sites of Jesus' life, the earliest Christian traditions about those sites were often based on imagination and long-forgotten guesswork.

As long as Christianity remained an unrecognized religion in the Roman Empire, the wish to locate the New Testament sites of Palestine was the preoccupation of a relatively small group. But in the fourth century A.D., when the Emperor Constantine officially established Christianity as the Roman state religion, the land in which Jesus had lived and preached suddenly took on significance to a great part of the western world.

Barely a year after the first Ecumenical Council at Nicaea in A.D. 325, Constantine's mother, the Empress Helena, assembled a lavish retinue for an imperial progress eastward through the land of her newly recognized Savior's birth. Unlike earlier Christian pilgrims, who were satisfied with the sometimes contradictory local traditions, Helena sought not merely to tread humbly in the legendary footsteps of Jesus, but to determine their actual locations and to enshrine them forever.

Accompanied by a large entourage of bishops and monks, the dowager empress roamed over the desolated countryside, searching for the authentic sites of the manger of the Nativity, of the hill of Calvary, and of the Holy Sepulcher, the rock-hewn tomb in which Jesus' body was placed before the Resurrection. Her mission was deemed a complete success. With the help of divine inspiration and extensive excavation, she located those sites to the satisfaction of all concerned, and when the Emperor Constantine received word of her discoveries, he ordered that imposing basilicas be built to memorialize them. The name "Jerusalem" was once again restored, and the city again became the center of religious veneration, though not for the Jews, who were still barred from visiting it. During the centuries of Byzantine rule that followed, countless sacred shrines rose over the length and breadth of the entire country, marking not only New Testament sites, but Old Testament sites as well.

Increasing numbers of pilgrims from every corner of the Christian world journeyed to Palestine, where they traveled along formalized routes of pilgrimage, prayed, and presented their offerings to the monasteries and convents that sprang up beside the holy sites. The former rebellious Jewish provinces of Judea and Galilee were transformed. They were now, in Christian eyes, lands of metaphysical splendor and holiness. While the Jews, now mostly scattered in exile, continued to hope for an eventual restoration in "the Land of Israel," the Christian world employed its own substantial resources and determination to maintain that same country as a physical validation of its piety.

Despite the collapse of Byzantine rule in Palestine and the military conquest of the country by the forces of Islam in A.D. 638, Christian pilgrims continued to brave the dangers of the journey to visit the holy shrines. This went on throughout the Middle Ages. The rise of the cult of relics in Europe had sparked an even greater fascination with the physical remains of Christian antiquity, and the inhabitants of Palestine were quick to recognize the possibilities of trade in pieces of the True Cross, phials of Mary's milk, and even locks of Jesus' hair. So popular was the cult of relics in Europe that many churches there were sustained by the local veneration of precious artifacts brought back by countrymen who had made the pilgrimage to Jerusalem. The Holy Land itself had become a relic, and to symbolize this special connection, Charlemagne concluded a treaty in the eighth century with the Abbasid caliph Harun ar-Rashid to ensure Christian "protection" over the ancient shrines of Palestine.

In the meantime, however, the Muslims had developed their own religious attachments to Jerusalem. It was there, according to the Quran, that Muhammad had performed a miraculous ascent to heaven from the sacred rock on which the Holy of Holies in the Jewish Temple had once stood. In A.D. 691, the Umayyad caliph Abd al-Malik constructed the Dome of the Rock on the site and established a tradition of Muslim pilgrimage to that shrine and the nearby al-Aqsa mosque. The monumental platform of the Jewish Temple became known as the Haram ash-Sharif —the Noble Sanctuary—thenceforth standing as a direct religious challenge not only to the traditions of the Jews, but to the primacy of the Church of the Holy Sepulcher as well.

As long as Christian pilgrimage was permitted, the western powers did nothing to oppose Muslim rule over the Holy Land. But the capricious destruction of the Church of the Holy Sepulcher in 1009 by the Fatimid caliph al-Hakim changed all that. From then on, the recovery of the ancient shrines of Palestine came to be an obsessive theme in the political and military machinations of the popes and princes of medieval Europe, the stimulus for wars and Crusades and considerable bloodshed. And though eight great military expeditions of knights and peasants ultimately failed to wrest Jerusalem from the hands of the Infidel except briefly, the saga of the Crusades themselves, told and retold for generations, added another layer of myth and veneration to the Christian conception of the Holy Land. The heroic struggles of Godfrey de Bouillon and Richard the Lion-Hearted became the national epics of France and England, and the original idea of the Crusades—the necessity for Christian possession and protection of the ancient shrines of the Holy Land —became a religious yearning that would, someday, surely be satisfied.

The fall of the Crusader Kingdom in 1291 marked the end of the great age of Christian pilgrimage, and little by little, the monasteries and convents that still dotted the countryside turned into tiny islands in a hostile sea. Significant native Christian communities remained, but their members, like the remaining Jews of the country, were required by the Muslim rulers to pay special taxes and wear distinctive dress. Venetian shipowners continued to carry groups of pilgrims to the Holy Land at Christmas and Easter, but overland travel within the country became increasingly hazardous as westerners were often subjected to harassment, robbery, and sometimes even death. By the beginning of the sixteenth century, the rise of the Ottoman Turks to ascendancy in the Middle East brought Christian pilgrimage to an almost complete halt.

After his conquest of Jerusalem in 1516, Sultan Selim I divided Palestine into several administrative districts and subjected them to the arbitrary exactions of official tax collectors serving as provincial governors with the rank of pasha. While the physical links between the Holy Land and the Christian world grew increasingly tenuous, western claims for the ancient shrines of the country became an object of bitter contention between the rising empires of the western world. In 1535, King Francis I of France became the first Christian monarch to conclude a treaty of friendship with the Ottoman sultan, thereby gaining for his country the right of "protection" over the holy sites. That right was eventually contested by the Russian Empire, which claimed to represent the Orthodox majority of the native Christians in Palestine. Added to the claims of the Catholics and the Orthodox were the contentions of a myriad of small denominations, Armenians, Copts, Syriacs, Abyssinians, all of whom demanded the right to maintain at least a token presence among the holiest churches of Palestine.

Eventually the Ottoman rulers of Palestine were forced to devise complicated schemes of partition within the churches of the Holy Land in order to head off confrontations among the competing Christian powers. At Jerusalem, in the Church of the Holy Sepulcher, the basilica and its subsidiary shrines were carefully parceled out to the competing sects, with complex rights of procession and passage between them. More often than not, these rights became the subject of fierce dispute as the simmering antagonisms of the various Christian sects erupted into full-scale disturbances. Even as the tide of mass pilgrimage all but ended, possession of the physical remains of Biblical antiquity became an issue of national prestige and sectarian honor.

One of the reasons for the decline in Christian pilgrimage was the Great Reformation which swept through northern Europe in the sixteenth century. The Protestant nations, burning with the fervor of a newfound faith, declared the actual journey to be nothing more than an empty ritual. Since for Protestants, pilgrimage would henceforth be one of the spirit rather than of the body, none of the Protestant nations saw the need to stake a claim in the traditional shrines of Palestine. But despite this voluntary separation—or perhaps because of it—the Protestant concept of the Holy Land underwent a profound and far-reaching conversion.

Encouraged by the wide distribution of the Bible and by the Puritan revolution in England in the seventeenth century, the names "Jerusalem," "Zion," "Canaan," "the River Jordan," and even "the Promised Land" blossomed into hymns, prayers, poems, and nearly every form of religious expression. Fiery sermons dwelt on the destruction of the wicked cities of Sodom and Gomorrah, rapturous odes sang the splendor of "Canaan's fair land," novels like *The Pilgrim's Progress* made commonplaces of Biblical allusions. The Protestant world took a logical step: it transformed the land of the Bible into a metaphor.

And so the various Christian traditions about the Holy Land grew and deepened over the course of centuries. Whether by physical possession of the holy sites or by theological interpretation and poetic use, the imagination and spiritual hopes of the entire Christian world became powerfully attached to that small strip of land on the southeastern shore of the Mediterranean. Yet so long as the strategic and commercial interests of the European powers remained focused elsewhere in the world, their competing claims for the Holy Land were of a strictly religious character. Now a new era was dawning.

This book is the story of the modern rediscovery of Palestine by the nations of the West, of its inextricable involvement with politics, religion, science, and empire from the dawn of the nineteenth century to World War I. Spurred on by the pressures of religious enthusiasm, national prestige, and diplomatic intrigue, the various nations of the western world struggled to gain political advantage in Palestine through an unlikely medium—Biblical archeology. Not until 1917, and the British conquest of Jerusalem, did the struggle end. Its lingering effects can still be felt in the Middle East today.

❖ 2 ❖

Rumblings in the East

NAPOLEON AND THE EUROPEAN STRUGGLE FOR THE MIDDLE EAST, 1798-1799

By the end of the eighteenth century, the forces of change in the Middle East could be held back no longer. From his opulent palaces and harems at Constantinople, Sultan Selim III ruled over an aged, crumbling empire.

Nearly five hundred years before, the founder of Selim's dynasty, a Turkish chieftain named Osman, had established a tiny principality on the eastern frontier of Byzantium in Asia Minor. By the sixteenth century, Osman's successors had spread their control over the entire Middle East, North Africa, and Eastern Europe. The vast Ottoman Empire, stretching from Morocco to the Persian Gulf and controlling the trade routes, raw materials, and tax revenues of three continents, was a powerful source of Islamic expansion for more than two centuries. By the end of the seventeenth century, however, the tide had begun to turn. Beaten back from the gates of Vienna in 1683 and suffering a series of disastrous defeats at the hands of the Russians in the following century, the Ottoman Empire ceased to expand. Without the infusion of new territories and tax revenues, it began to decline, and by the time that Sultan Selim III ascended to the throne in 1789, it seemed only a matter of time before it would die.

The disintegration of the Ottoman Empire would not occur in a vacuum; it threatened to provoke a dangerous scramble for territory among the rising empires of the western world. Russia's Romanov dynasty, its appetite whetted by the victories of Catherine the Great in the Crimea in the seventeen-seventies, was anxious to push its southern borders still farther, to Constantinople and control of the Dardanelles. The Hapsburgs in Austria coveted the sultan's fertile Balkan provinces, and the prosperous merchants of both Britain and France eagerly eyed the entire eastern Mediterranean as a potential market for their growing overseas trade.

Great Britain, in particular, had an important stake in the ultimate fate of the Ottoman Empire, for ever since the loss of her American colonies, the British economy had become increasingly dependent on commerce with India and the Orient. The most direct land and sea routes to those markets passed through the sultan's domains, and one of them—the overland caravan route through the Isthmus of Suez—was already considered vital for the transmission of urgent communications between London and its Indian outposts. So long as Suez remained free of obstruction, Britain's direct link to India was secure. But if ever it should be cut off, British commercial and strategic interests in India would undoubtedly suffer.

For the time being at least, the British were content to allow the sultan his tottering throne. Suez was safe and a far more pressing threat at home absorbed their thoughts of the immediate future.

In 1797, General Napoleon Bonaparte led the armies of revolutionary France across the Alps into Italy and soundly defeated the forces of the Hapsburg Empire that had massed against him. By the terms of the Treaty of Campo Formio, signed with Austria in October, the French Republic gained for itself important territorial concessions in both Europe and the Mediterranean. Further aggression by Napoleon's armies could be expected without delay; the young general seemed convinced of his invincibility.

Great Britain, France's only remaining opponent, was the obvious target for Napoleon's next adventure, and all through the winter of 1797–1798, the British people mobilized to fend off an expected French invasion. King George III and his ministers fretted over reports of an ominous French buildup at the port of Toulon, royal engineers hastily shored up coastal fortifications, local militia units assembled in villages and towns all over the country, and Admiral Horatio Nelson was dispatched to the Mediterranean at the head of a naval squadron to keep a close watch on the movements of the French fleet.

Taking advantage of the paralyzing fear he inspired, Napoleon found a way to strike a blow against his chief rivals that did not entail the passage of a single man-of-war across the English Channel. Secretly slipping out of Toulon with the massive invasion fleet that had been expected to converge on Dover, he unexpectedly headed eastward. The object of his secret plan, which had been formulated by Talleyrand and approved by France's revolutionary council, was to disrupt Britain's vital overseas commerce by establishing an extensive French colony in the Middle East.

The Ottoman province of Egypt was Napoleon's target, for it was there, he correctly realized, that the rule of the sultan was most vulnerable. For decades, this wealthy province had been held virtual hostage to the power of the local Mamluk beys, whose continual feuds and struggles for supremacy had kept both the rich tax revenues of the province and the strategic Suez caravan route beyond the effective control of the pitifully weak Ottoman administration. The sultan had long resigned himself to a state of constant disorder in Egypt, wresting halfhearted pledges of loyalty from the feuding beys, content that at least the fiction of Ottoman sovereignty was preserved.

Within a week of the French landing on the beaches of Alexandria that fiction was shattered forever. Napoleon's modern tactics and heavy artillery easily crushed the antiquated Mamluk cavalry that the sultan himself had been able to suppress only sporadically. For the first time since the fall of the Crusader Kingdom in 1291, a European army had pierced the defenses of the Middle East by the force of its arms, and it now marched virtually unopposed, in conquest.

Soon after his first glimpse of the Nile, Napoleon traveled upstream to Cairo, where his forces destroyed the last organized Mamluk resistance at the Battle of the Pyramids. Entering Cairo in triumph, he promptly settled into a palace belonging to one of the defeated Mamluks and began to put into action his grandiose schemes for the occupation of Egypt. Bonaparte saw before him visions of a prosperous French colony along the Nile, resurrecting the ancient grandeur of pharaonic Egypt. The forces of modern civilization, he believed, could overturn centuries of misrule and economic stagnation. So along with the siege equipment and heavy artillery that had been loaded aboard the ships at Toulon, Napoleon had also brought along a Scientific and Artistic Commission composed of France's most prominent scientists, engineers, naturalists, orientalists, and antiquarians. Their mission was to survey every facet of present-day Egypt and to propose the best means for its restoration. Like a new Alexander, in whose footsteps he fancied himself to be following, Napoleon sought to spread the light of his own civilization in the wake of his conquests.

"Forty centuries are looking down upon you!" Napoleon claimed, in his memoirs, to have shouted down to his soldiers as they engaged the Mamluk enemy within sight of the pyramids. The historical accuracy of that moment has been called into question, but it would not have been out of character for Napoleon, whose images of faded glories and future conquests were not always easy to disentangle. The lure of the past and the new science of archeology fascinated him and he was anxious to reap the rich harvest of antiquities that now lay before him.

In his campaign through Italy in 1797, Napoleon had sent back crate after crate of confiscated paintings and artworks to the museum being created at the palace of the Louvre. The *Mona Lisa* was but one of these glittering prizes, and now, he was sure, even greater treasures might be found. For the first time in history, the military might of a European power had cleared the path for the researches of antiquarian explorers. The artist Vivant Denon accompanied General Desaix into Upper Egypt, accurately sketching the monumental temples at Karnak and Luxor for the first time; in Lower Egypt, other savants attached to the Scientific and Artistic Commission unearthed ancient temples and palaces, compiled topographical maps, and assembled massive collections of ancient artifacts, including the Rosetta stone, which would, twenty-two years later, finally serve as the key to Egyptian hieroglyphics. The modern science of Egyptology was born, and with it a broad new interest in the scientific study of antiquities. Long after Napoleon himself had departed from the Middle East, this interest would continue to bear fruit in the form of large-scale archeological activity.

For the British, Napoleon's civilized invasion of Egypt was no mere antiquarian treasure hunt. A permanent French presence along the Nile was in itself intolerable, and the possibility that it might lead to an eventual attack on the British colonies in India could not be ignored. So, despite centuries of distrust and contempt for the Turk, the government of Lord Pitt saw no alternative but to conclude an official alliance with him. The ostensible object of that alliance was to uphold the territorial integrity of Selim III's empire; its immediate purpose was to cast Napoleon, his savants, and his revolutionary armies out of the Middle East.

On the evening of August 1, 1798, Admiral Nelson's naval squadron appeared off the coast of Alexandria. Nelson had been cruising the Mediterranean even before the French invasion, and only the chance occurrence of a dense night fog had permitted Napoleon's fleet to slip past him and land unopposed. The night of August 1–2 was clear, and rather than delay the inevitable battle, Nelson ordered an immediate attack. By day-break, all but three vessels of the massive French invasion force had been either grounded or destroyed. Napoleon's lines of communication and resupply back to France were effectively severed.

When news of Nelson's great victory in Abukir Bay reached London, the British government assumed it would be only a matter of time before the French invasion force was destroyed. A large Ottoman army was then massing in Syria while the British were setting in motion plans for an invasion of Egypt the following summer, and it was confidently believed that Napoleon, facing this combined threat, would recognize his strategic isolation and be willing to negotiate for the safe passage of his forces back to France.

That event, however, would not occur for more than three years. The British struggle in the Middle East was, in fact, just beginning.

The narrow land bridge of Palestine, hemmed in between the sea and the Great Syrian Desert, had long served as a highway of empires. Its fertile coastal plain provided the only convenient military route from Africa into Asia, and Egyptian pharaohs, Assyrian, Babylonian, and Persian kings, and even Alexander the Great recognized its importance to control of the entire region. Now that the British had come to the aid of the sultan, Napoleon saw no reason to continue paying even lip service to the myth of Ottoman rule. Palestine would provide a convenient buffer for his Egyptian enclave, and the defeat of the Ottoman forces there might even encourage a widespread rebellion in other territories of the sultan.

In January 1799, six months after the destruction of his fleet at Abukir, Napoleon ordered an expeditionary force of approximately thirteen thousand men to proceed from bases in Egypt into the Promised Land. His immediate intention was to destroy the army of the local Ottoman pasha Ahmad al-Jazzar before reinforcements could arrive from Syria. Further conquests to the north and east were not out of the question, even though the speed of the campaign was an extremely important factor. Napoleon knew that he would have to be back in Egypt by the summer in order to repulse the expected Anglo-Ottoman invasion.

The first obstacle encountered by the French was the small garrison at El-Arish in Sinai, manned by al-Jazzar's troops, which put up unexpectedly stiff resistance for ten days. Gaza, to the north, was the next objective of the French invasion, and it surrendered without a struggle. From Gaza, Napoleon's forces continued their advance into the Holy Land, following in the footsteps of the Crusader armies, but this time, it seemed, the stationary Turkish defense would be no match for the dynamic tactics of a modern European army.

There were other differences as well. At the time of Napoleon's invasion, almost no scientific information was available about current conditions in the Land of the Bible. The country had been visited by only a few adventurous European traders and explorers in the previous centuries, and their reports on the topography, population, and natural resources of the country were fragmentary at best. In order to gain this important strategic information, Napoleon brought with him a specially selected corps of scientists and mapmakers, under orders to extend their researches into Palestine. As the French invasion proceeded steadily up the coast, Napoleon's explorers branched off into the hilly interior of the country, busily collecting artifacts, sketching the prominent landmarks, and compiling the first modern topographical map of the country.

And, as he had been in Egypt, Napoleon in Palestine was well aware of the romantic notions of national rebirth that this exploration symbolized. From the stronghold of his general headquarters at Ramla, he issued emotional appeals to the Jews, Muslims, Christians, and Druze of the country to cast off the rule of their Ottoman overlords and establish their independence under the benevolent protection of the French Republic. Napoleon was soon to learn, however, that promises of liberty, fraternity, and equality were meaningless to a populace equally frightened by strange invaders and familiar oppressors.

The populace had reason for worry. At Jaffa, once the royal harbor of King Solomon, the Turkish garrison stubbornly refused to surrender. When the fortifications of the city were finally breached, Napoleon's forces streamed through the streets in a twenty-four-hour orgy of looting, rape, and slaughter. During the following few days, Napoleon ordered the execution of between three and four thousand unarmed prisoners of war. The expansive promises of French protection were quickly forgotten as the stench of unburied corpses began to rise over Jaffa, and as the true face of the Napoleonic invasion of the Holy Land began to emerge, some of the survivors of the siege saw nothing less than divine vengeance in a sudden outbreak of bubonic plague in the midst of the French camp.

Unburdened by superstitions and determined to maintain his momentum northward, Napoleon marshaled his exhausted and now plague-stricken forces for a march to the port of Acre, residence of the notorious pasha Ahmad al-Jazzar. Acre had been the last stronghold of the Crusader Kingdom, but long before the Crusades it had witnessed countless other invasions. Although it was far declined from its former splendor, its thick walls, surrounded on three sides by jagged rocks and unpredictable tides, posed a far greater challenge to Napoleon's forces than the crumbling fortifications of Jaffa.

"Al-Jazzar" was only the pasha's nickname; roughly translated from Arabic it meant "the Butcher." But Napoleon had already proved at Jaffa that there was more than one butcher in the Holy Land. Battering rams and siege equipment were on their way by sea from Egypt, and together with the modern artillery and infantry of his invasion force, Napoleon seemed determined to transform al-Jazzar's capital into a huge abattoir.

Napoleon arrived at Acre to discover an unpleasant surprise. A line of British battleships lay at anchor a few hundred yards off the rocky coast, and their unexpected arrival had resulted in the interception and seizure of his heavy siege equipment. Englishmen had fought and died at Acre under Richard the Lion-Hearted to defeat the infidel, but now, under Commodore Sidney Smith, hundreds more would give their lives to defend him. The British cared little for the internal politics of the Ottoman Empire, still less for the survival of Ahmad al-Jazzar, but they were determined to make the Battle of Acre Napoleon's last stand in Palestine.

Napoleon himself knew that without either battering rams or siege artillery he could not possibly take the city, except at the cost of tremendous casualties. But he had staked the destiny of his crusade in the Holy Land on the capture of Acre before early summer, and time was running out. Despite the continuing ravages of bubonic plague among his troops, the incessant showers of British grapeshot, and little possibility of reinforcement or resupply, Napoleon ordered repeated human-wave assaults on the fortifications of the city in the following two months. His troops breached the walls more than once, but could not succeed in destroying the combined Anglo-Ottoman defense.

On May 20, 1799, five months after his triumphant entry into the Holy Land, Napoleon ordered the pitiful remnant of his invasion force—now hacked down to a half of its original strength—to abandon the siege camp. Then, frantically summoning his scattered explorers, he began the humiliating retreat back to the relative safety of Egypt. He had suffered the first defeat of his career, and the initiative of his invasion of the Middle East had been lost. "In that miserable fort," a rueful Napoleon said of Acre, "lay the fate of the East."

Although Ahmad al-Jazzar and his Ottoman overlord could rest easily once again, the strategic land bridge of Palestine would never again be ignored by the great powers of the western world. Even before the last of the bodies had been cleared from the battlefield outside Acre, al-Jazzar vowed to massacre all of the native Christians in the country, whom he suspected of secretly aiding the French. Massacres had always been the Butcher's prerogative, but this one never occurred. British Commodore Sidney Smith, hearing of al-Jazzar's threats, issued a strong warning of his own. The British were Christians too, and the same guns which had turned away Napoleon could be trained just as easily on al-Jazzar. The French might have been defeated, but the West had come to stay.

In a clear demonstration of that fact, Smith subsequently landed a detachment of his sailors for an ostentatious march to Jerusalem, where they accepted the nervous appeals of the Catholic and Orthodox communities for "protection." So it was that even though Napoleon's explorers had made their way into many parts of the country, the British, not the French, were the first to bear Christian flags into Jerusalem since the time of the Crusades. And by the end of the century that was just beginning, both Christian flags and Christian explorers in Jerusalem would become a familiar sight.

❖ 3 ❖

The Land of the Butcher

HARSH ENCOUNTERS
IN A PROMISED LAND,
1801-1818

With British forces eventually driving the French out of Egypt, and British ships regularly calling at the ports of the Palestinian coast for supplies, the territory under the control of the pasha of Acre suddenly received a flood of curious visitors. While Sidney Smith and his honor guard restricted their exploration of the interior to Jerusalem, other British officers now toured the country on their own, making sketches and watercolors of the scenery and compiling journals of their visits to the various holy sites. These accounts of the current state of the Holy Land, together with the patriotic stories of the Battle of Acre, suddenly aroused the interest of the British public in the Land of the Bible, long idealized yet visited by only a handful of English travelers in the previous two centuries.

Part of this renewed fascination arose from the fact that the present reality of the land varied so greatly from its Biblical descriptions. The "land of milk and honey" was no longer so fruitful; the thick forests described in the Bible had long since disappeared, leaving the rolling hillsides of the interior rocky and barren. True, along the coast there were extensively cultivated areas, with orange groves, wheat, and cotton, but there were also malarial swamps and relentlessly drifting sand dunes, every year burying more and more of the precious arable land. Many of the ancient cities and towns mentioned in the Scriptures had seemingly vanished without a trace, and even the holy cities of Jerusalem, Bethlehem, and Nazareth were now little more than provincial market towns.

The authors of the first British accounts of the Holy Land were amateur explorers, but the protecting presence of the British fleet in the eastern Mediterranean quickly encouraged scientific research as well. Edward Daniel Clarke, one of England's most prominent geographers and world travelers, arrived in Acre in the summer of 1801 as a civilian passenger aboard a British supply ship, and in the course of seventeen days produced one of the most complete archeological reports on Palestine that had yet been compiled.

The thirty-two-year-old Clarke personified the spirit of scientific curiosity that marked the age in which he lived. During more than two years of wide-ranging explorations, he had observed and recorded the daily life of the Laplanders, ridden across the Russian steppes in the company of cossacks, and wandered alone over the plains of Asia Minor in search of the site of ancient Troy. Less a pilgrim than a skeptical scientist, Clarke had come to the Holy Land with an eye to discovery. Yet the religious significance of the country did not completely escape him; the admitted goal of his journey was a thorough examination of "all those places rendered remarkable by the life and actions of Jesus Christ."

At the head of an impressive cavalcade of armed soldiers provided by al Jazzar, Clarke first traveled through Galilee, cataloging plant life, searching out antiquities, and collecting geological specimens. Clarke also found, however, much to his (uncharacteristic) religious dismay, that the "true spirit of the Gospel is even less known in the Holy Land than in Caliphornia [sic] or New Holland." As he stopped at villages throughout Galilee, he noted that the native Christians were hardly distinguishable from their Jewish or Muslim neighbors, and that the ancient shrines so eagerly pointed out to centuries of pious Christian pilgrims were nothing more than "superstitious trumpery."

Clarke visited Nazareth at the time of an outbreak of plague and was horrified to see the Christian inhabitants flock to the Franciscan convent there for miraculous cures. He found no evidence that the site named as the "birthplace of the Virgin Mary" was anything more than an icon-laden grotto of questionable antiquity. After traveling southward through Samaria into Judea, Clarke was impressed with the outward appearance of the walled city of Jerusalem, but he was bitterly disappointed to find that the renowned Church of the Holy Sepulcher had the appearance of "any common Roman Catholic church."

Clarke's failure to discern the remains of any ancient tomb within the Church of the Holy Sepulcher caused him to make the first important advance in the scientific exploration of the Holy Land. Vowing "not to peer through the spectacles of priests," Clarke abandoned the traditional routes of pilgrimage within Jerusalem and began a search for the "true sites" of the tomb of Christ, Mount Zion, and the tombs of the Hebrew kings. On a hill several hundred yards to the south of the city wall, Clarke noted the presence of many ancient tombs cut into the bedrock and came to the conclusion, based on his reading of some fragmentary Greek inscriptions, that he had located the authentic Mount Zion of the Bible.

In the course of time, as more scientific explorers came and worked in the Holy Land, Clarke's "discovery" proved to be as fanciful as anyone else's, but that fact in itself had little significance. The important thing was his approach. Edward Daniel Clarke had been the first to utilize secular learning rather than ecclesiastical tradition in examining the ancient remains of Palestine. The real monuments of Biblical antiquity, he became convinced, lay scattered over the desolated countryside, untouched and unnoticed by the local Christian communities, which were still chained to the traditions of their unenlightened priests.

The year following Clarke's journey saw the travels of another western explorer in Palestine who would have an equally important effect on its exploration. This was Ulrich Seetzen, an adventurous Swiss physician who had taught himself the languages and customs of the Middle East, disguised himself as an Arab, and become the first European since the time of the Crusades to travel through and record the little-known regions to the east of the Sea of Galilee, along the winding course of the Jordan River, and across the mountains of the Sinai peninsula.

Although Seetzen visited many of the traditional Christian shrines of Palestine, the religious motive played a very minor role in his travels; his patron was the duke of Saxe-Gotha in Germany, who was anxious to acquire some "oriental curiosities" for his private museum. Seetzen's search for those curiosities was apparently successful, for before he had concluded his exploration of the Holy Land, he acquired the added patronage of another noted collector, Tsar Alexander I. For both the duke and the tsar, the crates of ancient and natural curiosities that Seetzen shipped back to Europe seemed but the smallest taste of the antiquarian treasures that the Land of the Bible might hold.

In the feverish wartime atmosphere of the Napoleonic era the exploration of remote and little-known lands took on overtones of patriotism and national pride. In Palestine, Napoleon himself had initiated the competition. Although the topographical map compiled by his savants was inaccurate in many respects, it had been a significant advance over the medieval pilgrims' maps, which saw Jerusalem as turreted and splendid, a city more heavenly than earthly. The horrors of the invasion of the Holy Land had been anything but heavenly, and long before Napoleon's explorers had the opportunity to gather even the most rudimentary picture of the country, they were forced to join the panic-stricken retreat back to Egypt.

For the British, the opening up of the country in the years following Napoleon's defeat provided the perfect opportunity for some official explorations of their own. Over the previous decades, the urge to expand their empire and open up trade routes and new sources of raw materials had given the impetus to the formation of British societies for the exploration of Africa, Asia, and the Pacific. Explorations backed by those societies had added greatly to both the scientific and commercial knowledge of the world by carefully cataloguing flora, fauna, topography, and geology. And despite the travels of Clarke and Seetzen, little was known of whatever natural resources or trade routes to the East Palestine might hold.

In 1804, a small group of wealthy Englishmen gathered together in London to form a private organization for the exploration of the Holy Land. Modeling their society on the enormously successful African Association, which had sponsored several expeditions to the "Dark Continent," the founding members of the "Palestine Association" promised the prompt publication of "such information as the committee can acquire as to the state of the country, its geography, its people, its climate, and its history."

Unfortunately for the Association's plans, 1804 was also the year in which Ahmad al-Jazzar died, and the territory formerly under his control quickly descended into chaos. Continuing battles between his would-be successors suddenly made the scientific exploration of the country by westerners an extremely hazardous enterprise. The first two explorers of the Palestine Association were at a stop-off in Malta when they received word of the disorders in the Holy Land and, valuing their personal safety far more than the scientific aims of their employers, they quickly retraced their steps to London and resigned their commissions.

This episode was undoubtedly embarrassing to the founders of the Palestine Association, but it would not be fatal to their cause. Among Edward Daniel Clarke's students at Cambridge in the fall term of 1808 was a young Swiss recruit for the African Association named John Lewis Burckhardt, who was destined to become the next major figure in Palestinian exploration. Burckhardt was a passionate enemy of Napoleon, whose forces had imprisoned his father, and he believed that Napoleon's defeat could best be brought about by the expansion of the British Empire. It was to that end that he had come to England and accepted an assignment to travel to the Middle East and discover a new trade route into Africa from the north, by secretly accompanying a caravan of return-ing Muslim pilgrims from Mecca.

After a year of study with Dr. Clarke and other prominent orientalists at Cambridge, Burckhardt set off for Syria disguised as an Indian Muslim merchant, taking for himself the name Ibrahim ibn Abdullah. Whether he believed that any Indian merchant had hair as blond as his, or eyes as blue, is uncertain, but he had at least the good sense to test his disguise in travels through Syria and the Holy Land before risking premature discovery in Arabia.

At Cambridge, Dr. Clarke had interested the young explorer in the antiquities of the Holy Land, and during the course of Burckhardt's two-year residence in Aleppo and Damascus, he spent much of his time exploring ancient ruins, copying hundreds of ancient inscriptions, and keeping up a voluminous correspondence with his former teacher. Burck-hardt was openly envious of the discoveries that Ulrich Seetzen had made for the German duke and the Russian tsar, and he expressed his astonish-ment in a letter to Dr. Clarke that "no English traveller has yet made his appearance in these parts since peace with Turkey; the moment is as favorable now as it ever will be."

Whether or not the moment was in fact favorable, the British interest in Palestine was steadily growing. Dr. Clarke himself had received a considerable advance from a London publisher to write of his travel experiences, and the Palestine Association, recovering from its humilia-tion, published an English translation of one of Seetzen's journals enti-tled *A Brief Account of the Countries Adjoining the Lake of Tiberias, the Jordan, and the Dead Sea.* The small pamphlet offered the British public its first glimpse of the Biblical lands of Hauran, Bashan, Gilead, and Moab, a fact which almost made up for its foreign origin.

By the spring of 1812, the time had come for John Lewis Burckhardt to end his period of training in Syria and proceed southwards toward Africa. In order to protect his disguise, he would have to avoid the more well-traveled routes through the Holy Land, but he had also gained another motive in the choice of his itinerary. "Even after the publication of Seetzen's travels," he had written to Dr. Clarke, "there is still so much to be discovered in Palestine." He would use his journey southward to follow in the footsteps of Ulrich Seetzen, and, he devoutly hoped, to contribute some major discoveries of his own.

Burckhardt set off from Damascus and briefly toured some of the traditional sites around the Sea of Galilee, showing little patience with the stuffy, candlelit chapels and cramped pilgrims' hostels there. His mission was of discovery, not pilgrimage, and, donning his disguise, he set off

again with a pair of Arab peddlers who were on their way back to the
eastern shore of the Dead Sea. "Sheikh Ibrahim" was determined to
travel down the Jordan Valley and, if possible, locate the ancient caravan
city of Petra which his competitor Seetzen had failed to identify.

As the journey progressed southward, Burckhardt filled his journals
with sketches and transcribed inscriptions from scores of hitherto undis-
covered ancient sites. Despite the prudent reluctance of his companions
to expose themselves needlessly to Bedouin attack, Burckhardt insisted
on stopping time and again at the slightest sign of ruins. More interested
in what he could discover than in what he probably ought to have feared,
he finally succeeded in locating the remains of Petra in a remote gorge
south of the Dead Sea. The site had only minor Biblical associations, but
the magnificence of its monumental necropolis, carved from the native
red sandstone, would attract generations of future western travelers and
tourists.

As word spread of Burckhardt's explorations, other British travelers
were encouraged to come out to Palestine to see what they themselves
might find for the honor of their nation. A handsome young writer and
adventurer on his way to India was the next explorer of note in the Holy
Land, but, unlike Seetzen or Burckhardt before him, James Silk Buckingham sought not the ancient treasures of the country, but its contemporary
riches and future prospects.

Trade routes to the Orient were a vital reason for British imperial
interest in the Middle East, and Buckingham was confident that Burckhardt's route from the Sea of Galilee to the Gulf of Aqaba had inadvert-
ently revealed a new one. Following his predecessor's example and dis-
guising himself as an Arab sheikh, Buckingham set out to retrace
Burckhardt's steps. The results of his explorations, however, were inconclusive, for he was not able to travel southward from the Dead Sea: the
region was embroiled in a war between neighboring Bedouin clans.
Nonetheless, by the time that he was ready to proceed on toward Calcutta, Buckingham was able to boast that he had explored the Holy Land
more completely than any previous traveler, and his hopes for the trade
route, although unconfirmed, remained very much alive.

Back in England, the public's interest in Palestine was growing still
more intense. The third volume of Dr. Clarke's travels was published, so
moving Lord Byron that he wrote to Clarke of his desire to go there
himself. By 1815, the wars which ravaged Europe were over, and Great
Britain emerged as the unquestioned leader of the western world. The

fabulous adventures of "Sheikh Ibrahim" and the other British explorers in the Holy Land had aroused the patriotic pride of many of their country-men, but they had also excited the envy of one of the most fascinating personalities of the time: an ambitious, haughty, and proud aristocrat who would soon become the first archeological excavator in the Land of the Bible.

Lady Hester Lucy Stanhope had come to the Middle East in 1810, after the death of her favorite brother in the Napoleonic Wars, and the breakup of her settled existence in England. As the granddaughter of William Pitt the Elder and the niece of Prime Minister William Pitt the Younger, she was born at the pinnacle of British society, yet her abrasive, impetuous disposition had gained her many enemies, mostly silent. After the younger Pitt's death, those enemies were no longer so silent, and with no family left to speak of, Lady Hester, like many other romantics of her time, tossed away the comfort and complacency of London society for the lure of distant shores.

Lady Hester's choice of a destination for her travels was as unique as her own personality. As a younger woman, fond of creating sensations among her aristocratic peers, she had paid a visit to the London insane asylum known as Bedlam, after hearing that one of the inmates there had reportedly seen a vision of her future. The inmate, possibly mad but nevertheless convincing, proclaimed that Lady Hester was destined to lead the Jews of the world back to the land of their forefathers—to become a queen of the desert and recapture Jerusalem. The memory of that prophecy never left her, and when she finally made up her mind to become an expatriate, it was inevitable that she would travel to the Holy Land.

A chance meeting with John Lewis Burckhardt at Nazareth convinced her that the path to her destiny lay in exploration. Not that she was impressed with "Sheikh Ibrahim"; Lady Hester resented the fact that the African Association had sent out a foreigner to do its important work, and was as skeptical of Burckhardt's achievements as she was scornful of his unkempt disguise. She herself had no need to hide her identity, except perhaps in dressing as a man; that was a habit she had adopted in the Middle East, she claimed, to ensure being treated with respect.

And as if to make good on her boast that her own daring was no less than that of the Swiss explorer, she assembled a lavish desert caravan to visit the magnificent remains of Palmyra at the headwaters of the Euphra-tes. The fear of attacks by Bedouin had kept other, less reckless western travelers from attempting such an expedition, but Lady Hester plunged into the desert fearlessly. Instead of being attacked, she was entertained by the notorious sheikhs of the region, who were undoubtedly amused by both the costume and the behavior of the strange Englishwoman.

Returning from her triumphant visit to Palmyra, Lady Hester took up residence in Tripoli on the Syrian coast, where her wanderlust was unfortunately restrained by an outbreak of plague in the countryside. Falling ill herself, Lady Hester received the sympathy of many local well-wishers who were fascinated by the tales of her exploits in the desert. During one of these visits, the monks of a nearby Franciscan monastery presented her with a copy of an intriguing ancient document that was to lead this most impressionable explorer into yet another adventure.

The text of the document described a fantastic treasure of gold bullion said to have been secretly buried in the ruins of the ancient city of Ashkelon on the Mediterranean coast, giving precise details of its location. Lady Hester was at first skeptical, and demanded that the monks bring the original document from which the text was copied. When they promptly did so, she was convinced of its authenticity and decided that the recovery of the treasure might gain her the undying fame she assumed was her destiny.

Lady Hester had no particular interest in the treasure itself; her dreams were of far greater things than mere riches. She believed that if the treasure were to be recovered by the efforts of an Englishwoman and duly presented to the sultan as a token of British esteem, the friendship of the two great nations would be cemented forever. As soon as she had recovered from her illness, Lady Hester dashed off an imperious letter to the British ambassador at Constantinople revealing the details of her plan to recover the treasure and requesting the services of a British frigate to scout out the shore. Unfortunately, Lady Hester's political influence with the British government had died with her distinguished uncle. When a mere sloop arrived some time later with a message saying that the plan was foolish and impracticable, she became even more determined to carry it out herself.

Sending word of her intentions directly to the sultan in Constantinople, Lady Hester began the journey down the coast to Ashkelon. A special representative of the Ottoman government, which apparently had more faith in Lady Hester and her treasure than did the British government, joined her caravan en route, as did the pasha of Jaffa, Muhammad Abu Nabbut. Arriving at the ruins of the Philistine city, Lady Hester settled into a comfortable cottage in a nearby village and conscripted hundreds of local fellahin to begin the work of the excavation. The treasure map indicated that the gold was buried beneath a ruined mosque, and it was there that the digging began.

At the end of the fourth day of excavation, several huge pillars were discovered lying side by side as if to conceal a secret hiding place. The sultan's representative hastily summoned special winches and ropes, but as the huge stone cylinders were lifted and removed, it became clear that the treasure they concealed was of neither silver nor gold. It was the huge, headless statue of a Roman emperor—the first archeological artifact ever discovered by excavation in Palestine.

But beneath the statue was nothing, and Lady Hester was seeking gold, not classical art. Ordering the statue to be set upright—and out of the way—she ordered the workers to resume digging for the treasure at another part of the site.

After several more weeks of excavation, a maze of empty trenches and haphazard piles of overturned earth testified grimly to the fruitlessness of the search. Lady Hester's tantrums grew more frequent as her workers exhausted every possibility. Rather than admit to herself that the treasure map was a hoax, she became convinced that the late al-Jazzar had himself removed the treasure only a few years before. All that was left to her was the Roman statue.

Lady Hester was determined to demonstrate, however, that unlike other British antiquarians she had no interest in filling a museum; *her* search had been undertaken unselfishly, with regard only for the friendship of the Ottoman ruler. She had seen for herself the aftereffects of Lord Elgin's removal of the Parthenon frieze while in Athens several years before, and she did not want her excavations to encourage similar plundering in the Holy Land. With a wave of her hand, she ordered the workers to destroy the monumental statue and cast its fragments into the sea.

With that act, Lady Hester Stanhope ended her brief but memorable archeological career. Within a few days she once again headed northward with her caravan along the coast. At Jaffa, she bade farewell to the pasha, Muhammad Abu Nabbut, who was less disappointed than she at the expedition's results. He would make his fame in the reconstruction of his city; the tons of ancient marble and building stones he recovered from the dig at Ashkelon would soon beautify the palaces and bathhouses of Jaffa.

The sultan's representative was equally undisturbed about Lady Hester's failure to find any treasure; he had enjoyed the luxurious outing immensely and could faithfully report that the interests of the sultan had been preserved. For Lady Hester, however, the expedition to Ashkelon had smashed her dreams. Returning to her mountain retreat in Lebanon, she remained in virtual seclusion until her death more than twenty years later. The woman whose destiny it had been to reign as Queen of the Jews became known to travelers and natives alike as the Mad Nun of Lebanon.

Fragmentary reports of Lady Hester's unsuccessful hunt for treasure quickly made the rounds of London society, but any amusement these might have inspired was quickly dispelled with the receipt of other, more sobering dispatches from the East. Ulrich Seetzen was finally unmasked, and poisoned by order of the imam of Yemen; John Lewis Burckhardt succumbed to malarial fever in Cairo in 1817, before he had even begun to achieve the real object of his mission in Africa. One more British expedition, led by two naval officers, Charles Irby and James Mangles, set off for the Holy Land in the same year; but even their successful travels through the Dead Sea region could do little to counteract the negative image of the country and its people created by the experiences of their predecessors.

By 1809, the Palestine Association had already suspended its regular meetings, and after the publication of Seetzen's journal it seems to have disbanded altogether. The Land of the Bible no longer lived solely in the romantic idealization of preachers and poets; through the efforts of the early explorers, vivid images of desolate terrain, spurious shrines, and uncivilized inhabitants had begun to clash unpleasantly with the more attractive religious images. And as the ambitious hopes of the early scientific explorers crumbled, it was plain that the first great wave of Palestinian exploration was over.

❖ 4 ❖

Visions of the End of the World

PROPHETIC DREAMS
AND MISSIONARY HOPES,
1818-1833

Like brilliant red flares fired into the inky blackness of the future, the Old
Testament Book of Daniel and the New Testament Book of Revelation
offer frightening glimpses at the events surrounding the End of the
World. Over the course of centuries, in times of natural disasters, political upheavals, and sinfulness, pious Christians of almost every denomination and nationality have looked to these two works for the comforting
reassurance that their faith would ultimately be rewarded, and wickedness and misery ended. At the "time of the end," prophesied Daniel,
"many of those who sleep in the dust of the earth shall awake, some to
everlasting life, and some to everlasting shame and contempt." Following
a period of unprecedented wickedness and tribulation, the righteous
would do battle with God's enemies, and the world would be transformed
into a state of heavenly splendor.

The Holy Land was thought to be central to this final, cataclysmic
period of earthly history, and many believed that it was there that the
forces of the Antichrist would finally be defeated at a place called "Armageddon," the Heavenly Jerusalem would descend to earth, and Jesus
Christ would return there to rule over his faithful followers for a thousand
years.

The belief that this millennium was imminent gripped large segments
of the Protestant world during the final decade of the eighteenth century.
Never before, it seemed, had the world gone through a period of such
upheaval and tribulation. Ominous reports of beheaded kings and angry
mobs provoked fears for the traditional basis of European civilization. Yet
to some, the current age of revolution and secular science seemed actually to be that divinely inspired phase of human history scheduled to

28

occur immediately before the final redemption of the world. Daniel himself had prophesied that the "end of times" would be preceded by a period in which "many shall run to and fro and knowledge shall increase."

In 1792, an Anglican cleric named James Bicheno published *The Signs of the Times,* a book in which he drew a series of eerie yet believable parallels between the prophetic timetables of Daniel and Revelation and the events of his own day. According to Bicheno, the revolution in France and the disenfranchisement of the French Catholic Church seemed to be a clear fulfillment of the destruction of the "Fourth Beast" foretold by Daniel. More tribulation and trials might be expected in the near future, and Bicheno even ventured to speculate that the sultan of Turkey, seen by many as an "eastern" Antichrist, would be the next to suffer.

Napoleon's invasion of Egypt and the Holy Land seemed to prove Bicheno right and added many converts to the belief that the End was indeed at hand. But even before Napoleon's invasion, millennial expectation in England had already been directed toward the Land of the Bible by Richard Brothers, a former naval officer turned pacifist, who harangued huge crowds in London with confident predictions that he would soon lead the Jews of the world back to the land of their forefathers. The conversion of the Jews and their return to the Holy Land was long seen as one of the characteristic signs of the imminence of the millennium, and it was to provide one of the prime motivations for missionary work among the Jews throughout the nineteenth century. Brothers' preaching gained him many fervent followers all across England, but it also brought him under the nervous questioning of the British government, which was unsettled by the excitement among the lower classes that he inspired. (Brothers was eventually arrested and confined in Bedlam, where he gained his most unlikely convert. For it was he who first turned Lady Hester Stanhope's eyes eastward, advising her that her "royal" destiny lay in Palestine.)

Across the Atlantic in America, interest in Biblical prophecy and the expectation of the imminent millennium was even more widespread. Spurred on by the religious enthusiasm that would soon give rise to the "Second Great Awakening," certain American religious leaders even offered exact dates for the fulfillment of the prophecies of Daniel and Revelation. The Reverend David Austin, a graduate of Yale College, solemnly announced to his New Jersey congregation that the world would end on May 15, 1796. The failure of anything unusual to happen on that day, however, merely changed Austin's focus. He promptly returned to New Haven, city of his alma mater, and began to solicit funds for the

construction of wharves and harbor facilities for the transportation of the
Jews back to the Holy Land.

How the scattered Jewish people might be gathered in Connecticut,
and how they might be persuaded to pile aboard ships hired by a Congregationalist minister, was apparently not given much serious thought. But
one general point had been established: it was no good waiting passively
for the millennium; it would have to be brought about by deliberate
effort, "human instrumentalities." Not only the Jews, but all the non-
believers and pagans of the world would have to be converted to the
enlightened gospel of Protestantism before the Second Coming could
occur, and it was the sacred duty of all true Christians to help bring this
about. Numerous private missionary societies thereupon began to spring
up on both sides of the Atlantic, sending off pious workers to establish
missions and distribute Bibles all over the world.

The wave of exploration that followed Napoleon's invasion of Palestine clearly showed how much remained to be done there if the Heavenly
Jerusalem were indeed to manifest itself within current lifetimes. The
accounts of the early explorers confirmed every detail of the poverty,
oppression, and seemingly intractable grip of ignorance over all the
people of the country. Not only the "fanatical" Muslims and "stiff-
necked" Jews would have to be converted, but also the local Christians,
bound to the dogmatic teachings of the Catholic and Orthodox churches.
Thus, although the attentions of the English missionaries were increasingly drawn to the spiritual needs of India, Africa, and the Orient, where
the path of their nation's empire lay, the missionary restoration of the
Holy Land was plainly an obligation that could not be shirked. It was not
to be long before their religious cousins in America would take up the
challenge and be the first to dispatch a sacred mission to the Earthly
Jerusalem.

The first Puritan settlers of New England, fleeing from the persecu-
tions of the Anglican High Church in favor of the imperatives of their own
austere dissenting religion, cherished a unique veneration for the Land
of the Bible. Cutting the thick forests and clearing the rocky hillsides for
farms, villages, and towns, the early New England Puritans saw themselves as the true successors of the ancient Israelites. The Old World was
their Egypt; the great American wilderness was their Promised Land.
Their theology, as articulated in the fiery sermons of Increase and Cotton
Mather, of John Winthrop and Nathaniel Ward, revealed little of the
mercy and compassion of the New Testament. They saw the stories of the

Exodus from Egypt, the Forty Years' Wandering, and the Conquest of Canaan as being far closer to the realities in which they lived.

The towns that they founded bore such names as Bethel, Hebron, New Canaan, Jericho, Bethlehem, and Zion. The names that they bore and passed on to their children—Josiah, Moses, Jonathan, Ebenezer, Abigail, Rebecca, Ahab, Sarah, and Rachel—were drawn straight from the pages of their well-worn family Bibles. Nowhere else in the Protestant world did the idealization of the Holy Land have a more tangible reality than in New England. New Englanders saw in it a vision of how the world should be. More particularly, they saw in it a vision of themselves.

The missionary activities of the New England Congregationalists began almost as soon as those of their Anglican counterparts. These efforts had consisted mostly of sending off pale young ministers to the wilds of the western frontier and into the slums of growing cities to convert the savages of the New World and the Jews to the "pure and primitive" gospel of Christ. But despite the numbers of Indian schools established, despite the numbers of missionary tracts distributed among the Jews of Boston and New York, and despite the participation of twelve of their own missionaries in the sacred work of their English brethren among the masses of India, in the early nineteenth century the New England Congregationalists were eager to spread the Word of their own faith to the land of its inception.

In the fall of 1818, the prayers of the faithful were answered at last. The American Board of Commissioners for Foreign Missions, established in 1810 to fulfill the millennial aspirations of its devout followers, announced plans for a historic extension of the holy work. "Resolved," the public announcement read, "that Reverend Messers. Levi Parsons and Pliny Fisk be designated for Jerusalem and such other parts of Western Asia as shall be deemed eligible, and that they should be sent out as soon as shall be found convenient. . . ."

To many of the Congregationalist communities scattered across the new nation of the United States, long nurtured by visions of the Holy Land and hopes for its millennial transformation, the mere mention of an American mission to Jerusalem stirred up great excitement, considerable national pride, and a sudden flow of contributions to the treasury of the American Board of Commissioners for Foreign Missions. The two young men who had been selected for the assignment in Palestine, both recent graduates of the Andover Theological Seminary, toured the country in the months that followed the official announcement, giving sermons and collecting funds at church meetings from Georgia to the northwest frontier. Secretary of State John Quincy Adams pledged the full protection of the United States government for their mission, and even the Stockbridge Indians, late of Massachusetts and now resettled in Ohio, who had been taught by earlier missionaries that they were the descendants of the Ten Lost Tribes, contributed "$5.67 and two gold bracelets for their forefathers in Jerusalem."

On Sunday evening October 31, 1819, a solemn convocation was assembled in Boston's Old South Church to pray for the success of the American missionaries on the eve of their departure. The Reverend Samuel Worcester of Salem, looking out over the tightly packed pews, read the official instructions of the "Prudential Committee" to the two young men who had been selected for the sacred task. They were to make contact with English missionaries at Malta, learn the languages of the countries through which they would travel, investigate the possibilities for the circulation of Bibles and religious tracts, and, most important of all, establish a permanent "station" at Jerusalem.

Then, turning from the congregation to the young men themselves, the Reverend Worcester expressed his own feelings at such an auspicious moment. "From the heights of the Holy Land," he told them, "from Calvary, from Olivet, from Zion—you will take an extended view of the widespread desolations and variegated scenes, presenting themselves on every side to a Christian sensibility; and will survey with earnest attention to the various tribes and classes of fellow beings who dwell in that land and in the surrounding countries. Two grand inquiries ever present in your minds will be 'What good can be done?' and 'By what means?' What can be done for the Jews? What for the Pagans? What for Mohammedans? What for Christians? What for the people of Palestine?"

Before the hushed audience, one of the missionaries, frail, bespectacled Levi Parsons, twenty-one years old, rose to deliver a sermon of his own. His subject was "The Dereliction and Restoration of the Jews" and he struck a responsive chord in the minds of his audience by linking the success of his own mission with the prophecies of Revelation. His colleague, Pliny Fisk, handsome and self-assured, followed with an address more to the point, more a lecture than a sermon, entitled "The Holy Land, an Interesting Field of Missionary Enterprise." But even Fisk was aware of the danger of that enterprise, and he concluded his remarks with an ominous quotation from the Book of Acts: "And now behold I go bound in spirit unto Jerusalem, not knowing the things that shall befall me there."

The path that lay before the two young American missionaries was uncertain. In 1815, the British Church Missionary Society had received discouraging reports from the Holy Land, stating that the work there would be difficult, owing to the fanaticism of the Muslims, the hostility of the Jews, and the tight grip of the Catholic and Orthodox churches on the native Christian population. Beyond such general reports, however, there was little hard information on the present state of the country. Parsons and Fisk's journey would become, therefore, a sacred exploration. Like Seetzen and Burckhardt before them, they would travel through regions rarely visited by westerners and provide new information about the Land of the Bible. Within two days of the service in the Old South Church, aboard the Boston brig *Sally Ann*, they began their long journey eastward, armed only with steamer trunks of religious tracts and Bibles.

Fisk and Parsons arrived in the bustling commercial port of Smyrna in Asia Minor in February 1820, and suddenly saw their prospects for converting the people of "western Asia" in a far more realistic light. Their first task was to learn modern Greek, which would allow them direct access to the members of the Orthodox Church in the Middle East, and after six months of study on the island of Chios, Parsons and Fisk embarked on a wide ranging journey through Asia Minor, to visit the sites of the Seven Churches of Asia, the ancient communities to which John had addressed his Revelation. There was still a great deal to learn before proceeding with the primary objective of their mission, but urged on by increasingly impatient directives from Boston, it was decided that Pliny Fisk should remain in Smyrna to establish a missionary station for the benefit of the local Christians and that Levi Parsons should proceed alone to Jerusalem to assess the difficulties and establish a beachhead.

As the first Protestant missionary ever to visit Jerusalem, Parsons found himself viewed as something of a curiosity. He was received warmly by the Orthodox patriarch of the city. He then toured the Church of the Holy Sepulcher and the other ancient shrines, distributed tracts, and made numerous contacts among the native population in the hope of "rekindling the flame of primitive piety on the crumbling altars of a long corrupted Christianity." Few of those contacts, however, produced the desired results. Even the Orthodox priests with whom Parsons was lodged apparently felt so unthreatened by his preaching that on his departure from the city, their patriarch cordially wished him farewell and expressed the hope that he would soon come again.

It was not to be. The rigors of his sojourn in the Holy Land had severely weakened Parsons' health, and after returning to Smyrna in the winter of 1822 he died, leaving Pliny Fisk to carry on the work alone. Fisk quickly abandoned his activities in Smyrna and sailed to Malta, where English missionaries were already well established. It was from Malta that Fisk sent urgent word to Boston for the immediate dispatch of more missionary workers, and within a few months gained the services of the Reverend Jonas King, a fellow graduate of the Andover Theological Seminary, who had been studying oriental languages in Paris. Then, late in 1823, the American missionary effort was further augmented by the arrival of Isaac Bird and William Goodell, and their wives, who established a new station at the port of Beirut.

After a preliminary visit to Jerusalem, Fisk and Bird staked out a permanent residence in the city, hired a deacon from the Orthodox community to serve as their Arabic teacher, and began the wholesale distribution of tracts and Bibles. This time, however, the Americans' work aroused serious opposition. Protestantism was not an officially recognized religion within the Ottoman Empire, and while the brief visit of Levi Parsons to Jerusalem had gone more or less unnoticed, the establishment of a permanent American missionary station posed a threat to the traditional religious status quo.

When word reached the Vatican through its representatives in the Holy Land that Protestant missionaries had arrived in the country and had begun distributing Bibles and tracts there, Pope Leo XII issued an angry declaration condemning their work and forbidding all native Catholics to read their heretical works or scriptural translations. The strictures of the Vatican soon had their echo in Constantinople as well, where Sultan Mahmud II issued a decree forbidding the circulation of all foreign Bibles and psalters within his domains, in order to prevent what was in his view potentially dangerous religious unrest among the Christian minorities. For Fisk and Bird, this meant trouble. The official Ottoman policy eventually resulted in their arrest in Jerusalem, and the seizure of their literature. Although the men were quickly released through the intervention of the British vice-consul in Jaffa, the battle lines had been drawn. It seemed, in Protestant eyes, that Pope and Sultan were in league against them. The hopes of the New England missionary effort in Palestine were dealt yet another blow in the autumn of 1825, when Pliny Fisk, on his way from Jerusalem to Beirut, was ambushed by bandits; he never recovered from his wounds.

With the second of the original two missionaries dead, and the newer recruits left without a leader, it was felt prudent to transfer all activities to the port of Beirut, where the presence of a British consulate and a large cosmopolitan community could ensure the Americans' personal safety. The missionaries established a church and school there, and continued with the distribution of Bibles and religious tracts. The Holy Land itself would have to wait. It was now clear that the real enemy was not the ignorance or superstition of the people, but the vested interests of the Catholic and Orthodox churches.

The Napoleonic invasion of Egypt and Palestine had been only the first chapter in the long chronicle of the Ottoman Empire's nineteenth-century woes. By the eighteen-twenties, a national uprising threatened to overthrow Ottoman rule in Greece, where rebels, inspired not only by the example of the French Revolution but also by the romantic obsessions of European antiquarians and classical scholars, formed an independent Greek government. European volunteers streamed into the country to join the rebel militia, engaging the troops of the sultan in a series of bloody battles. The war went badly for the Turks, whose poorly paid and poorly fed soldiers could not cope with the fiery passion of the Greeks, and the sultan was forced into the humiliating position of having to ask for assistance from one of his vassals, Mehmet Ali, the pasha of Egypt.

The arrival of the Egyptian fleet in Greek waters turned the tide of the hostilities, but the brutality of the Turkish counterattack, however successful in terms of enemy soldiers killed and territory recaptured, mortally damaged the sultan's chances for victory. One by one, convinced they were defending a Christian nation against Turkish barbarity, the nations of Europe rushed to the side of the Greek rebels. In 1827, the European powers presented an ultimatum to the sultan to acknowledge the independence of the Greeks or face the consequences of his refusal. Stubbornly determined to maintain the integrity of his empire at any cost, Mahmud II refused—then watched helplessly as his entire fleet and the fleet of the Egyptian pasha were destroyed by a combined European armada at the Battle of Navarino.

The European intervention in Greece had immediate effects on the American missionaries who still clung to their small foothold in Lebanon. The disintegration of Ottoman authority and the arrival of a Greek fleet, which shelled the port of Beirut, brought every westerner under suspicion both of the Turkish officials and of the mobs that roamed unchallenged through the streets. In 1827, the American mission house was itself besieged for a time, and by the following year, conditions in Beirut had become so dangerous that the remaining New England missionaries agreed to be evacuated aboard an Austrian ship to the relatively safe haven of Malta. The mission to Jerusalem was officially "suspended." Yet

the religious imperative for the further exploration and eventual transformation of the Holy Land remained as strong as ever.

Biding their time in the company of the English missionaries in Malta,
the Americans prepared for an eventual return to the Land of the Bible.
The prohibition against the importation of foreign Bibles could be
evaded by printing Protestant works locally in the Middle East, and with
the arrival of an experienced printer from Boston, they began to stockpile
a wide array of religious literature for later distribution. Since translations into Arabic would be required to reach an even wider audience of
potential converts, another graduate of the Andover Theological Seminary, a young man named Eli Smith, was sent out from Boston to begin
a period of travel, exploration, and linguistic training.

The international difficulties of the Ottoman Empire eventually
played into the hands of the American missionaries. In 1821, the pasha
of Egypt, outraged that the destruction of his fleet for the defense of the
sultan had not earned him a sizable reward, marched his armies northward from the Sinai with a speed and determination that Napoleon himself might have envied, and wrested the provinces of Syria and Palestine
from the sultan's grasp, easing the restrictions set up by the Ottoman
authorities. Once again, the American missionaries returned to Jerusalem
to take up their sacred work.

Eli Smith's efforts in learning the languages and customs of the Middle East were progressing admirably, but the ideal of missionary exploration in the Holy Land would need yet another protagonist before it could
truly claim a victory. A decade earlier, in the autumn of 1821, an unassuming young scholar from Connecticut had arrived at the Andover
Theological Seminary in Massachusetts, training ground for the American Board of Commissioners for Foreign Missions. Although he had
come for work quite apart from the missionary restoration of the Holy
Land, he would, in cooperation with Eli Smith, eventually pave the way
for one of its greatest triumphs.

❖ 5 ❖

The Evolution of a Dream

EDWARD ROBINSON AND THE
BIRTH OF BIBLICAL
ARCHEOLOGY,
1821–1842

Edward Robinson was born in Southington, Connecticut, in 1793, son of a stern Congregationalist minister who had given up the pulpit for the responsibilities of running a large, prosperous farm. Despite his father's practical turn of mind, Robinson showed an exceptional interest in books and learning from an early age, and by his late teens it had become clear that he had no interest whatever in spending his life farming the harsh New England soil. After working for several years as a schoolteacher and apothecary, Robinson was able to persuade his father to entrust his future to an uncle who was on the faculty of Hamilton College in upstate New York. At Hamilton, Robinson proved his brilliance, showing an outstanding aptitude for both Greek and mathematics. Upon his graduation he was himself appointed to the faculty.

There seemed to be no bounds to Robinson's talent for success. Marrying well and wealthily, he no longer needed the meager salary of his teaching position and was able to retire to pursue his private studies at home. There were few classical scholars of Robinson's caliber in the new nation of the United States, and when he was unexpectedly widowed at age twenty-seven, Robinson found himself with a large inheritance and an unrestricted future. After several years of private study, he felt himself ready to publish his own revised translation of Homer's *Iliad,* and it was for this purpose that he sold his late wife's farm in upstate New York and made his way to the Andover Theological Seminary in Massachusetts, the most suitable place, he thought (considering his own strict Congregationalist upbringing), to engage in a serious academic endeavor.

Andover soon proved to be something less than the island of scholarly tranquillity that Robinson had hoped. The Andover Seminary was on the front lines of an intense religious controversy within New England itself. Even before the American Revolution, the dangerous specter of liberalism had begun to undermine the granite-like theological foundations laid down by the Puritan fathers. An influential group of Boston Unitarians had attacked the traditional leadership of the New England church, and began to examine both ritual and Scripture with a decidedly revisionist approach, analyzing and rejecting much of the traditional dogma of Puritanism, which to their minds had become outdated and empty.

To the conservative ministers of the outlying towns of New England, whose faith was grounded in the unquestioning observance of traditional ritual, such views were nothing less than heresy; if one part of the Scripture or liturgy were to be discarded, then the whole could well be suspect, and that was a thought that could not be countenanced. Unfortunately for the conservatives, however, the Unitarians had powerful support in Boston, which enabled them to appoint a liberal professor to the chair of divinity at Harvard College in 1803. For the conservatives, this was a declaration of war. Removing themselves, their support, and their sons from Harvard, they founded a rival seminary at Andover. The new conservative school would provide both manpower for missions all over the world and a conservative defense against the heretical liberal attack at home.

Soon after Robinson arrived at Andover and began work on the *Iliad,* he fell under the influence of the Reverend Moses Stuart, one of the most charismatic and influential conservative theologians of his day. Stuart was greatly impressed with Robinson's self-taught linguistic achievements and his iron self-discipline in the decipherment of ancient texts, and he suggested that it might make an interesting experiment for Robinson to use the same techniques that he had employed in his Greek translations in the study of the Bible.

Needless to say, the experiment worked. Robinson so completely mastered the grammar of ancient Hebrew in just two years that Stuart wholeheartedly recommended his appointment as an instructor at the seminary. In Robinson, Stuart believed, he had found the perfect conservative scholar to refute the blasphemous Bible criticism of the liberals in Cambridge.

Unfortunately, the resources of Andover were not sufficient, in Stuart's view, for the complete education of his protégé, and in 1826 he arranged for Robinson to further his Biblical studies in Europe. In the great centers of learning at the universities of Paris, Göttingen, Halle, and Berlin, such scholars as Silvestre de Sacy and Wilhelm Gesenius were making great advances in the analysis of ancient texts by the classification of grammatical forms and the study of comparative linguistics. Although the theological attitudes of European Biblical scholars—who regarded Scripture as little more than an interesting ancient document—made the liberalism of New England Unitarians seem downright conservative, Stuart believed that Robinson could use the revolutionary European techniques to validate the authenticity of the Bible.

Robinson spent four years in Europe, gaining for himself not only a traditional European education but also a German professor's daughter for his second wife. By 1830, his period of training was complete, and he returned to Andover to wage theological war. Gaining the chair of professor of sacred literature, he became the moving force behind a conservative academic journal called *The American Biblical Repository*. As a counterweight to the numerous liberal periodicals, the *Repository* fearlessly and confidently defended the literal accuracy of the Bible, utilizing, on the one hand, the reports of Eli Smith and other missionary explorers to confirm its geographical details and, on the other, Robinson's own textual analyses to clarify many obscure and hitherto misunderstood passages.

Robinson's reputation quickly spread beyond his conservative readership, and in 1837 he was recognized as one of the leading Biblical authorities in America and offered the great honor of appointment as the first professor of biblical literature at the new Union Theological Seminary in New York City. For most scholars, such an appointment would be seen as the crowning achievement of a distinguished career, yet Robinson himself was troubled about his own future prospects in his chosen field of scholarship. Despite his years of training and study, despite the dozens of articles and treatises he had written on Biblical geography, he felt deficient, in that he had never been to Palestine himself.

In 1832, he had spent some time at Andover with Eli Smith, then on home leave from the Beirut mission. Smith had fired Robinson's imagination with the great prospects for Palestinian exploration under the current Egyptian occupation. Now, to the immense gratification of Union Theological Seminary, Robinson accepted the appointment to its faculty, but countered with some terms of his own. He asked that the beginning of his tenure be delayed for three or four years so that he could pursue the one objective in his career that had eluded him so far. He would take up Eli Smith's offer of cooperation and assistance and travel to Palestine to see for himself that ancient and holy land.

.   .   .

By 1837, the former Ottoman provinces of Palestine had been under the control of the Egyptian pasha, Mehmet Ali, for six years. During that time, the pasha and his son Ibrahim had ruled the country strictly. Official state monopolies controlled all commerce, the administration was reformed, and for the first time a large measure of public security was established along the formerly bandit-ridden roads and caravan routes. Although the people of Palestine bridled at the changes and even rose up in a short-lived revolt in 1834, a flood of western travelers took advantage of the improved conditions to add yet more knowledge to the western understanding of the Land of the Bible. During the eighteen-thirties, a number of explorers from France, Germany, England, and America had roamed among the ancient sites of Palestine, recording their impressions and theories. None, however, had the background that Edward Robinson possessed, and the achievements of all of them would soon pale by comparison.

Setting sail from Boston, Robinson traveled first to Europe, where he left his wife in Berlin with her family, and at the same time renewed his old university acquaintanceships, proudly announcing his forthcoming trip and soliciting questions on Biblical geography that he might profitably seek to solve. From Germany, he traveled down the Danube to Trieste, and from there, after a brief stop in Athens, on to Cairo, where he had arranged to meet Eli Smith.

The plan of their trip was simple: like the ancient Israelites, they would leave old Egypt and set out across the rugged wilderness of the Sinai peninsula. After visiting the site of Mount Sinai, where Moses had received the Ten Commandments, they would make their way into the Promised Land, spending some time at Jerusalem, traveling northward through Samaria and Galilee, and ultimately conclude their journey at the headquarters of the American mission at Beirut.

The spartan traveling conditions that Robinson and Smith had decided on allowed little in the way of excess baggage. Robinson had brought with him three compasses, a thermometer, telescopes, measuring tapes, Bibles in English and the original languages, and a few books of earlier travelers and explorers in Palestine, as well as a recently written tourist guide entitled *The Modern Traveller*. Since it would be impossible to acquire additional supplies until they arrived in Palestine itself, they hired camels to carry their provisions of rice and biscuits, coffee, tea, sugar, butter, dried apricots, tobacco, wax candles, and charcoal. Their camping equipment included a tent, canvas ground cloths, two old muskets, and two pistols. Most important of all was their official firman, or traveling document, and only slightly less so their Bedouin guides and

Egyptian servants. And when all was assembled to the satisfaction of Eli Smith, the two men set off toward Suez.

After speculating on the exact site of the passage of the Children of Israel through the Red Sea and confidently recording its probable location, Robinson and Smith made their way to the Monastery of St. Catherine in the heart of the Sinai, where they were accommodated by the resident Greek monks. The patriarch of the fifth-century monastery insisted on personally guiding the two Americans to the traditional pilgrims' shrines on Mount Sinai, but the steep climb up the rocky mountainside proved a disappointment to Robinson, who resented the general ignorance and unreliability of his guide's descriptions.

For centuries, Christian pilgrims to Mount Sinai had provided the monastery with its chief source of income, and Robinson could see that the patriarch had a greater interest in encouraging a generous offering than in correctly and critically identifying the historic sites. In place of the grandeur of Sinai's summit that Robinson had always imagined, there was only a dirty, flea-ridden shrine to mark the place of the Giving of the Law a place that Robinson quickly concluded, on the basis of his own knowledge of the Biblical text, could not possibly be the correct location.

From Sinai, Robinson and Smith proceeded to Aqaba with hopes of following the route of the Israelites northward into Transjordan, but once again modern realities interfered. The commander of the Egyptian garrison at Aqaba refused them permission to proceed, warning them of Bedouin wars in the region. Robinson interpreted his refusal as an attempt to exact the payment of a "protection" fee, and stubbornly refused to submit to such blackmail. A change in route was decided on, to take the travelers northeastward through the largely unexplored Negev desert. Robinson tried to make the best of the situation, hoping that he might be able to contribute some reports on previously unknown territory. But the trepidation of their Bedouin guides made the traveling unpleasant and at a pace too rapid for the liking of the Americans.

As they proceeded northward toward the heartland of Palestine, the countryside through which they passed was extremely barren and hot even then, in the early months of the spring season. Arriving at the small well of Bir es-Seba' at the conclusion of the first stage of their journey, Robinson reflected on the great events of history that had taken place at the spot when it was known by its Biblical name of Beersheva. "Here then is the place where the Patriarchs Abraham, Isaac and Jacob often dwelt!" he noted in his journal. "Here Samuel made his sons judges; and from here Elijah wandered out into the southern desert and sat down under it every day and every night. Here was the border of Palestine proper,

which extended from Dan to Beersheva. Over these swelling hills, the
flocks of the Patriarchs once roved by the thousands; where now we found
only a few camels, asses and goats." Entering the more fertile regions of
southern Judea, Robinson and Smith dismissed their quarrelsome Bedouin guides and made their way quickly on horseback to what they hoped
would be a more pleasant visit to the Holy City of Jerusalem.

   The barren countryside around Jerusalem was no more attractive to
Robinson than the land through which he had already passed, but as he
approached the walls of the ancient city, a startling realization came to
him. It was as if the reality of present-day Palestine had suddenly become
insubstantial, nothing more than a mirage; a deeper essence rose up,
billowing into his consciousness and filling it.
   "From earliest childhood," Robinson later wrote, "I had read of and
studied the localities of this sacred spot; now I beheld them with my own
eyes. And they all seemed familiar to me, as if the realization of a former
dream. I seemed to be again among the cherished scenes of childhood,
long unvisited, indeed, but distinctly recollected." The very nature of his
journey to Palestine would soon change completely; no longer a mere
pilgrimage, it would become a history-making exploration. He would
retrieve for the world the lovely vision of the Holy Land, so revered in
his native New England, snatching it, if he must, from its present filth,
degradation, and poverty.
   After entering the Holy City and meeting with a small group of American missionaries, several of whom had been his students at Andover,
Robinson immediately set off, measuring-tape and compass in hand, to
rediscover the forgotten glories of Biblical antiquity in the back alleys and
courtyards of the modern city. He quickly came to the conclusion—like
Edward Daniel Clarke almost forty years before—that the traditional site
of the Holy Sepulcher was nothing more than a "pious superstition."
Unlike Clarke, however, Robinson had a broad background in Biblical
and post-Biblical literature, and he was far more qualified to view all of
the remains of Jerusalem with the eye of a critical observer. Using the
most modern techniques of Biblical scholarship on physical remains,
Robinson attempted to separate fact from fantasy, ancient from modern,
and to compile a comprehensive picture of the walls, gates, water supply,
and topography of Biblical Jerusalem. And the industrious New England
scholar slowly began to piece together, like a vision God-sent for the eyes
of the righteous, the true splendor of the ancient city of Zion.
   Of all the landmarks of Jerusalem that had become familiar to the

western world through the travel books and watercolors of the earlier explorers, the monumental raised platform crowned by the gilded Dome of the Rock and the nearby silver-domed mosque of al-Aqsa had long been viewed as the center point of a unique and momentous antiquity. The Arabic name of this sacred enclosure, Haram ash-Sharif, meaning "the Noble Sanctuary," echoed the Muslim veneration for its sacred rock, site not only of the ancient Jewish Temple, but also of Muhammad's miraculous night journey to heaven.

A huge retaining wall surrounded the Haram, and for centuries Jewish pilgrims had gathered in prayer alongside its western face, mourning over the last remnant of their ancient Temple. Christian tradition also associated the Haram with the site of the Temple of the Jews; the Crusaders had renamed the Dome of the Rock Templum Domini, the Temple of the Lord, and the al-Aqsa mosque Templum Solomonis, the Temple of Solomon, during their short-lived occupation of the city, and the knights stationed there founded the Order of Templars. But since only a handful of non-Muslims had been able to enter its sacred precincts since the end of the Crusades, there was little hard scientific fact to support that identification.

Robinson was forced to restrict his investigations to the exterior features of the Haram, yet he was nonetheless able to make an important discovery. Among the striking yet hitherto unnoticed vestiges of antiquity that he observed were some odd-shaped stones projecting awkwardly from the southwestern face of the Haram wall. Earlier explorers had assumed them to be evidence of some ancient earthquake, but Robinson's familiarity with the writings of the first-century Jewish historian Josephus Flavius enabled him to identify them as the remains of a monumental entrance arch to the Temple, built by King Herod. Within a few years, guides would regularly point out this feature to western tourists as "Robinson's Arch," but it was in fact one of the first of a long series of discoveries leading to Robinson's conclusion that the platform of the Haram ash-Sharif was actually the foundation of the Herodian Temple.

By the beginning of May, Robinson was ready to extend his researches into the surrounding countryside of ancient Judea. Eli Smith's experience and advice were especially crucial now, for although Robinson had been successful in exploring Jerusalem, which was so fully described in the Biblical texts, the little-known countryside would provide a far greater challenge. In the course of his work as a missionary, Eli Smith had compiled a list of the Arabic names of the villages of Palestine, and this would enable Robinson, the Hebrew scholar, to compare their linguistic similarities to the various localities mentioned in the Bible. By matching place and name, Robinson was able to recognize accurate correspondences between the ancient Hebrew and modern Arabic place-names, and to identify dozens of ancient sites: the village of Anata seemed to be none other than the Biblical Anatoth, birthplace of the prophet Jeremiah; Jeba' was Geba, a city of Benjamin; Mukhmas seemed perfect for the site of Saul's battle at Michmas; Beitin was Bethel, stopping place of Abraham and the site of Jacob's famous dream; and el-Jib must undoubtedly be the Biblical Gibeon where Joshua made the sun stand still.

This trial excursion to Judea, Robinson later wrote, "had led us through scenes associated with the names and historic incidents and deeds of Abraham and Jacob, of Solomon and Saul, of Jonathan and David, and Samuel; we had been able to trace out the places where they had lived and acted, and to tread almost in their very footsteps." Robinson's hopes had been fulfilled beyond his wildest expectations. It was possible, he believed, to retrieve the splendor of the past from the midst of a wretched present.

For the next two months, Robinson and Smith's travels took them through nearly the entire land of Palestine, rarely crossing over the same terrain more than once. Descending into the Jordan Valley, they explored En-gedi and Masada and located probable sites for the cursed cities of Sodom and Gomorrah. In the evenings, by the light of the campfire, Robinson and Smith carefully recorded each day's findings in their journals, providing continuous proof of the veracity of geographical descriptions in the Bible.

Traveling northward through the hilly countryside of Samaria, they rediscovered dozens of additional Biblical sites, every day adding more points of interest to the hitherto empty map of Palestine. In Galilee as elsewhere, Robinson avoided the traditional shrines, preferring to explore the remote villages where traces of genuine antiquity might be found. As elsewhere in Palestine, Robinson was able to reconstruct the ancient geography of that region, identifying and recording the remains of ancient churches, synagogues, and Biblical sites.

Following the coast northward past Acre and Tyre, on the twenty-seventh of June the two travelers finally reached Beirut, where they were welcomed into the comfortable headquarters of the American missionary station. Robinson's first journey in the Holy Land had been completed. Unfortunately, his health had been on the decline during the latter part of his travels, and in Beirut a violent attack of fever confined him to bed for several days. Mere illness, however, could not stand in the way of his compiling and publishing the results of his researches. By early July, his health had recovered sufficiently for him to take a steamer to Alexandria, and from there he went back to Berlin, where he hoped to spend some time reviewing the copious notes, sketches, and observations that he had compiled in the Holy Land.

Here, in company with Eli Smith, Robinson gradually realized the importance of their discoveries. In a sense they had successfully superimposed the map of ancient Palestine upon the present map of some backward provinces of the Ottoman Empire, in consequence discovering Palestine's hidden treasure: the hundreds of Biblical sites scattered all across its desolate countryside. The present inhabitants of the country, pending the advances of the American and English missionaries, were hopelessly enslaved in either ignorance or barbarism. Industry was practically nonexistent, and much of the land itself was too barren to be farmed. The real riches of Palestine, Edward Robinson was convinced, lay in the past.

During the year following Robinson and Smith's journey through Palestine, the Egyptian pasha and the Ottoman sultan renewed open warfare. At the decisive Battle of Nezib in the highlands of Asia Minor, the Turkish army was completely routed, leaving the way open for an Egyptian advance to the gates of Constantinople. The sudden death of Sultan Mahmud II further shocked the crumbling empire and brought a frail sixteen-year-old named Abdul Medjid to the throne. Goaded by his hovering ministers, Abdul Medjid vowed to avenge the humiliations inflicted upon him by the Egyptians. But to drive the invaders out of Asia Minor and regain possession of Syria and Palestine, he would be forced to ask for military assistance from the Europeans, whose own territorial ambitions in the area were by now well known.

In the summer of 1841, a combined armada of British, Austrian, and Turkish warships converged off the rocky coast of Acre. Within three days, under merciless shelling, the fortress was taken and its Egyptian occupiers were put to flight. A general rebellion of the Palestinian peasantry against the Egyptian occupation forces raged in the interior of the country, and paved the way for a Turkish invasion from the north. With the help of his European allies, the young sultan was able to destroy the might of Mehmet Ali and regain Palestine once more. The humiliating period of Egyptian occupation was over, but the resumption of Turkish control over the Holy Land would certainly not spell a return to its former isolation.

In 1839, Great Britain had become the first of the western powers to establish a permanent consulate in Jerusalem, and in the years that immediately followed the Ottoman reconquest, France, Prussia, Sardinia, Austria, and Spain were also granted the right of official representation there. For centuries, few westerners had ever been allowed to reside in the Holy City, but now top-hatted European diplomats strolled through the streets of Jerusalem with their native bodyguards, or kawasses, anxious to promote the interests of their respective countries in the Holy Land.

Under the terms of the ancient "capitulations" treaties between the sultan and the various western powers, these consuls were granted a status equal to that of the pasha of the city, with rights to control the legal and administrative affairs of their countrymen within their geographical jurisdiction. But although the French consul could claim the right of "protection" over the local Catholic Church and its possessions, and the Russians could claim similar rights over the possessions of the Orthodox Church, the Protestant nations had no tangible possessions, except for the small establishments of the various missionary societies. In 1839, special permission had been granted by the Egyptians for the construction of an Anglican church on Mount Zion, but it was only in cooperation with the other great Protestant power, Prussia, that the British were able to found a Protestant bishopric in Jerusalem, enabling Protestantism to compete on an equal footing with the older churches in the Holy Land. The Americans, in the meantime, had abandoned all their efforts in Jerusalem, leaving it to the British and the Prussians, in order to concentrate exclusively on Beirut.

In 1841, the year of the Ottoman reconquest of Palestine, Edward Robinson returned to the United States to take up his teaching duties at the Union Theological Seminary, and Eli Smith returned to the mission at Beirut to continue saving souls. But the appearance of their book, *Biblical Researches in Palestine, Mount Sinai, and Arabia Petraea,* suddenly brought them before the attention of the entire Christian world. So great was the excitement over Robinson and Smith's rediscovery of the Biblical geography of Palestine, both in America and in Europe, that one British commentator was moved to speculate that the Hand of Providence might have played a role. "The gratification of their own curiosity was the only motive perhaps of which they were conscious," he wrote. "Little did they think that they were obeying an impulse from on High, and that Jehovah meant them to be witnesses of His truth to the after-ages of the world."

The first Protestant missionaries had tried to save the souls of the native population of the Holy Land, and their more established successors would continue that quest. Robinson and Smith, however, had begun to save the historical soul of Palestine itself.

In 1842, Edward Robinson became the first American to receive the coveted gold medal of the Royal Geographical Society in London. Scientists and geographers, as well as Biblical scholars and clerics, hailed his achievement. And as surely as he had completed a process, Edward Robinson had begun one. The return of Ottoman control to the Land of the Bible would soon bring a wide penetration of the country by the sultan's European allies, and the continued search for Biblical sites and relics would provide a tangible object for that penetration.

The pioneering work of Edward Robinson and Eli Smith had far transcended both missionary goals and the New England battle for the authenticity of the Bible. In their stubborn search for the past, they had laid the groundwork for an entire new scholarly, religious, and political enterprise in the Holy Land. The art and science of Biblical archeology was born.

❖ II ❖

POWER AND PRESTIGE

❖ 6 ❖

Conquering the Wilderness

LIEUTENANT W. F. LYNCH AND THE AMERICAN EXPEDITION TO THE DEAD SEA, 1847-1848

In the two decades that followed the publication of Edward Robinson's researches in the Holy Land, Palestine witnessed an unprecedented flood of western travelers intent on following in the footsteps of the learned American professor and recovering the splendor of the Biblical past. In the eighteen-thirties, regular steamship service reached the port of Jaffa, and by the eighteen-forties, with the beginning of an established tourist industry, a journey to Palestine no longer entailed the hardships and danger common at the start of the century.

The Ottoman reconquest of Palestine marked the opening of a new era in the entire Middle East, and in the wake of the European intervention against Mehmet Ali, western traders and explorers roamed the length and breadth of the rejuvenated Ottoman Empire, mapping, investigating, and seeking out new raw materials and routes of trade for the industrializing world. The resuscitation of Abdul Medjid's crumbling empire had been made possible only at great expense to the sultan, for while England and France continued their traditional rivalry for Suez, the great western powers now sought more than the mere right of passage through the sultan's domains. The Middle East was a potential treasure trove of unexplored resources and strategic outposts, and the once placid halls of the Ottoman bureaucracy in Constantinople, the Sublime Porte, now resounded with the frantic chatter of European ambassadors and commercial agents eagerly bidding for trading concessions, telegraph lines, canals, and railroads—to be built with Ottoman tax revenue by foreign entrepreneurs.

The United States, despite the considerable achievements of individual explorers such as Edward Robinson, was among the last of the major western powers to enter the international scramble for economic advantage in the Middle East. The first American-Ottoman friendship treaty had been signed by President Andrew Jackson and Sultan Mahmud II in 1830, but because the primary interests of the United States still lay in the New World, the tangible results of that agreement were little more than the customary trading privileges and rights of port calls enjoyed by every other commercial power in the Mediterranean. By the time of the Mexican War in 1846, a number of enterprising American cotton growers had established experimental plantations on the outskirts of Constantinople and along the Nile, but though American cotton indeed flourished in the soil of the Middle East, the political realities of the region allowed little room for expansion. An exclusively American trade route would have to be developed through the Middle East to enable the United States to compete with the other great western powers for the lucrative commerce of the Ottoman Empire and the Far East as well. And while France continued to expand its influence in Egypt and the British were showing an increasing interest in the possibility of river transport down the Euphrates to the Persian Gulf, American interest was turned to an intriguing alternative at the very heart of the Fertile Crescent.

As Edward Robinson and the earlier explorers had indicated in their reports, the Holy Land was bisected north to south by a continuous valley containing the Sea of Galilee, the Jordan River, and the Dead Sea. As a natural route of trade running from the Syrian heartland to the Gulf of Aqaba and the Red Sea on the south, it seemed a perfect prospect for the transshipment of goods from the Mediterranean coast to the Indian Ocean. As early as 1816, the disguised agent for the British East India Company, James Silk Buckingham, had traveled to the Holy Land intent on exploring just such a possibility, only to be balked by hostile Bedouin and the rigors of the region's climate.

The Dead Sea, one of the most puzzling and mysterious geological features of Palestine, posed the greatest obstacle to the development of a trade route. There in the hot, dry, and desolate basin, where grotesque mineral formations rose up along the southern coast of a landlocked sea, few sources of fresh water could be found. The greasy, lukewarm waters of the sea itself held no visible life, and its barren, salt-encrusted shores offered little shelter from the wind and sun. In order for the trade route scheme to succeed, these difficult climatic conditions would have to be overcome. And it was necessary, first of all, to prove that the Dead Sea itself was navigable.

In 1835, an Irish adventurer named Christopher Costigan accompanied by a Maltese sailor attempted to sail on the surface of the Dead Sea in midsummer. Their timing was unwise: adrift in an open boat, they quickly exhausted their supply of fresh water and grew weak and drowsy from the relentless heat. Costigan himself lost consciousness, but his companion managed to bring the boat to shore and stumble toward the village of Jericho. After a considerable delay, help finally arrived and Costigan was carried up to Jerusalem, where he died after two days from the lingering effects of severe sunstroke. Costigan's gravestone in the small Protestant cemetery in Jerusalem stood as a stern warning to all other would-be adventurers to beware of the consequences of further exploration of the Dead Sea.

That warning was ignored. In 1847, a contingent of the British Navy under the command of Lieutenant William Molyneux resolved to challenge the Dead Sea once again. Enlarging on the initial object of the Costigan expedition and gaining the financial support of the Royal Geographical Society, Molyneux transported specially constructed boats overland from the Mediterranean to the Sea of Galilee. From that tranquil body of water, he proposed to sail down the entire length of the Jordan River, and from its outlet near Jericho to explore thoroughly the surface and shores of the Dead Sea.

Molyneux and his men succeeded in making their way down almost the entire course of the Jordan, but gradually fell victim to thirst and ultimately to sunstroke. They became an easy target for the marauding Adwan Bedouin who inhabited the region east of the river. Several of the British sailors were killed in a surprise attack. Molyneux himself lasted only a few more months before dying of the effects of a malarial fever. For the time being at least, the Dead Sea was to remain a mystery.

The author of the idea of an American naval expedition to investigate the possibility of a new trade route through the Holy Land, from the Mediterranean to the Red Sea, was a forty-six-year-old navy lieutenant from Virginia named William Francis Lynch. Lynch, while serving in the Mexican War, had taken part in the naval battles along the steep sea cliffs of Vera Cruz, and the success of those operations had encouraged him to contemplate the spread of his nation's glory to even more distant shores. In Lynch's native South, the Bible was as deeply venerated if not as closely scrutinized as in New England, and the excitement over the discoveries of Edward Robinson created a special American enthusiasm for further exploration in the Holy Land. The failure of the earlier Dead Sea explorers served not as a warning but as an irresistible challenge to Lynch, who was convinced that the sailors of the United States could succeed where an impetuous Irish adventurer and a small, poorly armed band of British Jack-tars had failed.

In May 1847, with the harbor and city of Vera Cruz safe in American hands, and Lynch immodestly claiming that "there was nothing left for the Navy to perform," he applied to a fellow Virginian, Secretary of the Navy John Y. Mason, for permission to undertake an official American expedition to the Holy Land. His ostensible object was the circumnavigation and thorough exploration of the Dead Sea with an eye toward opening up a new American route of trade. But there was also another motivation. There in that barren, salty valley, the wicked cities of Sodom and Gomorrah had been destroyed by the Lord. And it was there that Lot's wife had been turned into a pillar of salt. Nowhere else in Palestine did the physical geography so accurately mirror the surrealistic descriptions of the Bible. And it would be there, Lynch believed, that brave American sailors would prove their ingenuity and devotion in showing that the Bible could indeed be believed, and followed even in these sadly diminished latter days.

On July 31, 1847, Lynch received word that his application for a United States expedition to the Dead Sea had been enthusiastically approved by the War Department in Washington, and traveled to the Brooklyn Navy Yard to take command of the U.S. store ship *Supply* (formerly named, appropriately enough, *Crusader*). The plan proposed by Lynch followed closely the route taken by Molyneux earlier in the year: the explorers would transport boats from the Mediterranean coast to the Sea of Galilee, and from there they would row down the Jordan to the Dead Sea.

In order to prevent damage to the boats by the rocky rapids of the Jordan and the corrosive chemicals of the Dead Sea, Lynch ordered that one of them, the *Fanny Mason,* was to be fashioned from copper, and the other, the *Fanny Skinner,* from galvanized iron. And to facilitate their overland transport, Lynch had special wagons built, complete with custom-made harnesses for the draft horses that would pull them. To man the boats, he selected ten "young, muscular, native-born Americans, from each of whom I exacted the pledge to abstain from all intoxicating beverages during the whole course of the expedition." One of the seamen had the responsibility of supervising the dismantling and assembly of the boats. Lynch had him instructed in the use of the most modern types of explosives, "should such a process become necessary to ensure the transportation of the boats across the mountains of Galilee and Judea."

When the New York *Herald* got word of the proposed expedition, it loudly condemned the tremendous expenditure of taxpayers' money on a "pleasure trip." Lynch was satisfied that the dangers and obstacles to be surmounted in the treacherous passage down the Jordan Valley would make it anything but that. In addition to the climate and the physical difficulties of transporting the boats overland, a potential threat from the omnipresent Bedouin would also have to be considered, and Lynch made sure that the men under his command would be able to repulse any attack. To this end, the expedition was supplied with a blunderbuss, fourteen carbines with bayonets, four revolvers, ten pistols equipped with Bowie knives, ammunition belts, and swords for each of the officers. In November, after a final conference at Union Theological Seminary with Dr. Robinson himself, Lynch directed the crew of the *Supply* to weigh anchor and head out into the open sea.

According to Lynch's formal orders, the *Supply* was to proceed first to Asia Minor to obtain an official firman for the expedition from the Ottoman authorities in Constantinople. The customary procedure for the acquisition of such a firman was to apply through diplomatic channels and wait patiently for a response, but Lynch was not content to operate in the customary manner. He arrived in the port of Smyrna in mid-February 1848, left his crew aboard the *Supply* and journeyed alone to Constantinople, where he appeared at the gate of the imperial palace in full dress uniform, accompanied by an interpreter from the American Embassy.

Here he was ushered into a lavish reception hall, served coffee and tobacco by black slaves in billowing silk costumes, and after only a short delay—for he again adamantly challenged protocol by refusing to remove his officer's sword—was escorted down a long marbled corridor to the private salon of the sultan.

His Imperial Highness Abdul Medjid was seated behind a small desk, dressed in a military uniform of the latest European style. But despite the air of opulence and splendor that enveloped the palace, its master was no more than a sickly young boy. Abdul Medjid sat expressionless as Lynch stepped forward to present him with some gifts in the name of President Polk, including an expensively bound collection of lithographs showing the life and manners of the North American Indians. The young sultan leafed through the heavy pages with a vague lack of interest. "They exhibit the high state of advancement and science in your country," he said at length. The formalities of the visit were quickly concluded. Lynch

received his firman, and quickly left the palace to rejoin his men at
Smyrna and set off at once for the Holy Land.

At Beirut, the United States expedition was greeted far more enthusiastically. Eli Smith and the staff of the American missionary station
showed their eagerness to promote their country's endeavors in the Land
of the Bible, assisting Lynch in obtaining the services of a native guide
and introducing him to a local merchant who might be able to arrange
for the acquisition of pack animals. The merchant reacted to the idea of
the American sailors' journey with amusement, but Lynch had no time or
inclination for argument, and struck a bargain for horses to be supplied
en route. Then the *Supply* weighed anchor again and plowed through the
sea toward its final destination, the small village of Haifa at the foot of
the Biblical Mount Carmel.

Once there, Lynch ordered the men to unload the metal boats and
provisions through the surf, establishing a campsite close to the beach.
The mechanic supervised the assembly of the metal boats and wagons,
and sentries were posted around the perimeter of the camp to keep away
curious onlookers.

"For the first time, perhaps," Lynch wrote as he surveyed the encampment, "the American flag has been raised in Palestine. May it be the
harbinger of regeneration to a now hapless people." Someday, Lynch
hoped, this small village would bustle with the activity of merchant ships
and modern port facilities at the head of the new trade route he would
pioneer. As a missionary of the secular faith of science and commerce,
Lynch had arrived in the Holy Land to spread not only the benefits of
prosperity but the light of national restoration as well. As the *Supply*
sailed away with a skeleton crew and orders to return to Beirut to pick
up Lynch and his men at the conclusion of the expedition, they were now
left alone with their dreams in an alien land. And the conditions of that
alien land would soon leave the Americans dependent on their own
ingenuity.

In the middle of their first night, Lynch and his men were roused from
their sleep by the arrival of the draft horses from Acre, and the gathering
light of daybreak provided proof that the Americans had been cheated.
The expensive harnesses so carefully designed back in the United States
hung loosely over the horses' bony frames, and when Lynch ordered that
the animals be hitched to the wagons, no amount of beating or shouting
could persuade them to pull the heavy metal boats. Under the circumstances, the expedition would never even leave the coast. Frustrated and

angry, Lynch pulled on his officer's boots, dressed quickly in his formal uniform and sword, and rode off to Acre to seek redress from the pasha of the city, through whom the Beirut merchant had arranged the deal for the pack animals.

At Acre, Said Bey the pasha placidly regarded the American officer's fury. It was harvest time, he explained, and the animals were the best that could be obtained. Besides, the pasha informed Lynch, he had received ominous word of Bedouin raids in the area around the Dead Sea, and any attempt by the Americans to travel through that region might prove extremely unwise. As if to remove further doubts, the pasha invited Lynch to return to his residence later in the evening to hear the testimony of a local Bedouin leader named Aqil Agha, who dutifully recounted the recent incursions of the Bani-Sakhr clan with whom he was well acquainted. The pasha amiably informed Lynch that the only way he could in all good conscience allow him to pass through that region would be with an armed guard of the pasha's own cavalry. And the price of that favor would be eight hundred American dollars.

Lynch was outraged by this suggestion and warned Said Bey that the blame for the failure of his mission would rest squarely with him. Lynch reminded the pasha that his expedition bore an imperial firman and that he was duty-bound to lend every assistance. The Americans were well armed and could defend themselves; they were willing to pay for draft animals, but not a single cent for "protection." The meeting was at an end. As the principals adjourned to an outer courtyard, Aqil Agha warned Lynch through an interpreter that the Bedouin around the Dead Sea would eat the Americans alive. If that was the case, Lynch answered coldly, "They'll find us difficult of digestion."

Lynch was determined to find suitable transport for the boats even without the help of the pasha. Camels, he learned the following day, could be hired in profusion from the inhabitants of the surrounding countryside, and he ordered the sailors to alter the expensive harnesses while he bargained for the animals. Hitched to the wagons loaded with the metal boats, the camels at first refused to move, but after repeated beatings by the sailors and the native drivers they slowly got under way. Despite the derisive jeers of some of the pasha's supporters, Lynch took satisfaction from the experiment. He had solved the problem of the wagon teams. There still remained the distressing problem of the Bedouin war.

Leaving Acre and galloping ahead of his gawky caravan, Lynch proceeded alone to the village where he had heard that Aqil Agha could be found. He had correctly sensed the tension that existed between the

Ottoman pasha and the Bedouin leader, and Lynch offered Aqil a handsome subsidy to escort the American expedition through the Jordan
Valley in direct defiance of the pasha's warnings. Aqil apparently admired
Lynch's doggedness, if nothing else, and a deal was quickly struck. Aqil
and his men would accompany the Americans and negotiate for safe
passage with the various Bedouin clans along the proposed route. And
with the arrival of the caravan from Acre, Aqil and Lynch took their place
at its head. The United States expedition to the Dead Sea now took on
an odd yet noble appearance. Behind Aqil and Lynch were the camels
carrying the American sailors, with Aqil's Bedouin walking beside them.
At the rear of the procession came the shiny metal boats, pulled along
by more camels, with—what else?—small American flags fluttering from
their sterns.

Faithful to the original plan, the caravan made its way eastward to the
steep cliffs that surrounded the Sea of Galilee. The sailors unloaded the
camels and with great difficulty lowered the boats and other supplies
down to the level of the seashore with ropes. Temporary headquarters
were established in the lakeside town of Tiberias, and as the men prepared and calibrated the surveying instruments and barometers, Lynch
toured the town with Aqil, considering the challenges that lay ahead. On
the basis of discussions with a local boatman who had accompanied the
ill-fated Molyneux expedition, Lynch decided to split his own expedition
into two parties. One of the junior officers, Lieutenant John Dale, would
lead an overland caravan parallel to the course of the river, thus relieving
the boats of the necessity of carrying the heavier supplies. In the event
of any attack on the boats, two rapid discharges of the blunderbuss
mounted on the bow of the *Fanny Mason* would summon the land caravan
to proceed immediately to the riverbank with guns loaded and ready. And
in an effort to lighten the loads of the metal boats yet further, Lynch
purchased an old Arab fishing boat to carry the excess supplies. In this
capacity it was christened by the sailors *Uncle Sam*.

In the week that followed, Lynch and his men drifted down the unexpectedly narrow and winding course of the Jordan aboard the *Fanny
Mason* and the *Fanny Skinner*, sketching the scenery, taking botanical and
geological specimens, and making an accurate map of the river's course.
High on the bluffs above the river, the land caravan proceeded apace. As
the flotilla and caravan approached the site of the attack on Molyneux's
party, all hands became edgy despite the protective presence of Aqil and
his men. At night, when the Americans beached their boats on the river-

bank and established their campsites, their security precautions took on the character of a scene from the American frontier. "It was a strange sight," wrote Lynch. "Collected near us lay all the camels, for security against a sudden surprise; while in every direction, but ever in close proximity were scattered lances and smouldering fires, and bundles of garments, beneath each of which was a slumbering Arab, with his long gun by his side."

But no attack ever came. By April 27, the flotilla had reached the green oasis of Jericho. Beyond, to the south, lay the barren mountains surrounding the Dead Sea. The first part of the expedition had been successfully completed. In the course of the previous eight days, the United States expedition had traveled nearly the entire length of the Jordan River and had mapped it accurately for the first time. No longer would the river be known strictly as an element in pious church hymns. Every turn and natural feature had been measured and recorded by Lynch's men.

Unfortunately, the results of that mapping clearly indicated how chimerical the trade route scheme really was. To cover a direct distance of only sixty miles, the Americans had actually traveled more than two hundred; and in many places the tortuous course of the shallow stream made the passage of even rowboats difficult. Yet Lynch, ever the duty-bound officer, was still committed to accomplishing the complete program of his expedition. Assembling the preliminary scientific findings and dispatching a report to Secretary Mason from Jericho, Lynch sent off Aqil and his men to bargain safe passage with the Bani-Sakhr Bedouin and ordered his own men to break camp, sail down to the outlet of the river, and move out upon the smooth, greasy surface of the Dead Sea.

Aboard the *Fanny Mason,* Lynch sailed southward along the western shore of the sea, making a preliminary reconnaissance of the coastline. Noting the presence of thick clumps of vegetation at various points, Lynch correctly presumed them to be evidence of freshwater springs, and at the end of the first day, he established a campsite at the Biblical spring of En-gedi, patriotically yet incongruously naming it "Camp Washington." It was to serve as the headquarters for the exploration of the entire region.

Although the plan for the trade route was by now obviously impractical, there was much scientific data for the expedition to gather about the Dead Sea and its immediate environs. The sea itself was only forty-five miles long and only about ten miles wide at its widest point, but there had never been a successful attempt made to determine its depth, map its coastline, and discover the geological reasons for its unusual salinity. In order to achieve at least these basic scientific goals, Lieutenant Dale in the *Fanny Skinner* began to take depth soundings at the northern end of the sea, while Lynch and the others continued southward along the western shore to begin the meticulous mapping.

All was going according to plan, but from the very start the American sailors, exhausted by the long trip down the Jordan and the oppressive temperatures, began to show distressing symptoms. Unused to the sulfurous fumes that perpetually hung over the surface of the water, they began to experience headaches and drowsiness that hindered the strenuous work of rowing. The heat of the daylight hours often grew so intense that buttons and rifles became too hot to touch, and the interminable drowsiness that had come over the men seemed to dull their reactions and lull them into a walking stupor.

One day, out in the center of the sea, under the burning rays of the early summer sun, the men of the *Fanny Mason* began to drop off to sleep in the hot shade of the canvas sail. Lynch's own mind began to wander in the salt haze, bringing forth dreamy, warm visions of slumber and death. He imagined himself to be none other than Charon of Greek mythology, faithfully ferrying the bodies of the dead across the River Styx to their new home in the underworld. A growing horror gripped him in his hallucinations: he feared that he would surely die, along with his men, if he could not regain full control of himself. Shaking off the weight of his drowsiness, Lynch roused his sleeping sailors and ordered them to pull down the sail and begin to row. Only the physical action of the oars, he believed, could save them from the same fate that took the life of Costigan. "Prudence urged us to proceed no further," wrote Lynch, "but to stop before some disaster overtook us; but the thought of leaving any part of our work undone was too painful and I resolved to persevere."

Persevere Lynch did, for the southern basin of the Dead Sea still remained uncharted. Proceeding along the southern shore, the sickly Americans explored ruins which they believed to be the sites of the ancient cities of Sodom and Gomorrah and eventually made contact with a messenger from Aqil, who led them up through the mountains of Moab to the town of Kerak, an ancient fortress of the Crusaders. After a brief stay there, during which the sailors were given a temporary respite from the insistent prodding of their commanding officer, they returned to the boats and mapped the strange peninsula on the eastern shore, naming its two projecting "capes" after their unfortunate predecessors, Costigan and Molyneux. One more trip, to the Herodian fortress of Machaerus, and the circumnavigation of the Dead Sea was completed. With the assistance of Aqil Agha and at the cost of considerable suffering by the American sailors, the United States expedition had assembled a large body of scientific information about the geology, hydrology, zoology, and archeology of this inhospitable region. Its oppressive climate, they found, was due to the fact that it was the lowest point on earth, nearly thirteen hundred feet below the level of the Mediterranean. And the lack of an outlet to the south and the effects of evaporation explained the incredible saltiness of its waters.

Leaving a raft bearing an American flag moored in the center of the sea, Lynch and his men disassembled the boats and traveled overland to Jerusalem, where they were received warmly by the British consul and visited the various holy shrines of the city. All that was left was an investigation of the sources of the Jordan River, so Lynch dispatched his trusted aide, Lieutenant Dale, and a small surveying party to explore the swampy area to the north of the Sea of Galilee.

Lynch and the rest of his men traveled to Nazareth, where they bade farewell to Aqil at a festive Bedouin celebration. But when he rejoined the survey party, Lynch was shocked to see that the ravages of malaria had spread among the men and disabled them. Dale himself had fallen ill, and it was only with the greatest difficulty that they were able to travel to Beirut, where they hoped that Eli Smith and the American missionaries could provide the sick sailors with proper medical attention. But by the time of their arrival, Lieutenant Dale's fever was too far advanced, and the French doctor whom Eli Smith summoned could do nothing for him. His death a few days later dramatized the cost of his commander's scientific curiosity.

In December 1848, thirteen months after its original departure from New York, the U.S.S. *Supply* anchored off Hampton Roads, Virginia. The United States expedition to the Jordan River and the Dead Sea had successfully completed its mission, and Lynch submitted his final report to the Secretary of the Navy. Little was ever heard again of the proposal for the American trade route through the Holy Land, although Lynch himself remained an outspoken advocate of it, apparently overlooking the conditions which he had endured; in 1860 he published a pamphlet entitled *Commerce and the Holy Land.* The cause for which he spoke out— the extension and prosperity of the economy of the American South—was the cause for which he ultimately fought, commanding Confederate naval forces at Vicksburg and later along the Potomac.

Apart from the failure of its commercial hopes, Lynch's mission had a lasting effect. The publication of Lynch's personal account of the expedition and the appearance of a book by another member of the crew aroused intense public interest in the further exploration of Palestine. Transcending the religious preoccupations of the missionaries or the Biblical scholars, the drama of the struggles of the American sailors in the Land of the Bible sprang vividly to life in the popular consciousness.

The Biblical wilderness quickly became an object of great appeal to the western world, and on both sides of the Atlantic the popular interest in the Holy Land reached a fever pitch in the years that followed. In 1851, the Broadway Georama in New York City responded to the public demand by presenting a "moving painting" by the renowned panoramist John Banvard entitled *Pilgrimage to Jerusalem and the Holy Land* in which the audience watched in rapt amazement as scenes of Biblical sites, the Dead Sea, fierce Bedouin, and the rugged landscape were unrolled before their very eyes.

In 1852, the illustrated edition of *The Land and the Book,* a detailed travelogue of Palestine written by an American missionary in Beirut, sold tens of thousands of copies all over the English-speaking world. And by the following decade, no less an expert in popular taste than P. T. Barnum had dispatched the director of his American Museum on a journey to the Holy Land to collect Biblical antiquities and curiosities for public display.

A new wave of Palestine exploration was under way, and among the adventurous travelers who set off for the Holy Land in the years that followed the Lynch mission were some of the most prominent figures in the Protestant world. Dr. Robinson returned to Palestine in 1852 to rejoin Eli Smith in more researches; the dean of Westminster, A. P. Stanley, traveled through the country and compiled a comprehensive work on Biblical geography; and the venerable Dr. William Smith, rising to the occasion in the compilation of his enormous *Dictionary of the Bible,* incorporated many of the latest discoveries amid the theological definitions and articles on church history.

The rediscovery of the long-forgotten regions of Palestine where many of the most famous chapters of Biblical history had been written was beginning to take on a religious significance of its own. Lynch had discovered a way for the Protestant world to stake a claim of its own in the Holy Land; the wilderness could be conquered and its Biblical past revealed.

❖ 7 ❖

For the Glory of France

LOUIS-FELICIEN DE SAULCY
AND THE TOMBS
OF THE KINGS,
1850-1863

Eight miles to the south of Jerusalem lay the small town of Bethlehem, famous for the fine work of its craftsmen in mother-of-pearl and olive-wood, and for its Church of the Nativity, built originally by the Emperor Constantine in the fourth century to commemorate and enshrine the place where Jesus was born. Never, in all the centuries of Christian pilgrimage to Bethlehem, had the authenticity of the site been questioned, and the competition between the various Christian sects for possession and maintenance of the lucrative trade in religious articles and offerings connected with it led to a complicated scheme of partition enforced by the Ottoman administration.

The priests of the Eastern Orthodox, or "Greek," Church had held title to the basilica itself since 1672; but the Catholics, or "Latins," had been granted the right to construct an adjoining church of their own, with rights of free passage through the Greek-held basilica to the sacred grotto beneath it. It was there, according to the time-honored tradition, that the Manger had been located, and to mark the precise spot, a silver star had been set in stone. King Louis XV of France, as official protector of the Catholic Church in the Holy Land, had been permitted to donate the star in 1717 and, most galling to the Greeks and their own Russian protectors, that silver star bore the fleur-de-lis.

On Christmas Eve 1847, the long-standing antagonism of the two sides finally flared into open fighting. The decline of religious interest in France and the domestic crises of the final days of King Louis-Philippe apparently convinced the Greeks that the time was ripe to expand their own claims to the exclusive possession of the holy shrine. On this night, as the Catholics began their yearly midnight procession from their adjoining church into the basilica, they found that the Greeks had walled up their only route of access. The Catholic priests began to tear away the freshly mortared partition and Greek priests suddenly appeared to stop them. Bloody brawling soon broke out all over the basilica.

In the course of the melee, a single Catholic monk managed to slip into the sacred grotto, where he discovered, much to his horror, that the silver star had been pried up and removed. This ecclesiastical larceny was immediately interpreted as a serious challenge to the Catholic claims over the sacred shrines not only of Bethlehem but of all the Holy Land. As Christmas morning dawned, the French consul in Jerusalem arrived to defend Catholic rights. A renewed struggle for the holy sites had begun.

The altercation at the Church of the Nativity was likewise a clear challenge not only to French Catholic interests but to French political interests as well. French prestige in Palestine had for centuries been a barometer of French prestige in the entire Middle East, and the agreement concluded more than a millennium before between Charlemagne and Caliph Harun ar-Rashid had set the precedent for the French claims of protection over the holy sites. In the wake of the Crusades, which had understandably left a lasting impression on the local population, all westerners had come to be known as Franks. And now that France was emerging from the aftereffects of the Napoleonic defeats to claim its place in the struggle for economic advantage in the Middle East, it once again recognized the importance of its claims to the holy shrines. Not only could France counteract Russian territorial ambitions in the Ottoman Empire by reasserting those claims, but it could also firmly establish French islands of influence in Palestine. The matter of the stolen star at Bethlehem, therefore, quickly became an issue of international diplomacy, and after the establishment of the Second Republic in 1848, the French ambassador at Constantinople, General Jacques Aupick, was instructed to press the issue in continuing direct appeals to the sultan.

Christian discord at the holy places was in itself nothing new in the Holy Land. But in addition to their competition with the Greeks, the French also had to contend with the new threat from the Protestant world. The rise of Biblical archeology had brought a new wave of British and American penetration into the Holy Land, and had also placed in jeopardy the traditional shrines themselves. For from the very dawn of Protestant exploration in Palestine an increasing conviction had been taking hold in scholarly circles that the pilgrim sites so adamantly defended by the power of France were, simply put, frauds.

Edward Robinson had not even bothered to enter the Church of the Holy Sepulcher in Jerusalem. On the basis of his own knowledge of the Biblical descriptions, any church standing within the city walls, where no Jewish tomb could possibly have been located, could not be the authentic tomb of Christ; the Gospels explicitly state that the sepulcher was *outside* the city walls. Robinson did not suggest an alternative to the traditional site, but his skepticism convinced other Protestant scholars that it could be found. And if the true location of Christ's tomb and the various other sacred places could be determined, the fierce competition of the Greeks and Latins for possession of the traditional sites would be robbed of all significance.

In the eighteen-forties, many British, American, and German travelers had come to Palestine in search of the actual sites of the Gospel events and, by the end of the decade, had formulated a number of ingenious theories with regard to their locations within Jerusalem. And in 1849, the British consul in Jerusalem, James Finn, established the Jerusalem Literary Society to bring together all those involved in the scientific study of Biblical archeology for regular meetings to discuss their latest theories and discoveries.

In other parts of the Middle East, however, the French were already at the very forefront of archeological discovery, bringing honor and artifacts to the resurrected French Republic—soon to be the Empire of Napoleon III. In Athens, the École Français, established in 1846, was already hard at work uncovering remains of classical antiquity. In Egypt, Auguste Mariette, on special assignment from the Louvre, was beginning extensive excavations at the Serapeum at Memphis. And in the mid-1840's in Mesopotamia, where the press of diplomatic business was apparently minimal, Paul-Émile Botta, the French consul at Mosul, had been the first to uncover the monumental remains of the Assyrian civilization. Botta's excavations, ultimately financed by the French government, filled the galleries of the Louvre with impressive finds from a site called Khorsabad, which he adamantly—and incorrectly—believed to be the site of the Biblical city of Nineveh.

Whether by design or chance, this diplomat and erstwhile explorer was suddenly transferred from Mosul to Jerusalem in 1848 and burdened with the responsibility of defending the rights of the French nation and the Catholic Church in the Holy Land. Consul Botta's duties would now involve mainly the fate of the modern inhabitants and the traditional sites, but his appointment at Jerusalem clearly symbolized the growing French interest in Biblical archeology as well. Before long he would have the honor of welcoming an official French archeological expedition to the

Holy Land, an expedition led by an individual who would later be described by Prosper Mérimée, confidant of the Empress Eugénie, as "a strange combination of a gunnery officer and a scholar."

Louis-Félicien Caignart de Saulcy was born to a noble Flemish family at Lille in 1807, and, like his father and grandfather before him, chose a career in the army. As a young cadet in the artillery corps, however, de Saulcy was drawn to such relatively unexplosive fields as archeology, geology, botany, and entomology. After publishing numerous scholarly treatises in his spare time, he was ultimately appointed curator of the Musée d'Artillerie in Paris.

De Saulcy was suddenly widowed in 1850, at age forty-three, and the shock of his wife's death made him "anxious to absent [himself] from Paris and familiar scenes." He had visited the classical sites of Greece, Italy, and Asia Minor in the previous decade, and another tour of those countries now seemed an attractive possibility, to further his own antiquarian researches and dissipate his grief. "But while meditating our route," de Saulcy later wrote, "I reflected that it would be no advantage to science were we to tread again the beaten paths already traced by hundreds of tourists." Palestine, however, scene of the recent Lynch expedition, still remained only partially explored and offered de Saulcy a unique opportunity to make some important discoveries of his own. "Mystery and danger sufficed to fix my resolution," de Saulcy wrote, "and I determined to proceed at once to Jerusalem."

In order to raise the funds necessary for his expedition, de Saulcy agreed to serve as a chaperone for the rebellious sons of several prominent French families who were being sent on a *voyage en Orient* in the hope that it would help them to mend their prodigal ways. The long journey to Palestine, however, apparently had little of the desired effect. They arrived in Jerusalem on December 23, 1850, were warmly welcomed by Consul Botta, and settled into one of the city's few European-style hotels. At that point one of de Saulcy's charges, Edouard Delessert, son of the former French prefect of police, managed to obtain some hashish for his own holiday celebrations in the Holy City. As a result, de Saulcy and the young men were peremptorily requested to leave their comfortable accommodations and fend for themselves.

But rather than seek out other quarters in the city, de Saulcy announced to his groggy wards that they would set off at once to the Dead Sea to begin the important scientific work of the expedition. The region around the Dead Sea, even in winter, was adequate to test the endurance of any would-be explorers, and de Saulcy's young men soon found little time for rebelliousness, disagreements, or hashish. For twenty-one days de Saulcy relentlessly led his companions around the southern end of the Dead Sea, disputing many of the findings of the Lynch expedition and blithely tossing off Biblical identifications for many of the scattered ruins he saw along the way. Then, confident that he would have no more trouble from his young traveling companions, and convinced (quite incorrectly) that he had located the authentic sites of Sodom and Gomorrah, de Saulcy returned to Jerusalem for a minute investigation of the ancient remains there.

After inspecting the masonry of the retaining wall of the Haram ash-Sharif and declaring certain sections—on the basis of no clearly defined criteria—to be Solomonic rather than Herodian, de Saulcy was drawn to a ruin outside the city walls, traditionally known as the Tombs of the Kings. This ancient rock cutting, on which traces of a carved frieze were still visible, offered him a tantalizing opportunity to verify the scientific reliability of the traditional religious identifications. If the Tombs of the Kings did in fact contain the mortal remains of the Hebrew kings, then an important blow could be struck against Dr. Robinson and his fellow Protestants.

De Saulcy ordered his companions to dig away some of the debris from the entrance of the ancient crypt and crawled into the muddy darkness of the interior chambers himself. Being a man who possessed the enviable talent of finding precisely what he was looking for, he managed to drag out the broken cover of a limestone sarcophagus which he exultantly identified as the coffin of King David. Loading the precious relic, other antiquities, and botanical specimens that they had collected onto pack animals, de Saulcy and his party of delinquents-turned-archeologists departed Jerusalem, traveling north through Samaria toward Beirut, where they boarded a ship for their return to France.

Even before de Saulcy's arrival back in Paris, word had spread of the results of his journey. In reports sent from Jerusalem and Damascus to the French minister of public instruction, he had boasted of his discoveries in Jerusalem and at the Dead Sea. "Even while treading in the footsteps of the learned Dr. Robinson," de Saulcy later wrote, "I have gleaned much new and interesting information." Not only had he established (to his own satisfaction) that the traditional sites of the Holy Land were capable of scientific validation, he had also collected tangible artifacts as proof.

It was as if de Saulcy were some sort of latter-day relic monger, bearing pottery and sarcophagus fragments from the Tombs of the Kings back to Europe for a new generation of credulous worshippers. Upon his return in April 1851, the curators of the Louvre were grateful to accept his finds as the nucleus of a "Jewish Court" to be opened in the great French museum. Other French explorers had traveled through Palestine before de Saulcy, but none of them gained such great public acclaim so quickly. Critical Biblical archeology was no longer the exclusive domain of the Protestants. And a sudden turn of events within the Ottoman Empire would lead to a still greater French archeological fascination with Palestine.

The tragicomic chain of events that began with the priestly brawls on Christmas Eve 1847 in the Church of the Nativity in Bethlehem was to culminate in the bloody battles of the Crimean War. The French government, seeking to reinforce its influence in the Holy Land at the expense of the Russian-sponsored Orthodox Church, had angrily demanded that the sultan allow exclusive Catholic protection over many of the formerly divided shrines. Tsar Nicholas and his ministers reacted with understandable outrage, but their invasion of the neighboring Danubian provinces of the Ottoman Empire was something more than a strictly religious protest.

The British ambassador at Constantinople desperately tried to mediate to avert a large-scale war, but England itself was soon drawn into the conflict on the French side. Tension over the "Eastern Question" developed into war. The Light Brigade charged into the Valley of Death, Florence Nightingale tended the sick and wounded, and with the storming of the Russian fortress at Sevastopol in 1855, a new balance of power in the Middle East was established. The Peace of Paris, signed in the following year, forced Russia to yield up its Ottoman conquests and recognized the victorious English and French as the legitimate protectors of the integrity of the sultan's empire.

In Palestine particularly, French influence reached new heights after the war, and a new interest in the country, symbolized by the growing collection of "Biblical antiquities" at the Louvre, spurred a new wave of French exploration. When Emperor Napoleon III dispatched troops to Lebanon in 1860 to suppress a civil war between the Maronite Catholics and the Druze, plans were formulated for an official archeological mission to accompany the invasion force. Félicien de Saulcy, by then retired to a comfortable life in Paris, was delighted with the idea of large-scale French excavations. He eagerly offered his own assistance, arranging for some of the guides and servants who had accompanied him during his own travels through the country to offer their services to the official French mission.

Under the supervision of a prominent theologian named Ernest Renan, hundreds of French soldiers armed with picks and spades attacked the sites of the ancient Phoenician cities of Byblos, Tyre, and Sidon. No archeological expedition to the Land of the Bible had ever before attempted such ambitious projects, and the result of those massive excavations was a new flood of artifacts for the exhibition halls of the Louvre and dramatic new information on the civilization of the Phoenicians, ancient neighbors and allies of King David and King Solomon.

De Saulcy's contacts proved to be of immense help to Renan during the course of his work and his subsequent visit to Jerusalem, but Renan was too stiff-necked to resist criticizing his predecessor. In several reports to the emperor dispatched to Paris en route, he bitterly ridiculed some of de Saulcy's more naïve archeological theories. The idea that the Haram ash-Sharif actually preserved substantial remains of Solomon's Temple, or that the Tombs of the Kings actually held the bodies of Hebrew monarchs, seemed hopelessly literal-minded to the free-thinking Renan.

De Saulcy was horrified when word of these jibes reached him. He considered Renan's criticism to be an act of kindness betrayed. Unable to bear the public humiliation, he resolved to prove that his theories were indeed correct. At stake now for Félicien de Saulcy was not only his archeological reputation but his social standing as well.

In 1853, Louis-Félicien de Saulcy had finally assuaged his grief over the death of his first wife by taking the hand of a second. The new Mme de Saulcy, daughter of the French minister to Copenhagen and close personal friend to the Empress Eugénie, provided her husband with entree to the very highest levels of French society. He was given the rank of major in the artillery in 1855, and four years later, after accompanying Prince Jérôme Napoléon on an official "exploration" of Greenland and the Faeroe Islands, he received the greatest honor of his career, an appointment as senator. Although de Saulcy's interest in the workings of the French political system was minimal, he faithfully attended the parliamentary sessions, "voting constantly," noted a contemporary observer, "for all the measures that were presented by the government."

Although the emperor was painfully aware of the criticism of de Saulcy's archeological theories, he had no alternative but to support a new expedition to the Holy Land by his faithful senator. Twenty thousand francs and full government sanction from the minister of public instruction were quickly forthcoming. The minister of war, Marshal Jacques-Louis Randon, obligingly provided the services of an experienced topographical officer from the general staff, and even the foreign ministry, through the French embassy in Constantinople, was instructed to use every influence to see that de Saulcy would be granted the protection of the sultan himself in his travels.

On October 9, 1863, Louis-Félicien de Saulcy, now aged fifty-six, set off once more for Palestine. Accompanying him, in addition to the topographic officer, a certain Captain Gélis, was his faithful friend and traveling companion the Abbé Jean-Hippolyte de St. Michon, who had gone along on the first expedition, as well as two young amateur archeologists. In the course of their journey eastward, the well-funded expedition was received with great pomp in Egypt by Auguste Mariette, now serving as head of the Egyptian Antiquities Service, who personally escorted them to view his massive excavations at the site of the ancient Temple of Sakkara. Arriving in Palestine on October 27, they were welcomed by officials of the French consulate, who quickly arranged an audience with the pasha of Jerusalem. The new French consul, Paul Barrère, offered every assistance, and it seemed to de Saulcy that conditions could not be better for his renewed assault on the mysteries of the Holy Land.

The first part of the itinerary was an excursion around the Dead Sea, during which de Saulcy had hoped he would be able to validate his earlier identifications of the sites of Sodom and Gomorrah. Unfortunately, a renewed outbreak of disturbances between rival Bedouin clans forced a change in route, and de Saulcy was prevented from reaching some of the most important sites. Then the winter rains arrived and traveling, even with an abbreviated itinerary, became extremely difficult. In addition, de Saulcy, no longer the young man he had been on his previous journey, was plagued by a flare-up of lumbago.

The results of the Dead Sea excursion might have been something less than de Saulcy would have wished, but he returned to Jerusalem with high hopes. He had witnessed for himself the fruitful results of Mariette's excavations in Egypt, and he would now turn his attention to the disputed site of the Tombs of the Kings and attempt a full-scale archeological excavation, for the first time, in Jerusalem.

On November 17, 1863, de Saulcy ordered his two young assistants to begin a systematic clearance of the debris that lay over the remains of the ancient site. Not since the time of Lady Hester Stanhope had any western explorer attempted large-scale excavations in Palestine, and no one had ever attempted to dig in the Holy City itself. But de Saulcy was convinced that, with the tacit protection of the Turkish governor, he would be able to dig without hindrance. For his own reputation and for *la gloire,* he would finally establish the sacred identity of the site through scientific excavation. And on the very first day of the work, de Saulcy's high expectations were rewarded with the discovery of a broad monumental stairway adjoining the courtyard next to the tombs.

Among the various fragments and shards removed from the layer of debris that covered the stairway was a large block of smooth, finished marble. Desperate to establish an archeological connection between his finds and the ancient descriptions of the royal tombs, de Saulcy immediately concluded that the stone fragment was a part of the monument set up at the site of the tombs of David and Solomon by King Herod in the first century B.C. De Saulcy had gained a reputation back in Paris as a brilliant and persuasive conversationalist, and it was not long before excited discussions of his excavations spread through the parlors and sitting rooms of the European community in Jerusalem.

De Saulcy's self-glorification, however, served him ill. On November 18, when he and his men returned to the site to continue the work, they were stopped by several angry locals who had already filled in all the excavation trenches and blocked access to the tomb itself. De Saulcy flew into a rage and sent word to the French consul, who soberly informed him that as word of his discoveries began to spread through the city, dozens of local residents claiming ownership of parts of the site had appealed in protest to the pasha for financial redress. One of them, who claimed to own the gateway, demanded a thousand piasters for the right of passage. De Saulcy angrily refused, threatening to give him "a hundred whacks with my walking stick" instead. Then he pulled his political weight. The expedition possessed the full authority of the French government, and with the leverage supplied by the French consul, de Saulcy was able to force the pasha to silence the public protest and allow the excavation to resume.

But he knew that he had no time to lose. He once again crawled into the musty tomb chambers and was relieved to find some relics that he had apparently overlooked in his previous visit. This time he managed to recover a complete stone sarcophagus, fragments of some others, some ancient pottery lamps, and some broken glass vessels. When the sarcophagus was brought out into the daylight, de Saulcy gleefully pointed out some ancient letters scratched on its upper edge. He was not a trained Hebrew scholar, but he could make out the word "Queen" in the inscription, and confidently announced to his staff that they had discovered the coffin of King Zedekiah's wife.

His identification of this artifact, as indeed his identification of the entire site, was badly mistaken, though the tomb was indeed royal. Later archeologists demonstrated that it was, in fact, the family tomb of Queen Helene of Adiabene, a Palmyran convert to Judaism in the first century A.D.—only about a thousand years later than the era of the first Hebrew kings. But any doubts as to the value of his finds were utterly disregarded as de Saulcy completed their clearance. As soon as he and his assistants had made plaster impressions of the elaborate frieze over the tomb entrance, he ordered his men to shift operations to the traditional site of the "Tombs of the Judges," where he hoped to make additional great discoveries. Other trenches were opened along the retaining wall of the Haram ash-Sharif and in the Kidron Valley below it. A few small and inconclusive finds were all that was recovered from these sites, but de Saulcy was confident that they confirmed his own theories.

Ironically, it was the success with which de Saulcy now managed to convince the public that he had discovered the authentic sites of Biblical history that aroused the outrage of the Jews of Jerusalem. Before de Saulcy's excavations, the local Jews had paid little attention to the efforts of the western Biblical archeologists, but the frenzied activities of the Frenchmen and the strange rumors of the discovery of ancient Hebrew coffins convinced the Jerusalem rabbis that the actual tombs of their kings had been desecrated. "The lust for the study of antiquities has become so intense here in recent days," charged an editorial in one Hebrew newspaper, "that its practitioners have not even shrunk from disturbing the ancient remains of our forefathers." The entire Jewish community was in an uproar, and its leaders dashed off angry protests to Constantinople to halt the excavations at once.

By the time the grand vizier had sent back instructions by the new telegraph line to halt the work, de Saulcy and his companions had already slipped out of Jerusalem with their finds. The point was now merely one of principle, but Consul Barrère stubbornly defended the French rights of excavation, and the Jerusalem rabbis continued with their protest, enlisting the support of the Jewish communities of London and Paris. News of de Saulcy's "sacrilege" began to appear in the British press, and even the staid London *Times* entered the fray, condemning the Frenchman for a "shameless profanation" of the ancient tombs.

The intense outrage over de Saulcy's excavation in Jerusalem gradually died down, but the tension lingered. While the French government sought to strengthen its claim on the traditional sites, individual British scholars were now becoming even more determined to show that those sites were false. The quest for the antiquities of Palestine would soon become a test of strength.

❖ 8 ❖

A Matter of Honor

CLAIMS AND COUNTERCLAIMS
FOR THE HOLY CITY,
1863-1864

The two huge volumes of *Jerusalem Explored*, bound in blue leather and embossed with gilt letters, appeared in the finer London bookshops in January 1864, selling for the unusually high price of five pounds. Consisting of one volume of text and another of plates, the set claimed to be a definitive and comprehensive compendium of the antiquities of Jerusalem, designed to put to rest forever the raging controversies and rival theories about the authenticity of the holy sites.

But if the book's suspiciously warm dedication to the patronage of Emperor Napoleon III were not galling enough to patriotic English sensibilities, then the seventeen apparent instances of plagiarism from the works of earlier British explorers would certainly seal judgment upon it. More horrifying still, the author appeared to have altered the plagiarized plans and photographs to support his own unquestioning belief that the traditional shrines of Jerusalem were indeed the Biblical sites that they claimed to represent.

The author of *Jerusalem Explored*, Ermete Pierotti, had mysteriously appeared in Jerusalem more than a decade before, in the years immediately preceding the Crimean War. Italian by birth, claiming to be a military engineer in the Sardinian army, Pierotti quickly found an outlet for his professional talents in the numerous building projects being sponsored in the Holy City by the rival Christian powers. Working as an architect and engineer for anyone who would hire him, he participated in the construction of the Austrian pilgrims' hospice commissioned by Emperor Franz Josef and in the renovation of the French Church of St. Anne, which had been presented to Napoleon III by the sultan, and he personally designed the huge compound of fortresslike buildings

73

financed by Tsar Alexander II to house the growing numbers of Russian pilgrims who came to Jerusalem every year. Pierotti's constant employment eventually brought him to the attention of Surraya Pasha, the Ottoman governor of the city, who appointed him to the quasi-official position of "Architect-Engineer, Civil and Military"—a title that he would later proudly place below his name on the title page of *Jerusalem Explored.*

The European fascination with Biblical archeology was growing more intense every year, and as an official employee of the Ottoman authorities in Jerusalem, Pierotti was offered advantages by the pasha that few western explorers had ever enjoyed. The task of repairing the water system of the Haram ash-Sharif enabled him to conduct a thorough examination of its ancient remains, and he was even allowed by the pasha to bring a local photographer with him into the sacred enclosure to take the first detailed photographs ever made of the Dome of the Rock and the al-Aqsa mosque.

The extent and value of the archeological information that Pierotti possessed became evident for the first time when he served as Ernest Renan's interpreter and guide during the French savant's visit to Jerusalem in 1860. Renan eagerly examined Pierotti's collection of maps and photographs, and was amazed at the tremendous amount of hard data that he had assembled in the previous six years. Even Captain Gélis, the French topographical officer who accompanied Félicien de Saulcy in 1863, was so impressed by the scope and precision of Pierotti's work that he made copies of some of his plans and encouraged him to publish them as soon as possible. Buoyed by visions of international recognition and possible profit, Ermete Pierotti packed up his few possessions and vast collection of maps and charts and left Jerusalem for Paris, hoping to find a publisher for his Biblical researches.

Pierotti's chances for success in this project were considerably strengthened by a renewed controversy that had sprung up in England over the true site of the Church of the Holy Sepulcher. The chief protagonists in this controversy were James Fergusson, a gentleman scholar who had amassed a fortune in the Calcutta indigo trade, and the Reverend George Williams, former chaplain to the British Embassy in St. Petersburg. In 1847, Fergusson had published a book entitled *An Essay on the Ancient Topography of Jerusalem,* in which he boldly asserted, on the basis of his own architectural expertise, that the Dome of the Rock—far from being a Muslim shrine—was actually the original Church of the Holy Sepulcher built by the Emperor Constantine in the fourth century A.D. The western memory of the original church, Fergusson contended, had been lost with the fall of the Crusader Kingdom and had subsequently

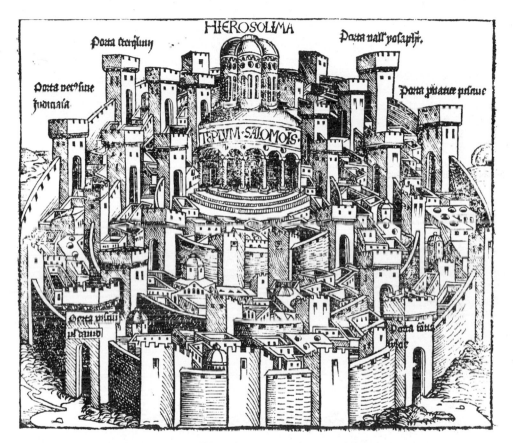

"Hierosolima": the traditional European image of Jerusalem, a city
more heavenly than earthly. From a late-fifteenth-century woodcut.

Detail from the official French topographical map drawn during the invasion of Palestine.

Napoleon Bonaparte rallies his forces at the Battle of Acre, 1799.

John Lewis Burckhardt as
"Sheikh Ibrahim."

James Silk Buckingham.

An early realistic view of Jerusalem, about 1815.

Lady Hester Lucy Stanhope, would-be queen and frustrated treasure hunter.

The Church of the Holy Sepulcher at Jerusalem, centerpoint of traditional Christian pilgrimage to the Holy Land.

The Reverend Pliny Fisk of Shelburne, Massachusetts, the first resident Protestant missionary in Jerusalem.

Dr. Edward Robinson.

"Robinson's Arch," a rediscovered vestige
of the Temple at Jerusalem.

Lieutenant William Francis Lynch, U.S.N.

The American navy in the Promised Land, 1848:
Top: The expedition makes its way inland with the help of Bedouin
and camels. *Bottom:* Rowing down the Jordan River toward the
Dead Sea.

Entrance to the Tombs of the Kings at Jerusalem, about 1855.

The Dome of the Rock, about 1842.

George Grove, secretary of the Crystal Palace Company.

The massive platform of the Haram ash-Sharif, supposed site of the "authentic" Church of the Holy Sepulcher.

The British survey of
Jerusalem, 1864–65:
Left: Captain Charles Wilson of
the Royal Engineers.
Below: "Wilson's Arch."

Modern inhabitants as anthropological specimens: a group of
Ashkenazi Jews photographed by Charles Warren, about 1869.

Warren works by the light of a candle in one of his underground
shafts, 1869.

The Moabite Stone.

The Great Survey of Western Palestine, 1871–77:
Above: Claude Conder at Jericho, in a photograph
by H. H. Kitchener.
Left: The official emblem of the expedition.

MR. SHARP-EYE-RA.

SHOWING, IN VERY FANCIFUL PORTRAITURE, HOW DETECTIVE GINSBURG
ACTUALLY DID MR. SHARP-EYE-RA OUT OF HIS SKIN.

Punch's venomous comment on the Shapira affair, 1883.

been transferred to the later, incorrect site. Fergusson's ingenious theory was seen as a powerful argument against the traditionalists and gained an influential following after being enshrined in Dr. Smith's *Dictionary of the Bible* in 1858.

The Reverend George Williams, however, remained unconvinced. He had long entertained the dream of uniting the Anglican and Orthodox churches, and was naturally inclined to believe in the authenticity of the traditional sites. Having accompanied the entourage of the first Anglican bishop to Jerusalem in 1842, he possessed considerable familiarity with the sites that Fergusson had seen only through lithographs and plans. Williams' own book, entitled *The Holy City*, had put forth a detailed reconstruction of the ancient courses of Jerusalem's city walls and concluded that the site of the Holy Sepulcher had in fact been outside the city in the time of Jesus. The traditional veneration of the spot was, to his mind, totally justified.

Williams first heard of Pierotti and his collected information from a wealthy Englishwoman, Lady Strangford, who had been guided by Pierotti in her tour of Palestine several years before. Intrigued by the possibility that Pierotti's plans might help him validate his position on the site of the Church of the Holy Sepulcher, Williams began a correspondence that eventually resulted in a visit to Paris to examine the plans more closely. He was excited by what he found, and quickly arranged for Pierotti to come to Cambridge to expedite the publication of the book.

Pierotti's plans showed the entire platform of the Haram ash-Sharif to be a single construction, and suggested that the Dome of the Rock, which Fergusson contended was the original Church of the Holy Sepulcher, was actually built above the remains of the altar of sacrifice of the Jewish Temple. The place where Fergusson argued that the Temple stood—the southwestern corner of the Haram—Pierotti revealed to be nothing more than a complex of ancient cisterns. Pierotti's carefully drawn plans, Williams hoped, would be the final destruction of Fergusson's claims. A publisher was quickly obtained, the text was written—with Williams' help—and the Sardinian engineer and the rebel Anglican prelate waited expectantly for the critical acclaim that was sure to greet their great and definitive work.

The first salvo in the battle of angry letters to the *Times* that attended the publication of *Jerusalem Explored* in early 1864 was fired by James Fergusson himself. On February 15, without even deigning to comment on the specific points raised by Pierotti's book, he announced to the public that he would soon be entering a suit of plagiarism against the book's publishers, the firm of Bell and Daldy, for the unauthorized reproduction of a plate from his own book.

Bell and Daldy did not take such an accusation lightly. After conferring with Williams and Pierotti about Fergusson's charges, the publishers announced that they had come into possession of Pierotti's original notebooks and pencil drawings from which all the lithographs had been produced, and they invited James Fergusson to examine them for himself. Fergusson did so at a tense meeting in the London offices of the publishers, but left unsatisfied. On February 29, he reiterated his original charges in another letter to the *Times,* calling the Italian's notebooks little more than forgeries, and haughtily predicting that when the matter was finally arbitrated in a court of law, "Our Jackdaw will be left with but very few of the fine feathers with which he has attempted to parade himself before an admiring public."

Outrage at the publication of *Jerusalem Explored* was not confined to Fergusson. One of Fergusson's most fervent supporters was George Grove, the tireless secretary of the Crystal Palace Company. Grove was interested in many different fields of human endeavor, and besides promoting the endless succession of expositions, curiosities, fairs, and concerts for the Crystal Palace, not to mention the single-handed compilation of his famous *Dictionary of Music and Musicians,* he also found time to pursue an active interest in Biblical archeology.

Grove had first become interested in the subject when James Fergusson was serving as director of the Crystal Palace Company (from 1851 to 1858), and he faithfully adopted Fergusson's theories about the unreliability of the traditional holy sites. Grove's meticulously compiled list of Hebrew place-names mentioned in the Bible had been of invaluable assistance to the dean of Westminster, A. P. Stanley, in the preparation of his comprehensive book about the Holy Land, *Sinai and Palestine,* in 1856. And after trips to Palestine in 1858 and 1861, Grove devoted much of his leisure time to helping revise the latest edition of Dr. Smith's *Dictionary of the Bible,* which incorporated many of Fergusson's theories.

By 1864, George Grove had established a fine reputation among the small circle of scholars and clerics in England concerned with the exploration of the Holy Land. It was that reputation more than anything else that he rushed forward to defend when he joined James Fergusson in the battle to discredit *Jerusalem Explored.*

With the publication of Grove's first letter to the *Times,* Pierotti mounted his counterattack. To refute the aspersions on his character, he produced expansive testimonials from Lady Strangford and Elizabeth Ann Finn, wife of the former British consul in Jerusalem. As for the charges of plagiarism, he categorically denied them, obtaining sworn testimony from his publisher's engraver to the effect that he had submitted original plans. And he maintained further that he himself had been plagiarized more than once in the hectic atmosphere of eighteen-fifties Jerusalem. When artists, photographers, and scholars flooded into the city in desperate search of new information about Biblical Jerusalem, he had lent his own plans to western visitors on many occasions; it was entirely possible that the plans in Fergusson's own book had been based on Pierotti's originals. Responding to Fergusson's threat of a lawsuit, Pierotti coolly advised all potential litigants that he had acquired the services of a prominent barrister with whom they could take up the matter —if they dared.

The counterattack was apparently successful, for Fergusson quickly backed down from his legal threats, suggesting instead a tribunal before the council of the British Institute of Architects. Pierotti recognized that he could never be given a fair hearing by a body of which Fergusson was himself a member and he was not, and he curtly declined the invitation, leaving the controversy at a deadlock. Both of the affair's chief protagonists might have been satisfied to allow the increasingly unpleasant public debate to fade away, but George Grove was intent on pursuing it further. The issues that had been raised directly challenged his own opinions about Jerusalem and its shrines, and Grove persuaded Fergusson to help him settle the controversy in another way.

Grove was determined to find out more about the mysterious Italian and probe for the motivation behind his researches. Why had he come to Jerusalem in the first place? What were his connections to the French Empire that had led him to dedicate his book to Napoleon III? With Fergusson, Grove traveled to Paris, where a personal meeting with Félicien de Saulcy failed to elicit anything but the most gracious admiration for the work of the Italian engineer. Professionally, at least, Pierotti's qualifications seemed beyond question.

It was only when they began to inquire into Pierotti's personal background that Grove and Fergusson finally uncovered the archeological evidence for which they were searching. A fifteen-year-old document buried in the archives of the army of the kingdom of Sardinia, which was then linked by alliance to the empire of Napoleon III, revealed that Captain Ermete Pierotti had been found guilty in 1849 of embezzling moneys belonging to his company in the Sardinian army, stripped of his rank, and banished for life from the country of his birth. That humiliating sentence was presumably the reason behind his mysterious arrival in

Jerusalem several years later, and it was presumably also the reason behind his contrite appeal to regain the good graces of Napoleon III. Viewed in the light of Grove's and Fergusson's hostility, the court-martial document could hardly be seen as anything but a complete condemnation of Pierotti's character, and it was a weapon that they could use to destroy him.

Grove and Fergusson returned to London with the precious and damning evidence against Pierotti, circulating it among the clubs and societies of English gentlemen that were just then converging on London for the upcoming social season. And in no time at all, the silent campaign against the Sardinian outcast had its effect. His archeological theories, once discussed with all earnestness, were now acknowledged only by derisive laughter. Pierotti had no defense against the vicious ridicule of London society, and he quickly dropped out of sight. The remaining copies of *Jerusalem Explored* soon became nothing more than amusing curiosities, rather difficult to sell.

Yet although Grove and Fergusson had destroyed the career of the Italian engineer and humiliated his Anglican patron, the archeological issue was not settled conclusively. So long as any doubt remained about the true location of the holy sites, the power and prestige of the Catholic and Orthodox churches in Palestine would continue to be bolstered by the veneration of the Church of the Holy Sepulcher and the other traditional shrines, and the scientific authority of critical Biblical archeology would remain unproven.

In another quarter of elegant London society, plans were being formulated for a mission to Jerusalem quite unconnected with the conflict over the holy places, but it would not be long before George Grove and James Fergusson turned it to their own advantage.

✳ 9 ✳

Building the New Jerusalem

MISSIONARIES
AND ROYAL ENGINEERS,
1864-1865

Every May, as the cold winds of winter receded for another year from the tree-lined walkways of Kensington and Hyde Park, London society came to life again. May was the month of the annual "Society Meetings," and aristocracy, clergy, civic leaders, and newly prosperous industrialists from every corner of the United Kingdom flocked back to their elegant London town houses to attend the yearly gatherings of the various philanthropic and charitable societies that were then so much in vogue. The religious enthusiasm of the Evangelicals had become very respectable; and whether it was by means of the British and Foreign Bible Society, the Ladies' Home Missionary Society, the Baptist Missionary Society, the Church Missionary Society, or the London Society for Promoting Christianity Amongst the Jews, the springtime task of sowing the seeds of enlightened Protestantism and industrial technology all over the world was seen as an important part of Victorian civic responsibility.

Ever since the establishment of the Protestant bishopric in Jerusalem in 1842, British missionaries had played a larger role than Americans there. Supported by the existence of a British consulate in the city, the "London Jews' Society" and the Anglican Church Missionary Society built schools, furnished hospitals, and, under the direction of the strong-willed Bishop Samuel Gobat, aggressively impressed all potential converts to Protestantism with the tangible benefits of western technology. Although the number of permanent conversions was small, the patrons of the two great missionary societies were buoyed by the belief that the prophecies of the Bible ordained their ultimate success. The Second Coming of Christ and the descent of the Heavenly Jerusalem still loomed large in the minds of the Victorians.

For the time being, however, a natural rather than spiritual obstacle stood in the way of Jerusalem's transfiguration. The early history of Protestant missionaries in Palestine, both American and English, had been punctuated by illness and suffering. Malaria and dysentery were common. Outbreaks of typhoid often occurred in times of famine and drought. Worst of all were the cholera epidemics within the walled city of Jerusalem, which, spreading across the quarters of the city like the shadow of death, left the Protestant missionaries as helpless and frightened as all the other inhabitants, fervently praying that they might be spared.

In the cities of England cholera had long been a problem, but by the mid-eighteen-sixties it was being controlled for the first time. Modern science had shown that cholera was carried in water contaminated with infected human waste, and the installation of effective and sanitary public water systems in British cities had already done much to stem the spread of the disease. In the mind of a prominent British engineer named John Irvine Whitty, who had compiled a systematic study of the hydrology of Jerusalem, the periodic outbreaks of cholera could be prevented if a new water supply system were established. His idea struck a responsive chord and in May 1864, at the height of the annual Society Meetings, a committee of prominent English aristocrats and churchmen banded together to put it into action.

The Jerusalem Water Relief Society, as they called their new organization, recognized that the central obstacle to improving the water system of Jerusalem lay caught on the twin horns of topography and tradition. Jerusalem, being a mountain city, was perched on steep ridges of land, and from ancient times it had drawn most of its water from underground cisterns that stored the winter rains. The only flowing waters were deep in the Kidron Valley at the "Spring of Gihon" and the "Well of Job," but these sources were contaminated with the runoff from the extensive cemeteries that sprawled over the Mount of Olives.

Because the barest public hygiene was observed in Jerusalem, the private cisterns within the city were rarely if ever cleaned, and were often themselves contaminated by the seepage of sewage beneath the ground. Modern hydraulic techniques might be employed to bring a plentiful supply of fresh water from "Solomon's Pools" near Bethlehem by means of a tubular aqueduct, in which case the need for unhealthy cisterns would be eliminated, and the incidence of cholera greatly reduced.

Before the new water system could be installed, however, an accurate topographical map of the city was needed. Several western travelers to Palestine during the previous decades had compiled maps of Jerusalem, but their findings, often based on hasty or imprecise observations, were in many cases contradictory. Before the new aqueduct could be laid out, the city would have to be surveyed using the most modern equipment and the most competent surveyors who could be hired.

For this purpose, the dean of Westminster, A. P. Stanley, who had enthusiastically joined the Jerusalem Water Relief Society, appealed to Miss Angela Burdett-Coutts, a member of a prominent banking family and a well-known philanthropist, for an initial contribution of five hundred pounds. By means of official contacts and influence, the committee members then communicated their plans to Earl de Grey and Ripon, Secretary of State for War in the Palmerston government, requesting the services of a party of Royal Engineers to execute the proposed survey. The missionary transformation of Jerusalem now entered the realm of official British governmental action, and with the consent of Earl de Grey and Ripon, the matter was quickly referred to Colonel Henry James of the Royal Engineers at Chatham, with the hope that he would assist in the immediate dispatch of a surveying party to the Holy Land.

In 1864, the Royal Engineers could look back on a long and glorious history of service to king and country. Beginning as early as the eleventh century, these faithful "military artificers" had played a crucial role in the progress of the British nation around the globe. The highly technical arts of siege warfare and fortification were their specialties, and they had gained glory in recent decades, serving with distinction at the Battle of Lucknow, in the Crimean War, and in the late conflict in China. The Royal Engineers' duties, in an age of increasing industrial technology, were indispensable to the colonial forces even after victory had been won. Roads, dams, bridges, communications, and public improvements were necessary for the maintenance of civilized British administration in even the most remote regions of the world. The maps of the Royal Engineers set the standard for the age. Whether it was the Ordnance Survey of England itself or the Great Survey of India begun in 1770, the meticulously drawn charts of the Royal Engineers recorded every house, tree, natural feature, and road in the territory they surveyed. Their efficiency was legendary, their competence unquestioned, and it was precisely those qualities that led the Jerusalem Water Relief Society to enlist their aid in the compilation of the first comprehensive map of the Holy City.

The agreement finally reached for the Royal Engineers' participation in the survey of Jerusalem, however, seemed something less than wholehearted. Since the project was private and philanthropic, Earl de Grey insisted that the costs of provisions and the salaries of the enlisted men would have to be paid out of Lady Burdett-Coutts' gift. Likewise, the personal expenses of the officer to command the survey could not be covered by public funds, and, officially at least, he would be required to take a leave of absence from the corps for the time of his work in Palestine. The task of finding an officer willing to undertake the mission at his own expense was entrusted to Colonel Henry James at Chatham, and it proved to be difficult.

In fact, it became a matter of open derision in the Royal Engineers' barracks at Chatham. The idea of a detachment of red-coated British surveyors wandering through the filthy streets of Jerusalem, carefully calculating the height and dimensions of every crumbling, disease-ridden building, was incongruous enough to be funny. Besides their reluctance to advance their own money on the daydreams of some aristocrats and churchmen, the young officers saw little to be gained from a leave of absence in the Holy Land. In their minds, the boundaries of the empire lay elsewhere—in India, Africa, and China—and it was there that medals would be won and promising careers advanced. Palestine, with its stuffy Sunday-school associations, was for petulant scholars and missionaries, not imperial heroes. Every officer approached by Colonel James politely declined the appointment.

One man, however, felt differently. Captain Charles Wilson had recently been transferred to Chatham. Bored with his routine duties there, he was anxious for almost any sort of escape. Six years before, he had been shipped off to the wilds of North America as secretary to the North American Boundary Commission and had supervised the work of the surveying parties that laid down the border between the United States and British Columbia. That project had lasted through four years of blizzards, isolation, and hard work. If, Wilson reasoned, he was capable of traversing prairies and forests from Puget Sound to the Rocky Mountains to mark a boundary decreed in London, he could surely surmount the perils and difficulties of Ottoman-ruled Jerusalem to compile an accurate map of the city.

His application was promptly accepted by Colonel James, and he was granted an official leave from his regular duties at Chatham. Financial support quickly came from an unexpected source: George Grove, still simmering over the Pierotti affair, arranged a meeting with the young captain and suggested that funds for his personal expenses would be forthcoming if he were willing to undertake some special investigations aimed at discrediting the Italian. He agreed. Grove arranged for the passage of the entire surveying party on the ships of the Peninsular and

Orient Steamship Company at "greatly reduced rates." In paving the way for the restoration of the modern city of Jerusalem, Captain Charles Wilson would also conduct a close and critical investigation of Ermete Pierotti's alleged discoveries.

On September 30, 1864, after a voyage of twenty days from Southampton, Wilson and his survey party, consisting of a sergeant and four corporals, landed at Jaffa. Time and resources were both in short supply, and while it was customary for arriving western visitors to spend their first night in an inn before traveling up to Jerusalem, Wilson saw no good reason to delay the start of his work by even a single day. Despite the dangers of highwaymen and unfamiliarity with the road, Wilson and his men set off through the Judean Hills after dark, arriving in the Holy City early the next morning.

Unlike all previous western explorers in the Holy Land, Wilson had not come to satisfy a personal obsession with Biblical archeology; his was a specifically outlined assignment, and as an officer of the Royal Engineers he represented his government. The first order of business was a meeting with the British consul, through whom he would make official contact with Izzet Pasha, the Ottoman governor of the city. The Turkish administrators of the city, however, were apparently well aware of Wilson's arrival. When he arrived at the pasha's residence the following day, he was greeted with a lavish ceremonial review by the troops of the local garrison and offered every assurance of assistance in the days to come.

The people of Jerusalem were suspicious of the red-coated Englishmen at first, but the proclamation of Izzet Pasha's official sanction and the generous wages Wilson paid local workers to carry the equipment were more than enough to allow him and his men to work quickly and without fear of interference. The engineers established a base line to the southwest of the city and, following standard topographic procedures, began to lay out a network of triangular measurements for a master grid. With the careful use of their brass theodolites, they established a mapping area of more than twelve square miles, within which every physical detail would be recorded and transferred onto the ordnance map of Jerusalem.

As the chief function of that map was to prepare the way for the installation of a new water supply system for the city, it was clear that it would have to take into account remains of ancient water systems as well. Wilson knew that Ermete Pierotti had noted the presence of a huge complex of subterranean cisterns within the Haram ash-Sharif. In order to check the accuracy of Pierotti's findings, Wilson gained the permission of the pasha to conduct some explorations there. This examination was far more thorough than any that had been done before; Wilson and his men carefully sketched all the surface features of the massive platform and descended into a series of underground vaults, incidentally discovering that in many cases Pierotti's measurements had been based more on imagination than on fact.

The presence of massive cisterns, however, was indisputable. The site of the ancient Temple seemed to be the centerpoint of an extensive water system, and Wilson felt obliged to trace its channels and aqueducts through the jumble of houses and buildings that surrounded the retaining walls of the Haram ash-Sharif. All previous explorers of Jerusalem had restricted their investigations to the remains visible above the surface. But Wilson and his men went underground. There, crawling through sewers and climbing down into disused cisterns, they unexpectedly came upon hitherto unknown evidence of the Biblical period.

In an underground chamber just north of the "Wailing Wall" of the Jews, they were able to distinguish the perfectly preserved span of a monumental arch attached to the exterior wall of the Haram. Similar in size to Robinson's Arch and parallel to it, Wilson's Arch, as it later came to be called, represented yet another entrance to the Herodian Temple. Hidden there in the sewer system of the modern Middle Eastern city was monumental evidence of the splendor of ancient Jerusalem.

It became clear to Wilson that much valuable archeological information could be gained by continuing the underground explorations, and he ordered the excavation of a vertical shaft into the layer of debris beneath the present-day city. Extensive digging, however, proved beyond the means of the small surveying party, and extensive digging was called for: the layer of deposits through which they penetrated reached a depth of more than eighty feet. Further excavation would have to be left to expeditions better equipped for the task.

As the weeks went on, Wilson expanded his explorations to the Dead Sea, where he hoped to gain additional information on the precise geographical position and elevation of the city of Jerusalem. His native guide was unwilling to make the journey through hostile Bedouin territory, so Wilson went alone, and the distinctive appearance of his red uniform gained him not only the protection but the friendship of the notorious Ta'amireh tribe. The survey of Jerusalem itself was nearing completion, well within budget estimates, and Wilson, proud of the success of his once-derided mission, began to send back detailed accounts of his discoveries to Colonel James at the headquarters of the Royal Engineers at Chatham.

James too had treated the projected survey of Jerusalem with indiffer-
ence at its inception, but Wilson's glowing dispatches from the Holy Land
converted him into a wholehearted supporter. In a letter to the London
Times on the eve of the new year 1865, he announced the success of the
Jerusalem survey, detailed Wilson's unexpected underground discoveries, and voiced his support for the extension of the Royal Engineers'
investigations in Palestine. James suggested that the expedition, having
virtually completed its survey for the Jerusalem Water Relief Society,
should now determine the absolute level of Jerusalem with regard to the
Mediterranean, and he concluded his letter to the *Times* with a wish that
the funds for such a project could be raised by popular subscription.

George Grove, of course, could not have been happier to hear of the
latest discoveries by Wilson in Jerusalem. Not only had Wilson demon
strated Pierotti's inaccuracy, but he had also added important new ele-
ments to the scientific knowledge of Jerusalem's Biblical remains. Grove
himself addressed a letter to the *Times* right after New Year's, in which
he warmly applauded the achievements of the survey, suggested some
additional problems of Biblical geography that might be tackled before
the party left Palestine, and finally offered an impassioned plea for continued public support for the exploration of Palestine. Perhaps, he suggested, the treasury of the now-defunct Assyrian Excavation Fund, which
had brought such great wonders to both the Crystal Palace and the British
Museum, could be used to sustain the work on a continuing basis.

The two polite letters to the *Times,* as with so many other subjects of
fretful Victorian discussion, evoked a large measure of public attention.
The Royal Society and the Royal Geographical Society enthusiastically
provided the two hundred pounds for the survey of the relative levels of
Jerusalem and the Mediterranean out of their own treasuries, and the
War Office officially extended the mission of the engineers to accomplish
this task. In addition, Sir Moses Montefiore, one of the Queen's wealthi-
est and most influential Jewish subjects, himself on a tour of the Holy
Land, sought out Wilson and interceded on his behalf with the several
leading rabbis of Jerusalem to allow him to explore the remains beneath
the Jewish Quarter of the city. Montefiore was already committed to the
ideal of Jewish restoration in Palestine, and he personally contributed a
hundred pounds to the support of Wilson's survey.

Public response to the official British exploration of Jerusalem was so
positive that George Grove decided the time was right to organize a
permanent society for the exploration of Palestine. The bitter antagonisms of the Pierotti affair had all but melted away in the excitement over
the work of Wilson. George Grove gathered together some of the most

prominent Biblical scholars and church leaders in Britain for an executive meeting in Westminster Abbey, at which they drew up plans to be presented to the public in May. Contributions soon began to flow into the treasury of the embryonic exploration society. A common cause would now unite the individual efforts of the past; the pieces were at last beginning to fall into place for the establishment of a British claim on the archeological exploration of the Holy Land.

On May 12, 1865, at the height of the busy London society season, a festive public meeting provided the backdrop for the official formation of the Palestine Exploration Fund. Seated on the podium along with the archbishop of York, who had been nominated president, and George Grove, who had been named honorary secretary, were some of the most prominent figures of Victorian society. The efforts of the fund's organizers had garnered the official support of the duke of Argyll, keeper of the privy seal in Palmerston's government, and of the foreign minister, Earl Russell, who would undoubtedly aid in negotiations with the Ottoman government. From the world of finance came Morton Peto, a railroad magnate, and Walter Morrison, a millionaire industrialist. Among the men of science were Walter Scott, president of the Royal Architectural Society, and Sir Roderick Murchison, president of the Royal Geographical Society. From the Church of England came, in addition to the archbishop of York and the dean of Westminster, the bishops of Oxford, London, and Ely, and the deans of St. Paul's and Christ Church. Even James Fergusson and George Williams had forgotten their previous differences, and joined the others in a society whose aim was the scientific investigation of "the Archaeology, Geography, Geology, and Natural History of Palestine."

After an opening prayer from the bishop of London, William Thompson, archbishop of York, rose to outline the goals of the new society in his capacity as president and clearly intimated the future directions of the work. "This country of Palestine belongs to *you* and to *me,* it is essentially ours," stated the archbishop to the crowded gathering. "It was given to the father of Israel in the words 'Walk through the land in the length of it and in the breadth of it, for I will give it unto ye.' *We* mean to walk through Palestine, in the length and breadth of it, because that land has been given unto us. It is the land from which comes news of our Redemption. It is the land to which we turn as the fountain of all our hopes; it is the land to which we look with as true a patriotism as we do to this dear old England."

At the conclusion of his expansive remarks about the special connection between the mighty British Empire and that small strip of land on the southeastern shore of the Mediterranean Sea, the archbishop announced that Queen Victoria herself had graciously consented to be the official patron of the Palestine Exploration Fund. Her contribution of £150 to the society's treasury, more than any other donation, symbolized the approval and interest of British society in what was seen as a national endeavor. Austen Henry Layard, the renowned Mesopotamian explorer, minced no words about the political importance of the work of the Palestine Exploration Fund. He expressed the hope that it might counteract the well-funded expeditions of "the French government, which is always more than ready to undertake researches of this character. . . ."

The religiopatriotic framework was set. Now all that remained was to raise the necessary funds and dispatch the first expedition to the Holy Land.

Barely a month after the official establishment of the Palestine Exploration Fund, Charles Wilson and the Royal Engineers under his command headed for home. In the course of ten months in Palestine, they had succeeded in accomplishing a task of survey that many had thought impossible, and they had exceeded their budget by only three pounds, due to a delay in Alexandria. In October, the official *Ordnance Survey of Jerusalem* was published, and it presented the public with a clear indication of the crisp competence of Captain Wilson. Included with the large volume of detailed text were two accurately drawn plans of Jerusalem, one to a scale of 1/25,000, and another, more detailed still, on a scale of 1/10,000. In addition, there were precise architectural plans of the Church of the Holy Sepulcher, the Dome of the Rock, and other notable monuments around the city. With his plans and photographs, Wilson had proved that exploration of Palestine was practicable, and that a capable officer of the Royal Engineers, with the official backing of his government and countrymen, was more than equal to the task of furthering it.

As a sidelight, for it had really become a sidelight by this time, the plan for the installation of a new water system for Jerusalem was quietly abandoned. The city council of Jerusalem had been willing to permit the Englishmen to measure their houses and streets, but the idea of letting them tamper with their cisterns was completely out of the question.

Of course, few people in England really cared by this point; the interest of the British public had been completely swept up by the past. The prospect of limitless discoveries from the sacred soil of the Holy Land spurred contributions to the Palestine Exploration Fund from the universities of Oxford and Cambridge, the Grand Lodge of Freemasons, the Syria Improvement Committee, and dozens of individual contributors. The exploration of Palestine, like the many other worthy Victorian endeavors, was seen as a noble cause, and local chapters of the P.E.F. began to spring up all over the United Kingdom.

In November, Captain Wilson and another party of Royal Engineers were sent off to Palestine to make a complete survey of the country, and, most importantly, to "locate such spots as might merit the further investigation of the Fund." The groundwork was set. A new crusade was about to begin.

✤ IO ✤

The Pastimes of an Empire

GEORGE GROVE,
CHARLES WARREN, AND
THE JERUSALEM EXCAVATIONS,
1867-1870

Despite the optimistic projections, Captain Wilson's preliminary survey of the Holy Land proved to be a bitter disappointment. Mapping and reconnaissance proceeded far more slowly than expected, owing to an outbreak of cholera in the north of the country. It was also running far above the allotted budget. George Grove conscientiously kept the patrons of the Palestine Exploration Fund informed of Wilson's progress all through the winter of 1865–1866, but the captain's long lists of geographical names and technical surveying problems offered them little satisfaction.

Contributions to the P.E.F. began to drop off as Wilson's survey dragged on through the spring, and, considering the heavy expenses it was incurring every month, the first expedition of the fund could now be seen as far too ambitious. The complete exploration and mapping of the Holy Land was clearly a task that could not be accomplished in a matter of only a few months. Rather than exhaust the fund's treasury, Grove ordered Wilson and his men to return to England immediately. Spectacular discoveries were what the P.E.F. needed now, and no other site in Palestine could provide as rich a treasure trove of Biblical remains as Jerusalem. Impressive results had already been obtained in Egypt and Mesopotamia by archeologists, and Grove was convinced that a well-organized dig in Jerusalem, staffed by competent Royal Engineers, would attract the public interest and private contributions that the Palestine Exploration Fund needed to survive.

The location of the holy sites was of course at the heart of Grove's own interest in Jerusalem. James Fergusson's theory, which he had so force-fully defended during the Pierotti affair, placed the site of Solomon's Temple at the southwestern corner of the Haram ash-Sharif. Robinson and other scholars had already identified remains of Herod's Temple in the southern and western walls of the Haram, and Fergusson believed that remains of the Solomonic Temple lay beneath them. As long as the ruins buried beneath the Haram ash-Sharif remained unexplored, Fer-gusson's theory lacked final confirmation. An official expedition of the P.E.F. could, however, provide just that.

George Grove understood that the Haram ash-Sharif was no ordinary archeological digging ground, but a zealously guarded sanctuary of Islam. No westerners had been allowed to enter its sacred precincts up to the time of the Crimean War, and the few non-Muslims who had managed to enter secretly before that time had done so only at the risk of their lives. Although the ban had been eventually lifted, even Pierotti and Wilson had been severely restricted in the extent of their explora-tions within the Haram. Grove understood that actual excavation there was likely to provoke considerable Muslim opposition, but he was confi-dent that the British ambassador at Constantinople had sufficient influ-ence with the sultan and his ministers to secure the appropriate firman.

James Fergusson himself offered to provide the necessary capital for the undertaking, which would conduct scientific investigations not only within the Haram but at many other of the sites crucial to an understand-ing of Jerusalem's history. Grove's application to Constantinople also included a request for permission to excavate near the Church of the Holy Sepulcher, among the underground cisterns and vaults discovered by Wilson, and at various locations in the city already excavated by de Saulcy and Pierotti. The exploration of the rest of the Holy Land would have to wait. Grove was taking a gamble that the validation of Fergusson's theory would provide the headlines and the flood of grateful contribu-tions that the Palestine Exploration Fund needed to survive.

Grove's first step was to get the use of another party of Royal Engi-neers from the War Office. The officer chosen to lead the team was a twenty-seven-year-old lieutenant by the name of Charles Warren, who had begun his career by scaling and surveying the dangerous rock face of Gibraltar at considerable risk to his life. He was also skilled in the art of military mining, which was at the time almost indistinguishable from standard archeological technique. Warren assembled a wide array of equipment for the excavations at Jerusalem including crowbars, ropes, jacks, handspikes, blocks, and wheels. He also secured the services of a photographer, a surveyor, and an old friend named Corporal Birtles, who had served with him at Gibraltar. Grove entrusted Warren with three hundred pounds as the first installment of a regular subsidy, and in February 1867, the lieutenant and his men set out from Southampton aboard a steamer of the Peninsular and Orient Steamship Company, determined to unlock the secrets of the Holy City.

Arriving at the port of Jaffa, however, Warren and his men encountered the first of many obstacles unanticipated by the P.E.F. bureaucrats back in London. The Ottoman customs officials, taking exception to the "warlike" appearance of the excavation equipment, detained the entire party until the British consular agent intervened. Finally reaching Jerusalem, Warren was further dismayed to learn that the firman from Constantinople had not yet arrived, and he appealed to the British consul in the city, Noel Temple Moore, to intervene. This was a mistake. The consul had apparently not been informed of either the firman or Warren's mission, and on hearing the details of the plan to dig up the third holiest site in the Islamic world, he angrily refused to endanger British interests in Jerusalem by supporting such an obviously provocative act.

Warren had his mission before him, and the honor of a Royal Engineer could not be tarnished by faintheartedness, no matter what the consequences. He insisted that the consul take him to a meeting with the pasha, and subsequently managed to convince the surprisingly compliant Turkish official that his excavations were not meant to harm the Haram ash-Sharif in any way. And since the imperial firman for those excavations had obviously been delayed en route from Constantinople, there would be no harm in anticipating the instructions slightly. Izzet Pasha was unwilling to sanction excavations within the Haram itself, but, much to the British consul's amazement, he granted Warren permission to begin digging anywhere he chose in the area immediately surrounding its massive retaining walls.

Hiring a small group of local workers, Warren established an excavation area against the southern wall and ordered his men to dig away a section of earth beneath an ancient gate which had first been examined by Félicien de Saulcy. Beneath the gate they uncovered a blocked passageway leading under the Haram itself, but as they began its clearance, the pounding of their sledgehammers disturbed the daily prayers in the al-Aqsa mosque above, a fact revealed to the engineers by a shower of stones hurled down at them by the angry worshippers. The soldiers of the local garrison quickly arrived to put down the disturbance, but as a result of the religious uproar, the pasha was forced to withdraw his permission and officially suspend the work until the firman from Constantinople arrived.

The document did, in fact, reach Warren's hands within a week, but it proved to be a disappointment. Its language not only confused the mosque at Hebron with the Haram ash-Sharif at Jerusalem, but it also expressly forbade any excavation in the vicinity of any religious shrines. Since Jerusalem made its greatest revenue from the thousands of pilgrims that streamed in every year, almost every building, landmark, and street had some sacred associations. Warren knew that if the details of the firman were made public, almost any excavation could be prohibited on the grounds that it infringed on the sanctity of some site. He therefore decided to keep the contents of the document secret, while making known the fact of its arrival, and to continue with the excavations in other parts of the city.

Warren again disregarded the nervous warnings of the British consul, who now refused to offer any more assistance. The young lieutenant was determined to proceed, convinced that the Ottoman officials would not dare to challenge the power of an imperial firman, even one they had not had the opportunity of reading. Choosing from the long list of excavation sites that had been suggested to him back in London, Warren ordered his men to remove the excavation equipment from the Haram wall and begin sinking some probes in the Christian Quarter. The leaders of the P.E.F. believed that the question of the authentic location of Jesus' tomb could be solved only by on-the-spot investigation, so Warren began digging close to the Church of the Holy Sepulcher, trying to determine whether its site lay inside or outside the city walls in the time of Jesus.

These scientific researches did not appeal to the commander of the Ottoman garrison, however, and he quickly dispatched soldiers to halt the British excavations. But no sooner had the soldiers closed down the work in the Christian Quarter than Warren began a new excavation on the unoccupied southern slopes of the city, where he hoped to tackle another problem of Biblical geography—the southern extent of Jerusalem in Biblical times. Warren's tactical flexibility wore down the Ottoman opposition, permitting him to continue by default.

Yet despite the tacit official sanction, it was clear that public sentiment concerning the British excavations was as negative as ever. Strange rumors, which Warren suspected the commander of the garrison had spread, stated that the Englishmen were planting small bags of gunpowder deep beneath the streets of the city. Within several years, those bags would grow into huge barrels, the story went, and the Englishmen would return to blow them up and destroy the Haram. Time and time again

Warren was forced to raise the pay of his local workers to prevent them from succumbing to the threats and curses hurled at them for cooperating with the infidels. Still, rumors and crude attempts at pressure were comparatively easy to deal with, and Warren felt confident that he would ultimately be permitted to excavate on the Haram itself. But returning from a brief excursion to the Jordan Valley and the Dead Sea at the beginning of May, he suddenly found himself facing a new problem that threatened to bring the excavations to a complete halt.

Nazif Pasha, the new governor of Jerusalem, symbolized the quiet wave of conservative reaction that had moved through the Ottoman Empire since the accession of Sultan Abdul Aziz in 1861. The previous governor, Izzet Pasha, who had been so reluctant to challenge Warren's right to excavate, had been called back to Constantinople under a cloud of suspicion of corruption, and the new pasha sought to disassociate himself from his predecessor's judgments in nearly every way. The status of Jerusalem was becoming an increasingly important matter of prestige, and the new governor, himself a militant Muslim, took up his duties intent on curbing western influence in the city and reasserting the Islamic basis of Ottoman rule. Nazif fully supported the hostility of the garrison commander, and announced that Warren would not be permitted to make any further excavations on public property. And any work on private property must not be closer than forty feet from the wall of the Haram ash-Sharif.

Nazif Pasha felt confident that he had successfully rid himself of the bothersome Englishmen, but the new directives were merely a challenge to Warren's ingenuity and commitment. Utilizing his experience in military mining, he leased some private plots of land on the southern side of the Haram, well beyond the forty-foot limit. From these points, he proposed to sink vertical shafts down to the bedrock, and from there dig horizontal galleries toward the foundation of the Haram wall. With his men working unnoticed far beneath the surface, he would locate and map all the ancient remains he encountered, hoping that the publication of his findings in London would demonstrate that the work could be done without disturbing the sacred shrines.

Warren opened the first shaft behind the cover of a huge cactus, but soon became acquainted with the difficulty of deep excavation in Jerusalem. While Wilson had estimated that the debris on which Jerusalem was built had accumulated to a depth of approximately 80 feet, Warren's men actually found that more than 130 feet of loose debris, collapsed cisterns, and disused water channels stood between them and the bedrock. Much

of this accumulation was composed of rock chips, loose gravel, and pock-
ets of hard, brittle earth, and the slightest disturbance, such as the shift-
ing of a ladder against the side of the shaft or the careless placement of
a shovel, would often cause uncontrollable cave-ins, burying the workers
up to their waists and filling the shaft with thick, choking dust.

Military mining, such as that which Warren now attempted, ordinarily
required timbers at regular intervals to reinforce the sides of the shafts,
but since wood was a scarce and expensive commodity in Jerusalem, he
was forced to make do with a few secondhand planks used only at the
most sensitive points. Thanks to the expertise of Corporal Birtles, Warren's galleries eventually reached the foundation of the great retaining
wall of the Haram, tracing an ancient pavement that ran along its base,
now more than a hundred feet beneath the surface of the earth.

Although Warren and his men had suffered no more than cuts and
bruises from falling debris, the danger of working underground without
enough mining frames was beginning to take its toll on the nerves of the
officers and workers. Warren feared that if a serious accident were to
occur, Nazif Pasha would have the perfect pretext to close down the
excavations permanently. With a sense of near-desperation, Warren
wrote back to George Grove urgently requesting additional funds to
purchase more wood; in the meantime he and Corporal Birtles continued
to enter the dangerous shafts to keep up the morale and initiative of the
workers. Corporal Birtles, Warren later wrote, was so fearless and so
determined to keep up the pace of the excavations that "every week [he]
had to act in such a manner as would, on active service, have ensured him
the Victoria Cross, or under other circumstances, the Albert Medal; but
here it simply came into the routine of our work." The recognition that
Birtles actually received for his efforts was much more humble: promo-
tion to the rank of sergeant.

Between March and June 1867, Warren and his men began more than
twenty-seven shafts at various points to the south and west of the Haram
ash-Sharif. In addition, they succeeded in locating the southern and
northern limits of the city, investigated an ancient subterranean aqueduct
on the southern slope, and unearthed a number of pottery jar handles,
stamped in ancient Hebrew with the words "Belonging to the King,"
which were the first genuine Biblical artifacts ever scientifically excavated
in the Holy City.

In July, the galleries were finally extended to the southeastern corner
of the Haram wall. That imposing rampart, which already rose 80 feet
above the level of the ground, was found to extend another 100 feet
beneath it. And at the corner, the excavators found traces of ancient

letters painted in red on the foundation course. These strange symbols, which Warren believed to be Phoenician masons' marks, reinforced his belief that the Haram platform itself was the foundation of the Temple of Herod. In the few probes that he had made within the city, which included a risky and unpleasant crawl through a sewer beneath the pasha's residence, Warren had found a striking uniformity in the shape of the stones of the four walls of the Haram. Like the huge ashlars visible in the western wall, at the place of prayer of the Jews, they were carefully drafted with smooth margins on all four sides. Warren noted the presence of these characteristic stones at the southeast corner as well.

With the measurements taken and the red letters carefully copied, Warren shut down the excavations for the summer. He assembled all the information he had gathered, drawing elaborate plans, cross sections, and architectural studies, and sent them to London in the hope that their publication would ultimately persuade the Ottoman authorities to allow him to expand the work. Then, confident that he could, in any case, resume the underground excavations in the fall, he left the city for an extended reconnaissance of the southern and eastern parts of the country.

It seems unlikely that Warren, as proud as he was of the results of his early investigations, actually realized their ultimate implications. All of the contemporary theories about Biblical Jerusalem were based on mere suppositions about the original topographic features of the city; but Warren and his men, penetrating the accumulated debris, had finally determined those features with accuracy. In the shafts that they had dug around the southern and western walls of the Haram, they had traced the levels of the bedrock and located the Tyropoeon Valley—the so-called Valley of the Cheesemakers—which had bisected the city from north to south in Biblical times. This ravine, they found, had been filled up with refuse and debris during the later Biblical periods, and by the time Herod constructed his massive Temple platform in the first century B.C., the Valley of the Cheesemakers had virtually disappeared.

In fact, the platform of Herod's Temple was built on *top* of the rubbish accumulation and extended completely across the ancient valley. The implications were clear. James Fergusson's location for the site of the earlier Solomon's Temple—at the southwestern corner of the Haram ash-Sharif—would have placed it at the bottom of the deepest valley of the city, in clear contradiction to both logic and the Biblical descriptions. If Fergusson's theory had been validated, Warren later wrote, his supporters would have "emblazoned it with the flourish of trumpets." But since the excavations had disproved it, and since Fergusson himself had contributed a large part of the budget of the P.E.F. expedition, the question of finances would soon become a burning one for Lieutenant Warren in Jerusalem.

From the very start of the mining operations, the few wooden frames had more than once saved the officers and workers from tremendous collapses of debris. Much more wood was needed, but the executive committee in London did not respond to Warren's repeated requests. He was forced to write to Malta and Alexandria, purchasing all the wood he could obtain, knowing that he was paying highly inflated prices and accumulating a huge personal debt. With the resumption of the excavations in the fall, and the beginning of the rainy season, the frames that Warren had sacrificed so much to obtain began to rot and had to be discarded. The situation was becoming impossible. Warren had finally lost his patience with George Grove, who had been "vacationing in Switzerland" and had not answered the increasingly desperate appeals from Jerusalem. Warren sent one last letter to the honorary secretary. Mining frames were absolutely necessary to the work with which he had been entrusted. If they were not forthcoming, together with sufficient funds to reimburse Warren for the amounts he had already advanced, he was fully intent on closing the excavations and returning with his men to England.

What Warren did not know at the time, as he later described it, was that "the Fund had become a Debt." The three hundred pounds that Grove had given Warren at his departure was the last of the treasury. It had been badly depleted by Wilson's costly survey. Grove had gambled with Warren's life in the hope that the results of the Jerusalem excavations would bring in a tide of contributions. Not only had no contributions arrived, but he had lost the support of James Fergusson as well. Faced with the dissolution of his society, Grove swallowed his pride and appealed directly to the public for funds in a series of letters to the *Times* in November 1867. As a result, he was able to dispatch to Jerusalem a bank draft for £850, which, although not entirely covering Warren's expenses, at least showed good faith and allowed the excavations to continue.

Warren had by this time despaired of ever being allowed to excavate within the Haram itself. The publication of his preliminary findings in London neither brought the public financial support that had been hoped nor persuaded the Ottoman government to grant unlimited access to the Muslim shrines. Now the shafts were public knowledge, and Nazif had begun sporadic harassment again. To make matters worse, by the beginning of 1868, Warren was receiving unmistakable indications of Grove's continuing problems. The sums remitted every month were beginning to shrink again. Besides that, Birtles had come down with a serious illness and had to return to England for recovery. The obstacles had become too great to continue. Requiring, at the very least, reinforcements of men and a steady supply of funds, Warren closed the excavations in April 1868 and returned to England to argue his case in person.

The consequence of Warren's return was nothing less than a total reorganization of the Palestine Exploration Fund. At a meeting of the executive committee, Warren provided the first detailed accounts of his ongoing battle with the pasha and revealed his deteriorating relationship with George Grove. Warren's forceful suggestions brought some wide-ranging changes. George Grove agreed to step down from the post of honorary secretary, leaving the day-to-day affairs of the fund in the hands of a full-time administrator. Given the assurance that £350 would be remitted faithfully every month, Warren went back to work. This time he brought his wife and daughter with him to Palestine, and instead of a bivouac or the hospitality of the Anglican missionaries, he rented the house of a former American consul, a well built residence outside the city walls.

Despite the earnest pledges of steady funding, however, the new leaders back in London were hard-pressed, try as they might, to supply the promised subsidy. By November they had been forced to cut his allotment to £200 per month, far below his actual expenses. If the P.E.F. were to continue as a truly scientific organization, they could no longer depend on the philanthropy of a few wealthy supporters with pet theories. The exploration of the Holy Land would have to become a truly national endeavor. The first great turning point in the history of the Palestine Exploration Fund had arrived.

From the very start of his excavations, Warren had always shown great patience and hospitality to the growing numbers of western tourists who stopped by the site of one of his shafts, those totally ignorant of Biblical archeology and those obsessed by it. Warren was thus able to gain private contributions at times when the money from England was not forthcoming, as well as strong support in times of conflict. One of Warren's own sketches from the period shows a proper Victorian lady being carefully lowered down one of the deep shafts lashed to an upright chair.

Travelers of every description returned from Palestine with glowing reports of Warren's daring labors, and in the course of time something of a legend grew up around him in Jerusalem as well. Even Nazif finally abandoned his harassment, and Warren's moral victory in this matter had raised his status in the eyes of many local residents. In fact, Warren often found himself besieged by people who wished him to intervene in some official matter, thinking him to be the powerful consul of a distant land called "Palestine Exploration Fund." The Jews of the city took great interest in Warren's discoveries, and a delegation of prominent rabbis was invited to descend into the shafts to examine "the magnitude of the works of their forefathers."

The details of Warren's most exciting underground exploits soon found their way into the popular British press, and they sparked great interest among sections of the public that had not even heard of the Palestine Exploration Fund. The noted adventurer John Macgregor, better known as "Rob Roy," visited Warren in Jerusalem and wrote a flattering account that was published in the *Times*. William Russell, the Irish journalist who had made a name for himself in the Crimea as the first great war correspondent, contributed his own description of the Jerusalem excavations, and the popular artist William Simpson brought them vividly to life in a series of dramatic drawings for the *Illustrated London News*.

In order to take advantage of this unexpected public interest, the leaders of the P.E.F. opened a Palestine Museum at the Dudley Gallery in London in June of 1869. Its exhibits included ancient pottery and other artifacts unearthed by Warren, as well as souvenirs of Rob Roy's canoe voyage down the Jordan River and a plan and model of Palestine lent by Sir Henry James of the Ordnance Survey. The modest display attracted upwards of six thousand visitors. Even the dispossessed George Grove, who still remained active in his support for Palestine exploration, was more than gratified to see the visitors stepping right up and purchasing annual subscriptions to the new *Palestine Exploration Fund Quarterly Statement.*

The idea of selling subscriptions, rather than asking for donations, immediately put the P.E.F. on a new footing. Many more local chapters began to spring up all over the country, including one in the far-off location of "Chicago, U.S.A.," and the individual subscribers could now follow the progress of the works at Jerusalem on a regular basis. As the editorial writer of the *Times* had proposed earlier in the spring, Biblical archeology took on the character of a national endeavor. The rediscovery of the antiquities of the Holy Land was no longer connected to the specific theories of a few interested aristocrats. The P.E.F. had staked a British claim on the archeology of Palestine, and the popular fascination with Warren's excavations had fixed that claim firmly in the British consciousness. "Our reason for turning to Palestine," stated the archbishop of York at the tenth annual meeting of the P.E.F., "is that Palestine is our country."

Warren himself continued to dig. He had accomplished the bulk of his work. But in the meantime there was another strange episode to be enacted, one in which Warren would play a small role. It was the affair of the Moabite Stone.

❖ II ❖

Race for a Relic

THE AFFAIR OF
THE MOABITE STONE,
1868-1870

The Reverend Frederick Augustus Klein had, by 1868, faithfully served the Anglican Church Missionary Society in Jerusalem for seventeen years. Although the city of his birth, Strasbourg, was legally within the boundaries of France, he felt little affinity for his native land. His native tongue was German, he had been educated in Switzerland, he was ordained in the Church of England, and he had devoted his life to the spread of Protestantism among the Arabic-speaking population of Palestine. Klein's duties often took him to the sparsely populated regions to the east of the Jordan and the Dead Sea where he would make the rounds of the small Christian villages in which missionary schools had been established, to perform the routine work of supervision, consultation, and conversion. The political concerns of Europe were of little interest to him, and he would spend weeks at a time completely isolated from civilization, absorbed totally in the great battle for souls.

On the evening of August 19, 1868, Klein was engaged in just such a mission. He was on his way from the village of as-Salt southward toward Kerak in the mountains of the Biblical land of Moab when he stopped to pay his respects to an encampment of Bani-Hamideh Bedouin near a place called Dhiban. Klein was accompanied on this journey by Sheikh Zattam, son of the great Bani-Sakhr chieftain Fandi al-Faiz, to whom the Bani-Hamideh were linked by alliance. Both clans had been engaged in sporadic hostilities for years with the clan of Adwan to the north, and the continual feuds of the two factions had both hindered the progress of western exploration around the Dead Sea and brought down the wrath of the Ottomans, who had carried out a brutal military campaign against both of them during the previous year. Klein was careful not to involve himself in the internal politics of the Bedouin, and by maintaining a friendly relationship with all the clans in the area, he was permitted to travel freely across the vague boundaries that separated them.

Because he had come with Sheikh Zattam, Klein was invited to sit at the campfire of the sheikh of the Bani-Hamideh, Ahmad ibn Tarif, who treated him as an honored guest. The territory of the Bani-Hamideh was rarely traversed by westerners, but Klein's Bedouin hosts were well aware of their growing interest in ancient artifacts and were anxious to tell Klein a strange story about a mysterious black stone "which no Frank had ever seen before." It was nearly sunset at the time, but Klein was intrigued by the possibility of finding something valuable, and he accompanied Sheikh Ahmad to an area of ruins at Dhiban, only a short distance from the encampment. There he was shown the artifact that had been described to him, lying on its side, partially exposed above the ground. The daylight was fading quickly, but Klein was able to make some quick measurements and notes. The stone was of polished black basalt, about three feet by five and two feet thick, rounded at the top, with a raised border.

Klein was a missionary, not an archeologist, but as he brushed away the dirt that covered the stone's face, he could clearly distinguish the delicate lines of writing engraved on one side. Assuming them to be ancient letters, he made a rough drawing of the forms of some of them before the gathering darkness prevented further inspection. The following day, Klein continued on his way to Kerak with Sheikh Zattam without returning to copy the entire inscription—missionary business was his first priority, after all. But upon his return to Jerusalem several weeks later, he gathered together his hasty notes and sought a professional opinion on the value of his find.

Later, long after the affair of the Moabite Stone was well known to the western world, angry critics accused Klein of a betrayal of "the claims of the country which gave him birth and of that which gave him bread" in not revealing his discovery to either the French consulate or the English missionaries in Jerusalem. Dr. Heinrich Petermann, however, expressed the feeling that it was only natural that "a German preacher should lay his discovery before a German consulate," and it was to Consul Petermann, the representative of the North German Confederation in Jerusalem, that Klein entrusted the news of the black stone. Petermann, an experienced linguist and scholar, quickly identified the few letters which Klein had traced as Phoenician. If Klein's observations were correct and the face of the stone was indeed covered with the same writing, it would undoubtedly be the most important artifact ever found in the Holy Land. No extensive inscription from Biblical times had ever been discovered, and Petermann, excited at the prospect of retrieving and deciphering the stone, dashed off a letter to his superiors at the Prussian Foreign Ministry suggesting that it would make a priceless addition to the collections of the Imperial Library in Berlin.

Petermann received his reply within two weeks. He was given official authorization by Professor Richard Lepsius, Keeper of the Imperial Library, to purchase the relic on behalf of the Prussian government for any sum up to one hundred napoleons. Utilizing that generous allowance, he gained the services of one of Klein's local converts and dispatched him quickly to Moab with a large quantity of felt for packing and a personal letter written by Klein to Sheikh Zattam's father, Fandi al-Faiz of the Bani-Sakhr, requesting that he use his influence to obtain the stone. Unfortunately, upon reading Klein's letter, the Bedouin leader did not view the proposed deal with very much enthusiasm. His clan had suffered greatly at the hands of both the Turks and their rivals the Adwan in recent years, and he was not anxious to arouse the jealousy or suspicion of either by accepting money from the Franks. Besides, the artifact was not his; it belonged, strictly speaking, to his allies, the Bani-Hamideh. He responded, after a considerable delay, that he could not help in the matter. Yet Petermann and Klein remained anxious to retrieve the stone, agreeing to keep the news of its discovery secret lest the agents of any other nation beat them to it.

By the spring of 1869, Klein had devised a new strategy. Among his local acquaintances was a man with close ties to the Bani-Hamideh. This man, a young teacher named Saba Cawar, assured Klein that he could arrange for the transportation of the stone to Jerusalem. Consul Petermann, for his part justifiably wary, gave Cawar fifty-three napoleons—fifty for the purchase of the stone and three for his traveling expenses—with fifty more to be paid him upon the successful conclusion of the mission.

Petermann waited impatiently as Cawar departed Jerusalem and headed toward Moab. The consul had given his emissary some tracing paper, in the hope that if the purchase were somehow delayed, then at least a copy of the entire inscription might be made. But Cawar's journey resulted in even more frustration. The Bani-Hamideh had not only removed the stone from its original location, but now demanded a thousand napoleons for its purchase and refused to allow any tracing of the inscription, saying that they believed the stone to be the shrine of a *jinn*, or spirit, whose power would vanish if any Frank were allowed to make a copy.

That summer, Petermann's term of office in Jerusalem was over. The fate of the black stone in Moab remained extremely uncertain, and several months passed without any new prospects for retrieving the relic. In early October, Saba Cawar, whose mission to Dhiban during the previous spring had been so singularly unsuccessful, now came before Herr Karl von Alten, the new German consul, with another proposal. He assured von Alten that he could purchase the stone for 120 napoleons: he had contacted Sheikh Ahmad ibn Tarif of the Bani-Hamideh directly, and the Bedouin leader seemed ready to conclude a deal. The sheikh had informed Cawar that the stone was indeed in his possession, and that he was willing to sell it for the named price. With such definitive assurances, von Alten offered the additional twenty napoleons out of his own pocket. But before he would hand over the money, he wanted Cawar to have a clear understanding of the terms. If he were to return with the stone in undamaged condition within thirty days, he could have the sum of 120 napoleons, with no questions asked as to how he got the stone or how much he had actually paid for it. If he could not bring the stone to Jerusalem within that time, the deal was off. Saba Cawar set off once again for Moab.

Cawar quickly made contact with Sheikh Ahmad ibn Tarif and duly signed a contract for the stone's purchase. The way seemed finally clear for the stone's removal, but the northern Adwan clan, which had so far refrained from involvement in the proceedings, now sent word to Cawar that if he were to attempt to transport the relic through their territory without their permission, he would pay dearly for it. Cawar returned to Jerusalem with only the contract for the purchase of the stone and not the stone itself, and with this Herr von Alten had finally come to the end of his patience with Middle Eastern intrigues: The Prussian government would no longer negotiate with desert sheikhs and native middlemen. The full power and force of the Ottoman government must now be enlisted to obtain Prussia's rightful prize.

The autumn of 1869, and in particular the month of October, signaled the beginning of a new era for the Middle East and for the world as a whole. Ferdinand de Lesseps' vision of uniting East and West by means of a sea-level canal through the Isthmus of Suez had finally become a reality. European heads of state, nobility, celebrities, and social gadflies came east in droves to be present at the official opening festivities for the Suez Canal. Only the British, who feared the strategic implications of a French-built canal, were less than completely ecstatic at this wonder of the age. The Ottoman Empire hoped to put on its best appearance for the expected flood of western visitors. In Palestine, the first proper carriage road was built from Jaffa to Jerusalem, and Nazif Pasha was judiciously transferred to another province, replaced by an older and more diplomatic official who could properly entertain the distinguished visitors expected in the Holy Land. Even Rashid Pasha, governor-general of the entire province of Syria, would be coming to Jaffa to greet personally the Austrian Emperor and the Prussian Crown Prince.

Karl von Alten was determined to use the festive occasion to break the deadlock over the acquisition of the relic from Moab, but his first meeting with Rashid Pasha proved fruitless. The governor-general had established a shaky peace in the Jordan Valley by a brutal military expedition into the region during the previous year, and the idea of provoking any of the local clans again was clearly not in the best interests of the Ottoman administration. Rashid informed von Alten coolly that he could do nothing in the matter, for the removal of the stone might result in renewed revolt. His answer was clear: no official Ottoman action would be taken.

As von Alten had hoped, the arrival of the Prussian Crown Prince markedly changed Rashid's attitude. Sailing into the port of Jaffa aboard the royal yacht *Sarona* on his way to the opening ceremonies for the Suez Canal, Crown Prince Frederick instilled a new respect for his country in the minds of the Ottoman bureaucrats. The visit made it obvious that the British and the French were not the only powers to be dealt with in the increasingly competitive international situation. Von Alten insisted on another interview with Rashid. With the imperial yacht lying majestically at anchor only a few hundred yards away, the German consul finally succeeded in getting a fair hearing from the governor-general. All of Rashid's objections to interference became groundless when von Alten showed him the duly executed contract between Saba Cawar and the sheikh of the Bani-Hamideh. It was not the sale of the stone that might provoke a rebellion, but its transportation through the territory of the Adwan. If the governor-general could not obtain the secure passage of private property along the public caravan routes of the country, could even the carriage road between Jaffa and Jerusalem be regarded as safe?

Rather than face the humiliation of another refusal, Rashid grudgingly agreed to intervene in the matter, and instructed von Alten to dispatch a copy of the contract to Damascus. If no further problems arose, a firman would be issued empowering Muhammad Said, pasha of Nablus, to arrange for the transportation of the stone. Von Alten had finally succeeded where Dr. Petermann had failed. The Imperial Museum in Berlin was alerted, and in Jerusalem, Saba Cawar waited impatiently for the official word to set off for Moab again.

Despite Dr. Petermann's wish to keep the Moabite Stone a closely guarded secret, it was not long before rumors in varying versions spread through Jerusalem. As early as the autumn of 1868, Charles Warren had heard of the strange discovery at Dhiban in Moab from one of his local workmen. But when Warren tried to find out more about the nature of the find, he received indirect yet clear intimations from Dr. Petermann that it was a private matter, and that he would do well to inquire no further.

Warren heeded the advice. There was more work than he could handle at the excavations, which were now generally left unhindered by the Ottoman authorities. Besides, he had no authority from the executive committee of the P.E.F. to purchase any relics or artifacts not connected with his excavations. He had spent nearly a hundred pounds of his own money on ancient coins and artifacts in his first few months in Palestine; but instead of being reimbursed for his assiduity, he was curtly informed that the artifacts were his own private matter, and that no money could be raised for their purchase.

In the spring of 1869, after all of the Prussians' initial attempts to purchase the stone from the Bedouin had failed, the matter was once again laid at Warren's feet. Dr. Joseph Barclay, head of the London Jews' Society Mission in Jerusalem, had heard of the Moabite Stone from one of the Reverend Klein's assistants, and was deeply worried that the relic might never be recovered. No complete copy had ever been made of the Dhiban inscription in all of the months that the Prussians had been negotiating for it. And in view of the hostility between the various Bedouin clans, Dr. Barclay appealed to Warren, as the most experienced archeologist in the city, to do something about getting a tracing or "squeeze" of the inscription as soon as possible.

Warren would not allow himself to interfere, or appear to interfere, with the Prussians' discovery, so independent action was ruled out from the start. As far as the relic itself was concerned, Warren did not care what museum it finally ended up in, so long as it was preserved for the benefit of science. He carefully and tactfully arranged a meeting with the Reverend Klein, at which he suggested that the Prussians obtain a plaster impression of the stone as soon as possible. He even offered to provide the finest-quality squeeze paper with which to take the impression.

Klein indignantly rejected Warren's interference. He did not need the lieutenant's help, or even his squeeze paper. Matters were being conducted privately and the German nation could get along perfectly well. Warren bowed out, leaving the Prussians to themselves. But as more rumors of failed negotiations and exorbitant Bedouin demands made the rounds of Jerusalem, Warren began to have serious fears for the safety of the stone. Before leaving for a summer rest in Lebanon with his family, he wrote a detailed letter to the P.E.F. in London, outlining all that he knew of the ancient Phoenician relic, describing the German interest in the affair, and suggesting that, in the case of their failure to gain its purchase, the British Museum should enter the competition.

While Warren was reluctant to interfere in the negotiations and arouse the wrath or displeasure of the Prussians, a young official of the French consulate in Jerusalem, also having heard rumors, felt no such scruples. His name was Charles Clermont-Ganneau, and although he was only twenty-three, he had already spent four years in Palestine and had gained for himself a fine reputation as a Biblical archeologist. Clermont-Ganneau was apparently unaware of the arrangement recently concluded between Rashid Pasha and Herr von Alten, and he considered the stone still open for bidding. His offer to Goblan, the sheikh of the Adwan, was 160 napoleons, 40 higher than that of the Prussians to the Bani-Hamideh.

The answer from Moab was favorable; quite apart from the money, the Adwan had been angered by the contract signed by the Prussians with their enemies. Clermont-Ganneau was now ready to make his first move. He dispatched some of his Adwan allies to make an impression of the inscription, arming them with squeeze paper and plaster and sending them off across the Jordan. The exact details of this secret expedition remain uncertain. In the later fierce arguments about the ultimate fate of the Moabite Stone, conflicting stories were told about who exactly Clermont-Ganneau's messengers were and how they knew where the stone was hidden. In any event, Clermont-Ganneau's men located the stone, and had begun to place the plaster-soaked squeeze paper on the face of the inscription when they were surrounded by an enraged band of Bani-Hamideh. Angry words were exchanged, then came blows, and then gunshots. One of Clermont-Ganneau's messengers, wounded in the attack, had the presence of mind to snatch the squeeze paper from the surface of the stone in the confusion of the battle and escape. Stuffing the torn shreds of the impression into his saddlebags, he galloped off to Jerusalem to present the hard-won treasure to his young French employer.

For the Bani-Hamideh, this was nearly the last straw. An innocent boast about an old black rock with some strange markings on it had caused a shower of misfortune to rain upon their heads. When the firman arrived from the pasha of Nablus ordering them to deliver up the stone to him at once, with no mention being made of any remuneration for themselves, they exploded in fury. The thought of the hated Ottomans robbing them of the 120 napoleons they were promised evoked rage and a call to action. The time had finally come to rid the tribe of the destructive influence of the *jinn* within the black stone.

The Bani-Hamideh could not understand the irresistible attraction that the stone held for the Europeans. Nothing of value could be seen on its surface, though perhaps it concealed something more valuable inside. The Bedouin hoisted the stone onto a blazing fire. When it became red-hot, they dumped it into a trough of water. Again and again this procedure was repeated. Cracks began to develop; the stone was beginning to reveal the secret of its contents. But when it finally split apart into dozens of fragments with a hiss of steam and a final splash into the water trough, the Bani-Hamideh found nothing. The stone, now nothing more than a water-soaked pile of black fragments, clearly contained no gold or treasure. The larger pieces were quickly distributed among the clan members for hiding in various places around their encampment. All that was left open to the light of day after the Bedouin had left was an innocent scattering of black gravel among the ruins at Dhiban.

Having discreetly absented himself from Jerusalem during the visit of the Prussian Crown Prince, Charles Warren returned with his family from Lebanon in the fall of 1869 to resume his excavations. On his way from Jaffa to Jerusalem his party was stopped on the road by a Bedouin of the Adwan tribe who had journeyed across the Jordan with a shocking story to tell the English officer. The Bedouin held a few small black fragments in the palm of his outstretched hand, and informed Warren of the destruction of the stone by the Bani-Hamideh and their subsequent dispersal of its many fragments. For Warren, concerned as he was with the progress of archeological discovery in the Holy Land, the time for the patient toleration of the Prussian claims was over. The entire inscription might be lost forever unless he acted quickly and so, laying aside his own strict neutrality, he dispatched the Adwan Bedouin at his own expense to make plaster impressions of all of the fragments of the stone that could be located.

Charles Clermont-Ganneau, in the meantime, was hard at work trying to make some sense out of the badly mutilated impression that had been taken by his own Adwan agent. The plaster-soaked paper, stripped from the stone while still wet and stuffed into a saddlebag during the escape, was not only torn into seven pieces but now badly crumpled also. The impression of the letters was barely perceptible, yet the young French scholar immediately recognized the significance of the find. The finely wrought "Phoenician" letters proved actually to be the long-extinct language of Moab, a kingdom previously known only from Biblical references to its idolatrous gods and rebellious kings. The capital of that kingdom was Dibon, and now, with the discovery of the "Moabite Stone" at Dhiban, the voice of ancient Moab had spoken again.

The text that Clermont-Ganneau managed to decipher from his mangled impression was written in the ninth century B.C. as an official chronicle of King Mesha, a notorious and sometimes dangerous rival to the contemporary Hebrew kings. The Second Book of Kings relates the story of the unsuccessful expedition of the armies of Judah and Israel to subdue Moab, and here for the first time was an independent account of the aftermath of their defeat. Clermont-Ganneau was able, despite the numerous gaps and illegible passages, to piece together an official Moabite description of Mesha's victory over the Israelites, the subsequent expansion of his kingdom, the reconstruction of his cities, and the plentiful blessings that the Moabite god Chemosh had bestowed on his people. The Moabite Stone was indeed the most important artifact so far discovered in the Holy Land. It not only confirmed the historical basis of a portion of the Bible with striking accuracy, but it also shed dramatic new light on a civilization that bordered on the Hebrew monarchies.

Still, the quality of the only impression of the inscription was poor, and efforts would have to be made immediately to retrieve the remaining fragments of the stone. By this time the Bani-Hamideh were willing to part with their artifacts rather than risk the the loss of any hope of recompense. Warren and Clermont-Ganneau, in their joint capacity as representatives of the scholarly world, met together frequently at the end of 1869, comparing and exchanging impressions of the various fragments that were slowly coming into their possession. The Prussians seem to have abandoned the entire matter at the news of the destruction of the stone, and so at the end of December both Warren and Clermont-Ganneau assembled all of the materials concerning the stone and sent them off to London and Paris for simultaneous publication. "Whether the stone gets to Berlin, London, or Paris," wrote Warren, "appears to me to be a small matter compared with the rescuing of the inscription from oblivion."

But Clermont-Ganneau had slightly anticipated Warren in the agreement for simultaneous publication. He quietly forwarded his own translation and description of the stone to the French ambassador at Constantinople, the Comte Eugène-Melchior de Vogüé, who had himself conducted several archeological expeditions to Palestine. De Vogüé was so excited by the discovery that he arranged for its immediate publication in the French government's *Journal Officiel.* On January 16, 1870, under the by-line of Charles Clermont-Ganneau, and under the title "La Stélé de Mésa, roi de Moab, 896 avant J.C.," the Moabite stone was introduced to the western world.

The London *Times* printed an article on the very next day containing the fantastic news of Clermont-Ganneau's translation. Excitement soon spread from the academic community to the general public. Article followed article in many of the popular periodicals. The dramatic proof of the historical accuracy of the Bible soon became a popular subject of conversation in drawing rooms, dinner parties, and garden receptions throughout England. "Like a lucky actress or singer," wrote one contemporary commentator, "it took us by storm."

The exciting story of the discovery of the Moabite Stone gripped the public imagination, but with the publicity came some unexpected complications. The questions of the priority of that discovery, the identity of its true discoverer, and the nation to which that discovery rightfully belonged would soon toss "an apple of discord"—in Warren's words—into the previously civil relationship of the foreign archeologists working in Jerusalem.

The sudden public excitement over the Moabite Stone was a new stimulus for the persistent involvement of George Grove in the affairs of Biblical archeology. Although he no longer played an official role in the Palestine Exploration Fund, and had himself coldly ignored Warren's urgent request for instructions regarding the stone several months before, Grove quickly emerged in England as the chief spokesman and publicist for the discovery. On February 10, while the preliminary reports of the stone were still based on the French translation, he responded to Clermont-Ganneau's premature publication with a long letter to the *Times,* crediting Warren alone with the discovery of the stone and mentioning neither the early Prussian negotiations nor the contribution of Clermont-Ganneau. At the same time, he dashed off a testy letter to Warren, requesting that he obtain even better squeezes than the "horrid" ones that he had previously sent. In complete disregard for the steadfast

policy of the P.E.F. discouraging the purchase of any relics, Grove demanded that Warren "leave no means untried to get possession of as
much of this unique Moabite relic as may survive."

Warren was still hard at work in Jerusalem and quite unaware of the
furor that was building in England when he began to receive some very
unsettling letters. While some of them lavished praise on him as the brave
discoverer of the stone, other, less benign correspondents accused him
of being directly responsible, by his negligence, for its destruction. When
Warren finally received a copy of the *Times* that contained George
Grove's first publicity release, he could barely contain his horror and
humiliation. Warren had attempted to maintain a nonpartisan, "scientific" reputation during all of the time that he had been in Jerusalem. He
had cooperated with the scholars of all nations, and through that cooperation he had been able to overcome many of the obstacles that stood in
his way, and for which he had received absolutely no cooperation from
home.

Charles Warren felt that he had no alternative but to sever all connections with the Palestine Exploration Fund. He had been promoted to the
rank of captain the previous fall, and the excavations in Jerusalem were
all but completed. The time had come for him to leave Jerusalem with
his last remaining shred of honor. Closing up the works for the last time,
he called upon the Prussian consul and officially offered his apology for
any inconvenience that might have been caused. Then he wrote a long
letter to the *Times* himself explaining that the true discoverer of the relic
was the Reverend Klein and emphasizing the part that Clermont-Ganneau had played in the affair. Warren sailed with his family from Jaffa in
April 1870. But before he left he performed one more act that was to have
even greater repercussions in the affair of the Moabite Stone. As a symbol
of his disgust for the whole shameful business, Warren handed over to
Clermont-Ganneau eighteen small fragments of the stone that had come
into his possession.

The reaction of the Prussian government was, as might be expected,
swift and angry. Dr. Petermann, writing from Berlin, expressed his righteous indignation that "the ordinary rules of discretion would seem to
have demanded that nobody should have interfered in the transaction
until it had regularly been brought to a conclusion or broken off." The
discovery was rightfully the property of the German nation, and in the
atmosphere of increasing military and political tension between France
and Prussia, the issue of Clermont-Ganneau's intervention in the affair
evoked strong feelings.

Clermont-Ganneau himself was well aware of the stir that the stone

had caused, and he set about immediately not only to refine his translation of the text of the inscription but to acquire the missing fragments
as well. He dispatched several expeditions to Moab during the spring,
and with considerable difficulty and a substantial amount of money was
able to locate several more pieces. Although nearly one-third of the
inscription was lost forever, a reconstruction of the remaining parts was
made, and through the summer Clermont-Ganneau worked tirelessly on
a revised and corrected translation. The young Frenchman had suddenly
become a national figure, and the articles he published in the *Revue
Archéologique* were avidly read in scholarly circles all over the western
world.

The affair of the Moabite Stone was not over, however. A flood of
academic papers poured forth from England, Germany, and France, ar-
guing both over differences in the text and over the circumstances of the
original discovery of the relic. Emanuel Deutsch of the British Museum
accused Clermont-Ganneau of "hasty and precipitous action" in acquir-
ing the remnants of the stone without due regard to the claims of the
Prussians. The tensions of the Franco-Prussian War of 1870 naturally
embittered the argument. On July 19, Napoleon III had declared war on
Prussia, but by September 2, the French armies had completely collapsed,
and Napoleon himself had been taken prisoner at Sedan. The Second
French Empire fell, and by January 1871, Paris had been occupied. It was
with unabashed national pride that the reconstructed Moabite stone was
put on display in the Louvre in 1873, as the symbol of one small triumph
against the Prussian enemy.

The Moabite Stone had unmistakably injected an element of western
politics in the search for the antiquities of Palestine, and the repercussions of its discovery sparked additional efforts by the British to defend
their national pride in the matter. With Warren back in England, repeated
attempts were made by the Palestine Exploration Fund to mount an
expedition to Moab to determine if more fragments of the stone might
be retrieved, but all these attempts met with failure. Two explorers sent
out by the P.E.F., Charles F. Tyrwhitt-Drake and Edward Palmer, who
visited the original site of its discovery at Dhiban, found only a few traces
of black gravel, and expressed their doubts that any more fragments
might be found.

But the important lesson of the affair of the Moabite Stone had little
to do with the affairs of the nations of the western world and their mania
for ancient stones. As Sheikh Ahmad ibn Tarif of the Bani-Hamideh

expressed it to Tyrwhitt-Drake and Palmer when they visited his encampment, "If you Franks had come down here twelve months ago and offered me a pound or two, you might have taken all the stones you chose, the Dhiban one included; but now you have taught us the worth of written stones, and the Arabs are alive to their importance at last."

✵ 12 ✵

Spying Out the Land

MAPPING, STRATEGY, AND IMPERIAL INVOLVEMENT IN THE MIDDLE EAST, 1871–1882

The exile of Napoleon III and the destruction of his empire in the Franco-Prussian War suddenly left Britain without a major competitor for control over the Suez Canal. With the danger of French influence in Egypt greatly reduced, the waterway became a lifeline of British trade to India and other parts of the Orient. The British representatives on the Suez Canal Commission pushed for ever-widening advantages for their country, and by the end of the canal's second year of operation, over three quarters of the heavy vessels threading the narrow passage between the seas flew the Union Jack. The Ottoman Empire continued to crumble, Khedive Ismail of Egypt was sinking ever deeper into debt, and although the ultimate fate of the Middle East remained very much in doubt, the British were content to maintain the international status quo at Suez so long as their freedom of passage was ensured.

But if Egypt and the canal were under control, the Russians were not. They were again making threatening gestures in the direction of Constantinople. Continuing disorders among the Orthodox Christian population in the Balkans provided Tsar Alexander II with a perfect pretext for delivering the *coup de grâce* to Ottoman rule there. An inevitable conflict loomed, for if the Russians began dismembering the Ottoman Empire, the scramble for territory, feared since the time of Napoleon, would ultimately pit the interests of the Russians in the Balkans against those of the British in Egypt. Where the dividing line would finally fall, no one could know.

Such ominous forebodings sent a chill through the membership of the

Palestine Exploration Fund. The time had come "for pressing forward discoveries," noted one member at the annual meeting of 1870. In light of the rapidly deteriorating political situation, "It was not likely that the Holy Land would remain in the hands of its present possessors; and if Jerusalem fell to another government, the exploration party would not be likely to receive the facilities at present given." Other grim prospects threatened the future of the P.E.F. as well. Warren had returned in disgust over the Moabite Stone affair, leaving his equipment and stores in the custody of an English missionary. The brief expedition to Moab to seek out more fragments of the Moabite Stone had been a complete failure. It was clear that a major new initiative must be undertaken, and its exact nature soon became a matter of intense debate.

George Grove was intent on continuing the excavations in Jerusalem, still hoping against logic and experience to salvage his badly battered theories. Other members spoke in favor of a continued search for more "Moabite stones." But a growing faction of the younger membership, led by Captain Charles Wilson, had other ideas entirely. When Wilson's preliminary survey of the country was called off in 1866, large areas of the Holy Land remained unexplored and uncharted. If the era of Ottoman rule in Palestine was indeed drawing to a close, it was even more important than before, strategically and scientifically, to achieve one of the most basic objectives of the fund: the compilation of an accurate, comprehensive map of Palestine.

Captain Wilson had continued to be active in the affairs of the P.E.F. even after the cancellation of his survey. In 1868 he had led a private mapping expedition to the Sinai peninsula, in search of the authentic location of Mount Sinai and the path of the Exodus. The construction of the Suez Canal had made the Sinai militarily as well as religiously significant to the British, and Wilson's survey, though private, was given considerable support by the War Office. By January 1869, eleven months before the official opening of the canal, Wilson completed his work of mapping more than four thousand square miles of previously uncharted territory and more than seven hundred miles of little-known trails and mountain passes around the southern approaches to Suez. Many of the persistent problems of Biblical geography remained unresolved, but there was no denying the strategic value of the work should hostilities over the Suez Canal ever break out.

The large-scale mapping of neighboring Palestine offered a similar strategic advantage to the British. Captain Wilson, now serving as executive officer of the Ordnance Survey topographical department, personally drew up a detailed plan of work and technique, which he presented to the executive committee of the P.E.F. A detachment of Royal Engineers would be entrusted with the mapping, which would take approximately four years. The Engineers would also assemble a list of native names and traditions, make tentative excavations where necessary, carry on a series of meteorological observations, make geological, botanical, and zoological notes, attempt to continue the work at Jerusalem, and examine and make plans of "interesting archeological remains." The objective was, therefore, nothing less than a complete inventory of every natural and historical feature of Palestine.

It was a huge and challenging undertaking, but it readily found support. "If you would really understand the Bible—which we circulate every year by the millions," the archbishop of York was quick to point out in support of Wilson's plan, "you must understand also the country in which the Bible was first written." A Great Survey of Palestine was the scientific obligation of the western world, for when completed, it would undoubtedly provide "the most definite and solid aid obtainable for the elucidation of the most prominent of the material features of the Bible." Unmentioned at the time, but no less significant, was its strategic significance in connection with the Suez Canal. The P.E.F.'s future course of action suddenly became clear. A resolution for a complete survey of Palestine was passed unanimously.

A fresh interest in the mapping of Palestine was growing in the United States as well. A new wave of American prosperity had come with the end of the Civil War, and American participation in the exploration of the Holy Land, which had lapsed since the time of Robinson and Lynch, began once more. As early as the summer of 1869, a group of prominent Chicagoans had established the first American chapter of the P.E.F., but it soon became evident that they could not be content with the mere financial support of a British organization. In the following year, an independent American Palestine Exploration Society was founded in New York, its organizers proclaiming their intention to compete on an equal footing with the British P.E.F. Subscribers were recruited, a periodical was published, and in July 1871, the Americans announced plans to dispatch a mapping expedition of their own to Palestine.

The discovery of the Moabite Stone had attracted great attention in the American press, and the organizers of the American society were anxious to take advantage of it. Although the P.E.F. had already concluded that additional explorations in the area around Dhiban would not be worthwhile, the Americans—perhaps out of inexperience or sheer stubbornness—did not agree. Disregarding the P.E.F.'s announced intention of mapping the entire Holy Land, the fledgling American society stepped forward to claim Transjordan for itself.

This claim posed the danger of outright conflict, but an accommodation was quickly worked out. In fact, the unexpected participation of the Americans in the mapping of Palestine proved to be a great advantage to the P.E.F. By dividing the country with the Americans along the boundary of the Jordan River, the Royal Engineers would be left with a much more manageable area to survey, and it was an area that included by far the most important sites of Biblical and strategic interest.

All that remained was the organization and dispatch of the British and American survey parties, and as might be expected, the British, with their considerable experience in mapping projects all over the world, had a far easier job of it. Charles Wilson quickly obtained the services of an officer and two engineers, equipped with instruments and other necessities by the Admiralty and the Ordnance Survey Office. By the fall of 1871, all was in readiness and emotional announcements appeared in the major British newspapers heralding the departure of the P.E.F. surveyors for their important work in western Palestine.

The Americans required considerably longer to get into the field. In fact, it took almost a year for them to raise sufficient funds for the expedition, and when those funds were finally raised, several more months were consumed by the search for a competent officer to take charge. The mantle finally fell on Lieutenant Edgar Z. Steever, a recent graduate of West Point, whose only experience in surveying had come during his brief service in the Indian Territory. The War Department in Washington gave him leave, and late in 1872 he departed from New York with Professor John Paine of the American missionary college outside Constantinople, who would serve as archeologist for the mission. Equipment and additional personnel, it was decided, would be acquired in the field.

Paine proceeded directly to Beirut to make the necessary preparations with the help of the American missionaries there, while Steever stopped off in London for a conference with the officials of the Palestine Exploration Fund. It was there that he first became aware of the utter unpreparedness of his own mission. The British plan of work, as explained to Steever by Captain Wilson, was topographical mapping of the highest accuracy; the Americans had planned only a preliminary reconnaissance of the area granted to them. With the limited financial means at his disposal, Steever could never hope to match the quality or comprehensiveness of the British work. The result of this meeting was an urgent request to New York for additional funds.

"It will be an everlasting shame," warned Steever, "if the American people allow this expedition to come to grief." The American Palestine Exploration Society had unfortunately bargained for more than it could reasonably accomplish. But by this time there was no turning back.

The Royal Engineers were already hard at work in Palestine, and despite the fact that the first officer sent out to lead them had been stricken with malaria and had to be returned to England, their mapping program was proceeding exceptionally well. With the noncommissioned officers taking charge of the technical work of the survey, Charles Tyrwhitt-Drake, the civilian archeologist attached to the mission, was called upon to handle the more practical concerns. He assembled a traveling party of six natives, a guard dispatched by the pasha of Jerusalem, eight horses, seven mules, and six camels to carry their heavy crates of instruments. They established base stations at a central location in each area to be surveyed, and conducted negotiations with the local sheikh or mukhtar for cooperation, protection, and temporary laborers.

A huge grid was laid down over each area by the determination of triangles, and after the work with the theodolites was completed, the smaller topographical details were filled in by hand, with the members of the survey party progressing across the hills and valleys with measuring tapes and drawing pads. The method proved extremely efficient, and by July 1872, Tyrwhitt-Drake was pleased to report to the officials of the P.E.F. back in London that he had accomplished the mapping of more than 560 square miles in the region to the north of Jerusalem.

Lieutenant Claude Conder of the Royal Engineers was eventually appointed to replace the invalided commander, and his term of office was destined to be far longer. Conder, in fact, would spend the rest of his life fully committed to the exploration of the Holy Land, writing dozens of popular and scholarly articles on the history of Palestine, translating the El-Amarna tablets from Egypt, and lecturing all over England on behalf of the P.E.F. about his discoveries and experiences in the Middle East. Like Wilson and Warren before him, Conder was an ambitious, meticulous officer, fiercely proud of the reputation of the Royal Engineers. Yet when he joined the surveying party in Nablus in July 1872, he was amazed at the precision and scope of the work that had so far been accomplished under Tyrwhitt-Drake and the noncommissioned officers.

With Conder in command, the expedition pushed ahead with even greater efficiency, surveying, mapping, and cataloguing more than 1250 square miles. By the summer of 1873, the party was occupying itself with the southern regions of Palestine, and their maps, sheets, and notebooks were being filled even faster than the committee back in London had expected. By fall, with the survey of Philistia complete, Conder and his men traveled northward through the Jordan Valley. In the notorious swamps of the area, however, both Conder and Tyrwhitt-Drake were attacked by malaria. Their illness forced the work to be stopped, but the amount of information that they had already sent back to England justified a temporary halt anyway, to give scholars a chance to sift through the mountains of reports, sketches, specimens, and dispatches that had flowed from Palestine during the previous two years.

The American Palestine Exploration Society was, in the meantime, all too short of results. Lieutenant Steever's urgent request for additional funding had been answered by a dispatch of ten thousand dollars to Beirut, but money alone was not enough to bring the Steever mission up to grade. When all the money had been spent, the sole product of the enterprise was a small chart of the region in which the Moabite stone was found, published in the journal of the American society. But being only a sketch map, it fell far short of the British standards for their maps of western Palestine.

Steever returned to duty in the Indian Territory at the conclusion of his mission, but the work of the American Palestine Exploration Society went on. They had pledged to the P.E.F. that they would complete the mapping of all territory to the east of the Jordan, and in 1875, they dispatched a somewhat more organized expedition to take up the work. This time, the American team included a competent surveyor, an archeologist, and a photographer—and at its head stood not a mere second lieutenant, but James C. Lane, noted railroad planner, frontier explorer, and hero of the Civil War.

The choice proved unfortunate. Almost from the start of the work, Lane's own view of how the American work should be carried out diverged widely from that held in New York. He felt that they should adopt the methods of topographic survey so successfully utilized for the construction of the transcontinental railroad in the American West. Immediately upon his arrival in Beirut, Lane began to dash off imperious memoranda to the committee in New York demanding additional funds. Unfortunately for Lane, the American society had already strained itself financially to mount the second expedition and had no additional resources. Told this, Lane angrily resigned his association with the society and returned to the United States, leaving his equipment and men in Beirut.

There was no alternative left to the stranded Americans but to press on without Lane. Under the direction of the staff archeologist, a former Congregationalist minister named Selah Merrill, the party proceeded to Transjordan, where it conducted intermittent explorations for the next two years, publishing an incomplete report of its findings in the journal of the American Palestine Exploration Society. Merrill himself later wrote a popular, highly romanticized account of his travels and ultimately won an appointment as U.S. consul to Jerusalem under the administration of President Chester A. Arthur. But the society that had given him that great opportunity did not fare so well.

A continual lack of funds and experience, to say nothing of results, eventually convinced the American society to abandon the work altogether. No more "Moabite stones" were found, no headlines garnered, and since the United States government had not yet developed any important commercial or strategic interests in the region, there was little hope of ever gaining any official support. The American Palestine Exploration Society unhappily became nothing more than a footnote to the history of Biblical exploration. Great Britain, with its considerable concern for the strategic balance of power in the Middle East, was destined to complete the mapping of Palestine all by itself.

In February 1874, after several months of convalescence in Jerusalem, Lieutenant Conder resumed the work of the P.E.F. survey, ordering his men to return to the point at which they had left off, continuing up the Jordan Valley to the Sea of Galilee. Unfortunately, Tyrwhitt-Drake, the archeologist, was attacked once again by malarial fever, and this time he did not recover. But the Survey of Western Palestine was now too important an undertaking to be halted even by the death of such a key figure, and in Tyrwhitt-Drake's place the P.E.F. sent out a twenty-four-year-old officer of the Royal Engineers who had been highly recommended for the post. The young lieutenant was Horatio Herbert Kitchener, and the mission to Palestine would be but the first of a long career of service to his queen and country in the Middle East.

With Kitchener joining the survey party, Conder renewed the work with increased speed and determination. By June 1875, they had surveyed more than 4400 square miles of the previously unmapped countryside, and by the end of the year, they hoped, the map of western Palestine would finally be complete. A compelling reason for this heightened urgency was the movement of political events in the Middle East. The Ottoman treasury was virtually bankrupt, and the raging inflation, black-marketeering, and widespread governmental corruption that resulted were creating unrest throughout the empire. The situation in Egypt was no different, for the Khedive Ismail was himself deep in debt to foreign investors, and it would only be a matter of months before the British government, at the instigation of Prime Minister Disraeli, would purchase Egypt's shares in the Suez Canal. The prospects for the future of the Middle East were even bleaker than at the time of the initiation of the survey, and with only a thousand square miles of Palestine left to survey, Conder and Kitchener girded themselves for the one final effort that would complete the work.

On July 10, 1875, Conder ordered the men of the survey party to establish a base camp opposite the Galilean town of Safed to serve as headquarters for the mapping of the northeastern region of the country. As they had done many times before, the servants unloaded the cases of equipment from the pack animals, unrolled and put up the tents for the officers, and began preparations for the evening meal. The official firman that they carried was dispatched by messenger to the Turkish governor of the town for his approval, and Lieutenant Conder retired to his tent, as was his custom, to relax in his shirtsleeves and slippers.

Suddenly, outside the tent, angry voices broke the evening stillness. A local sheikh, his face flushed with rage, was engaged in a furious argument with one of the servants, who accused him of stealing a pistol from one of the equipment crates. Conder emerged from his tent, determined to restore calm. During the entire survey he had been treated respectfully by the population as the official representative of a powerful nation. But now, as he approached the sheikh, the sheikh lunged for him, taking him by the throat with both hands, shaking him like a child.

The cause of this outburst was unknown to Conder, but he had his reputation to uphold, as an English officer and as a gentleman. He pushed the sheikh to the ground, and assumed a boxing stance, ready to accept the personal challenge of the Arab. But the sheikh apparently was unfamiliar with both the marquess of Queensbury and the art of fisticuffs. Seeing the Englishman tensed and ready to fight, the sheikh drew a knife and lunged toward him. Fortunately for Conder, the servants of the party rushed the sheikh and disarmed him. A rope was quickly brought and the sheikh was bound, kicking and screaming, on the ground.

A large crowd of local inhabitants had gathered in the meantime, brought down from the village by the sounds of shouting and disturbance. The sight of one of their number tied and under the control of the Englishmen clearly enraged them. A shower of stones descended on the campsite. Conder quickly ordered Kitchener to load the guns, and while retreating into the safety of his own tent ordered that the sheikh be released and that word be sent to the governor immediately.

The shower of stones and the crowd's angry shouts became more intense. Packing crates crunched and were looted. The tents collapsed, and Conder and Kitchener and the other officers were forced together in the ever-contracting circle of the mob. Kitchener pointed his gun toward the crowd, Conder flailed away with his riding crop, and the photographer jabbed at the crowd with the sharp points of his camera tripod. Word of the sheikh's humiliation had spread quickly through the village, and now several young men charged down the hill toward the camp armed with a battle-ax, clubs, and a scimitar, determined to take their revenge on the "Franks."

In the battle that followed, both Conder and Kitchener were badly beaten. All of their servants were wounded by stones, and the campsite was left in shambles. But rather than open fire on the crowd and take the risk of even greater violence, Conder ordered his men to retreat, leading the way himself barefoot through the thistles and thorns with blood streaming down his forehead, running for his life and for the lives of his men.

By evening, all was quiet in Safed again. The troops of the local garrison had arrived to disperse the crowd, and Conder returned with his bruised and battered men, requesting an urgent meeting with the qadi, the governor, and the British consular agent. He carefully detailed the injuries to his men and the damage to their equipment, and announced that the work of the survey would be halted pending the arrest and trial of the guilty parties. The official permission granted to the P.E.F. to survey the country without harassment had been transgressed, and it would be impossible to continue until the damaged honor of the Palestine Exploration Fund and of the Royal Engineers was vindicated by the full force of the Ottoman government.

After a fearful and sleepless night at the ruined base camp—since the sheikh had warned that he would return and "cut the throats" of the Englishmen—Conder ordered his men to pack up what was left of their belongings and begin a march to the coast. The men were weakened by their beatings, and by the time they reached Haifa, several of them had developed fevers. No other course lay open to Conder but to order them all back to England. The British consuls in Jerusalem and Beirut were duly informed of the matter and instructed to insist on bringing the culprits to trial. It had been a relatively minor incident by the standards of the Ottoman Empire, but imperial Britain regarded it as a serious affront. For the time being at least, pride was far more important than the completion of the survey of western Palestine.

Conder and Kitchener and their staff remained in London throughout 1876, working steadily in an office loaned to them by the government on the huge amount of material that had been gathered in the first four years of the survey. There was more than enough work preparing the preliminary maps, and the Safed affair had taken on a tremendous symbolic significance that had to be resolved before a return to Palestine could even be contemplated. The Ottoman authorities were at first reluctant to prosecute the case, but, under pressure from the British consuls, the suspects and ringleaders were eventually rounded up and brought to trial in Acre. Ali Agha Allan, the sheikh who had begun the disturbance (he proved to be an Algerian exile settled in Safed by the Ottomans, and claimed to be a relative of the notorious Berber rebel Abd al-Kader), was sentenced to nine months' imprisonment. The young men of the town who had actually attacked the surveying party were given sentences of several years at hard labor. And, to add insult to injury, the entire populace of Safed was ordered to pay an indemnity of £270 into the general treasury of the Palestine Exploration Fund.

"The affair has in the end proved a salutary lesson," noted Conder from the safety of a secure position in England, "and has shown the natives of Palestine that English subjects cannot be insolently treated with impunity." Then, as if to demonstrate that lesson in person, Lieutenant Kitchener left for Palestine at the beginning of 1877 to complete the still unfinished work of the great survey of the Holy Land. Despite the continued turbulence of the native population, Kitchener maintained complete discipline over the noncommissioned officers under his command and the natives in his employ. The return of the surveying party to Safed was triumphant; all the officials and dignitaries of the village came out to greet the Englishmen and pay homage. Ali Agha himself, recently released from prison, begged for Kitchener's forgiveness, and in an act of majestic condescension the young English lieutenant waived the last sixty pounds of the indemnity, in consideration of the recent drought and public humiliation that the apparently contrite inhabitants of Safed had already suffered.

By October 1877, the survey party had completed the remaining portions of northern Palestine, and Kitchener was able to inform the executive committee in London that every feature, road, ruin, and watercourse in Palestine had been faithfully recorded and plotted. No longer could the Holy Land be considered unexplored territory, more vivid in the pages of the Bible than in reality.

Back in London, George Grove and Charles Wilson supervised the publication of the *Memoirs* of the Palestine survey and in September 1878 issued them, to great excitement. They included, in addition to the huge, detailed map of Palestine and twenty-six volumes of memoirs, the special reports of Charles Clermont-Ganneau on Jerusalem and of Professor Palmer on Sinai, a huge collection of architectural photographs, and a large number of carefully drawn plans of archeological remains. While scholars pored over the wealth of scientific material, the results of the survey also went out to the general public in more popular forms—*Lt. Kitchener's Guinea Book of Bible Photographs,* and Conder's enormously successful personal account of the expedition, entitled *Tent Work in Palestine: A Record of Discovery and Adventure.* The Palestine Exploration Fund proudly rode a tidal wave of public enthusiasm and admiration. Future plans were excitedly discussed and projected, including a large-scale expedition to the Sea of Galilee meant to uncover many of the sites connected with the life of Jesus.

But one of the most lasting effects of the Survey of Western Palestine was as yet unrecognized. The Ottoman Empire still considered the Holy Land to be an integral part of the province of Syria. The time was approaching when it would become a separate state, and when that happened, its shape would have already been established. The northern limit was exactly that boundary along the hills of Upper Galilee where the P.E.F. mapping had stopped; so was the eastern line along the course of the Jordan River. The Survey of Western Palestine had defined the geographical future.

During the final years of work on the Palestine Survey, the British government viewed the "Eastern Question" with ever-deepening concern. Renewed revolts of the Christian populations in the Balkans provoked a brutal campaign of suppression by the Ottoman authorities, and news of the Turkish atrocities aroused sympathy and outrage throughout the Christian world. The Russians, always anxious to extend their own boundaries on the pretext of defending their Slavic brothers, invaded the Balkans in 1877, totally defeating the forces of the sultan and detaching Romania and Bulgaria from Ottoman rule. The loss of the Balkan provinces was the first step in the final dismemberment of the Ottoman Empire, and despite the considerable anti-Turkish feeling among the British, the government tried desperately to prevent the inevitable. In 1878, at the Congress of Berlin, the European powers acting in concert devised a complex scheme to patch the Ottoman Empire back together again.

Great Britain, mediating between the Turks and the Russians, confirmed the independence of Romania, Serbia, and Montenegro, but pledged in the future to protect the territorial integrity of the remaining regions of the sultan's empire. For that purpose, Britain was allowed to occupy the island of Cyprus as a strategic bastion of naval strength in the eastern Mediterranean and, more importantly, as a convenient base from which to guard the freedom of passage through the Suez Canal.

An increased British presence in the Middle East required the services of experienced officers and administrators, and such individuals could be found among the former explorers of the Palestine Exploration Fund. The proposed P.E.F. expedition to the Sea of Galilee was postponed and Kitchener, fresh from his work in Palestine, was appointed to survey the newly acquired island of Cyprus. Charles Wilson, the first explorer of the fund, was assigned to the Serbian Boundary Commission to chart the revised European boundary of the Ottoman Empire.

Both men performed their tasks admirably and were rewarded with even more sensitive appointments: Wilson became the British consul general in Asia Minor the following year, and Kitchener was appointed military vice-consul on Cyprus. The P.E.F., despite the loss of personnel to the more pressing demands of the nation, continued its activity in the Holy Land, though on a greatly reduced scale. Conder was dispatched to survey those regions to the east of the Jordan abandoned by the Americans; he worked there until 1882, when he was stopped by the increasingly suspicious Ottoman authorities.

Early in that same year, renewed British fears arose over the safety of the Suez Canal. Following a nationalist uprising of Egyptian army officers, the war minister, Ahmad Arabi Pasha, began to stir up anti-European sentiment as a prelude to open rebellion against the ineffectual British-supported Khedive Tewfik. Such a revolt was seen as a dangerous threat by the British government, which quickly formulated a plan to invade and occupy Egypt in order to ensure the security of the canal. The mutinous Egyptian army posed no significant military obstacle, but the same could not be said for the Bedouin of the Sinai peninsula. If they allied themselves with Arabi's rebellion, constant attacks on the British invasion force could be expected from the east. Some means would have to be found to determine their intentions, and for this purpose the British government appealed for the services of a former explorer of the Palestine Exploration Fund.

Professor Edward Henry Palmer had explored the Sinai twice—with Wilson in 1868 and with Tyrwhitt-Drake in the following year. As a prominent Arabic scholar and expert on the nomenclature of the Sinai peninsula and the customs of its Bedouin, Palmer volunteered for the potentially dangerous assignment, traveling to the east in the summer of 1882 in the character of a civilian journalist. His instructions were to make contact with the Sinai Bedouin and, if possible, to persuade them to remain neutral in the coming conflict.

After setting out from Gaza, Palmer met with a number of important Bedouin leaders, renewing old acquaintanceships and finding that there was no great sympathy for the cause of the Egyptian nationalists. This intelligence did not satisfy Palmer, the scholar now playing spy. Arriving in Suez, he convinced the admiral in command of British forces that the active cooperation of the Bedouin—not just their neutrality—was possible and that a second expedition into the Sinai could turn the trick. Accompanied by two officers of the Royal Navy, Palmer set off into the desert again with a bag containing three thousand pounds in gold. His instructions were to acquire a supply of camels for the British invasion force, cut the telegraph line that led out of Egypt across the desert, and, most important of all, convince the Bedouin to come over to the British side.

He set off, and vanished. The telegraph line remained in operation, and the British invasion force received no hint of the fate of the secret mission. As the weeks passed, the British forces—without the help of the Bedouin—gained complete, unchallenged control over Egypt. But Palmer was gone. The famous professor and the officers who accompanied him had mysteriously disappeared into the heart of the desert.

Charles Warren, the pioneer of Jerusalem exploration, had not returned to the Middle East since completing his excavations in 1870. He served with distinction in southern Africa, and was chief instructor in surveying in the school of military engineering at Chatham when the rebellion broke out in Egypt. Warren had suggested a plan of his own to the War Office for the pacification of the Sinai Bedouin, although it had been rejected in favor of the dispatch of Professor Palmer. He was now urgently requested to find out what had happened to Palmer and, if possible, to salvage his mission.

On September 1, 1882, Warren left Chatham for Egypt. Arriving at

Suez, he gathered information on Palmer's probable route, then set off into the wilderness with several noncommissioned officers. He firmly believed that Palmer was being held for ransom by the Bedouin. But after several days of travel and interrogation of the Bedouin that he met, Warren finally learned the grisly truth: Palmer had apparently overestimated his familiarity with the Bedouin; lured into a trap by a traitorous guide, he and his entire party had been murdered for the money that they carried.

On October 22, Warren and his search party discovered Palmer's remains in a desolate ravine in the midst of the Sinai. There was nothing to do but to raise a memorial pile of stones on the spot, offer some words of prayer, and carefully collect what was left of Palmer and his officers for shipment back to England.

In the meantime, the British forces were consolidating their control over Egypt. Charles Wilson had been summoned from his post in Asia Minor to serve as the British commissioner for the trial of Arabi Pasha and, together with Warren, to supervise the search and capture of the parties responsible for the murder of Professor Palmer. In time, the guide responsible for the ambush gave himself up and confessed to the crime. One bag, containing a thousand pounds, was recovered. By Christmas 1882, all the other suspects had been rounded up, tried, and executed in the presence—insisted on by the British—of the sheikhs of all the Sinai's Bedouin clans. Lieutenant Kitchener, who visited the country shortly afterward, commented with satisfaction that "Warren's energetic action in the capture and bringing to justice of the perpetrators of the crime has created a deep impression. . . . the whole peninsula is now, for foreign travelers, as safe as, if not safer than, it was previously."

In March 1883, Charles Warren received a knighthood and a campaign medal, in addition to the honors he had already received from the Ottoman government and the British-controlled government of Egypt. He returned to Chatham, where he quietly resumed his position at the military engineering school. His continued career in the service of the British Empire would ultimately take him to such remote posts as Bechuanaland and Singapore, and to command of the Royal Engineers in 1905. Curiously, his greatest notoriety in later years came from another attempt to track down a murderer, this time less successfully. Warren was chief commissioner of Scotland Yard at the time of the "Jack the Ripper" murders, a case which even his considerable experience as an investigator did not help to solve.

Charles Wilson became increasingly involved in intelligence matters. After the completion of his service in Egypt he participated in an attempt to break the siege of Khartoum and rescue General Gordon. Horatio Herbert Kitchener returned to Palestine briefly in 1883 to conduct an additional survey for the P.E.F., and he, more than any other of the fund's former explorers, was destined to play a crucial role in the formulation of British strategic policy in the Middle East. As secretary of state for war during World War I, he would lay the groundwork for the most effective and permanent means of defense for the Suez Canal: the conquest of Palestine.

The long procession of military explorers that had begun almost forty years before with Lieutenant William Francis Lynch was now over, and Palestinian exploration would in the future lie for the most part in civilian hands. Both the army and science had benefited from the cooperation; Palestine's general geographical and archeological outlines were now clearly drawn, and the maps of the survey of Palestine, printed at the expense of the British government, would be of crucial value some thirty years later, at the time of the final British campaign in the Holy Land

❖ III ❖

THE TRIUMPH OF
SCIENCE

❖ 13 ❖

One Million Pounds Sterling

THE RISE AND FALL OF
MOSES WILHELM SHAPIRA,
1883–1885

Throughout the decade of the eighteen-seventies, while the brave men of the P.E.F. survey determinedly paced their way across the wild and forgotten regions of Palestine, a steady stream of wealthy western tourists flowed along the better-traveled routes. With the building of the first carriage road from Jaffa to Jerusalem, the improvement of steamship communications, and the inclusion of the Holy Land in the group tours of Thomas Cook & Son, the tourist trade became an important element in the economy of Jerusalem. Unlike the poor Greek and Latin pilgrims, these travelers from England, Europe, and America had money to spare. And in the aftermath of the affair of the Moabite Stone and the great publicity given to Warren's excavations in Jerusalem, many dreamed of making earth-shaking discoveries themselves.

The inhabitants of Palestine quickly realized the financial possibilities of this obsession with antiquities. Ancient pottery, coins, and figurines soon replaced the more traditional souvenirs of a trip to the Holy Land. Everywhere the western tourists went in the country, they were besieged with ancient relics, and the high prices they were willing to pay for them soon gave rise to shops in Jerusalem specially catering to their desires. Clustered around the "Pool of Hezekiah," these European-style shops offered the wealthy visitor to Jerusalem the opportunity to purchase photographs of the holy sites and elaborately carved olive wood souvenirs, plus a whole range of ancient pottery and coins, gathered from the peasants of the country for a few piasters apiece and resold at a considerable profit.

One of these shops on Christians' Street, mentioned as "the best" in the 1876 edition of Baedeker's *Palestine & Syria,* was owned by Moses

Wilhelm Shapira, a Jew converted to Anglicanism, who had come to Jerusalem from his native Kiev in 1856 at age twenty-six. Shapira felt that he was a cut above the many purveyors of tourist souvenirs in the Holy City: he had married a German Lutheran deaconess, was an active parishioner of the English church, and devotedly waited upon the wealthy western visitors who happened into his well-kept shop. Although scorned by the Orthodox Jews of Jerusalem as a shameless social climber and apostate, Shapira was proud of the reputation he had established for himself in the European community of Jerusalem.

Shapira was more than a mere merchant. Through his dealings in antiquities, he came to consider himself something of an expert in archeology. And through his wife's connections with the German community in Jerusalem, he was thoroughly familiar with the unfortunate outcome of the attempt to purchase the Moabite Stone for the Imperial Museum in Berlin. Anxious to attract a serious European clientele to his shop, he maintained a network of peasant contacts throughout the country and was able to obtain a steady supply of ancient artifacts of the best quality. In 1873 one of Shapira's occasional suppliers, Selim al-Gari, brought into Shapira's shop a collection more important than anything that Shapira had ever seen before. Selim's collection, reportedly found by the Bedouin in the very same region where the Moabite Stone was uncovered, included dozens of complete pottery vessels, animal figurines, and stone busts. And unlike the ancient pottery that normally fell into Shapira's hands, many of these pieces were inscribed with ancient letters almost identical to those found on the Moabite stone. A collection like this was too important to be sold to the tourists. Armed with Selim's assurance that more pottery and figurines could be obtained for the right price from the same source, Shapira approached the German consul with the idea that he might obtain the lot for the Imperial Museum.

As Shapira had hoped, the Prussians eagerly jumped at the opportunity to make up for their humiliation in the Moabite Stone affair. Shapira's "Moabite potteries" quickly caused a sensation in Jerusalem and the scholarly world. Crate after crate of the relics was carefully packed in straw and shipped to Berlin, where German scholars studied the inscriptions and published their results in dozens of academic papers. The strange, often grotesque, sometimes erotic figurines were heralded as ancient likenesses of the gods of the Moabites, and both Shapira and the German consul in Jerusalem basked in the attention of the learned world.

During this same period, the Palestine Exploration Fund was plagued with troubles. The Survey of Western Palestine, still in its early stages, had been halted temporarily because of malaria, and while Captain

Conder and the other men were recuperating in Jerusalem, they heard the reports of the Moabite pottery. Both Conder and Tyrwhitt-Drake visited Shapira's shop to see the relics for themselves. Then, with the permission of the Prussian authorities, they made drawings and copied some of the inscriptions to be sent back to the P.E.F. in London. Though the Germans had carefully cornered the collection for themselves, effectively cutting out the British, Conder voiced strong support for its authenticity. Tyrwhitt-Drake, however, remained skeptical and privately informed Conder that he had heard rumors of some "salted" excavations going on in Moab, implying that they were the source of Shapira's relics.

Shapira considered such criticism to be underhanded and the result of pure envy on the part of the British. In order to disprove the charge of faked excavations, he personally conducted the German consul and Pastor Weser of the Lutheran mission across to Jordan to see for themselves the site of the find. By this time, Shapira himself was sponsoring the excavations there, and the two Germans concluded, after witnessing several vessels being unearthed, that the Moabite potteries were indeed genuine. This vote of confidence summoned up an even greater flow of antiquities from Moab into Shapira's shop in Jerusalem, many more of which bore the Moabite inscriptions that were so prized by the German scholars.

In December 1873, Charles Clermont-Ganneau returned to Jerusalem to make a special survey of the city's antiquities for the Palestine Exploration Fund. As the chief actor in the drama of the Moabite Stone, he naturally considered himself an expert on the subject, and since first hearing of the discovery of the Moabite potteries, he had taken more than a passing interest in them. The tensions between Clermont-Ganneau and the Prussians still remained, and it was only through the intercession of Tyrwhitt-Drake that the young Frenchman was even allowed to examine the pottery. The carefully supervised examination, under the suspicious eyes of both Shapira and the Prussians, did nothing to change Clermont-Ganneau's opinion. He had believed them to be forgeries from the start. Although there was much work to be done in his researches for the P.E.F., Clermont-Ganneau spent the last few weeks of 1873 determined to prove —even obsessed with proving—the Moabite potteries to be a fraud.

In a matter of days, Clermont-Ganneau was able to discover the exact origin of Shapira's collection. Coaxing a confession from a potter's apprentice who had been in on the scheme, he confronted the Prussian consul with evidence that the pottery had been manufactured in Jerusalem under the careful supervision of none other than Selim al-Gari. Selim, it turned out, had approached Clermont-Ganneau several years

before, with an offer to obtain the Moabite Stone. As if to convince
Clermont-Ganneau of his reliability, he had presented him with his own
tracing of some of the letters of the stone. Clermont-Ganneau refused
Selim's proposal, for he even then had known him to be a local artist fond
of creating "ancient" icons for sale to pilgrims. Noticing that the letters
on the "Moabite pottery" bore a suspicious similarity to Selim's tracings,
he had secretly stalked Selim's movements with the elegant stealth of a
Victorian detective.

The German consul was naturally thunderstruck by Clermont-Ganneau's charges. A special inquiry was held at which Selim fiercely defended his honesty, and the apprentice renounced his previous statements to Clermont-Ganneau, saying that they had been forced upon him.
Selim's house was searched by the order of the pasha, but no trace of
pottery manufacture was discovered. By February 1874, the matter remained at a deadlock. The conflicting testimony remained unresolved,
yet the whole matter of the "Shapira collection" was very much under a
cloud. Shapira staunchly defended the antiquity of the pottery and was
supported by Professor Konstantine Schlottman, a noted German Biblical scholar. But the tide had clearly turned. Fierce debates raged in the
Prussian parliament over who had been responsible for appropriating the
seventy thousand thalers that had already been spent on the "Moabite
potteries." Prussia, it was clear, had once again been humiliated in its
attempt to gain honor through the purchase of Biblical relics.

Although Clermont-Ganneau did not implicate Shapira—except for
naïveté—in the forgery of the pottery, Shapira felt that his honor had
been besmirched by the ambitious Frenchman. He returned to the routine of his shop on Christians' Street, but he longed for another discovery
that would restore his name and reputation in the highest circles of
European scholarship. His position in the Jerusalem Anglican community, always shaky because of his Jewish and Eastern European origins,
had been severely damaged. If he could only find another artifact of great
importance, he could regain his deserved position in society.

In the summer of 1878, by which time the affair of the Moabite potteries had been more or less forgotten, Moses Shapira finally found what he
was looking for. In July of that year, as Shapira himself later recounted
the story, he was visited in his Jerusalem shop by several Bedouin sheikhs
with whom he had carried on dealings for his ill-fated "excavations" in
Moab. The sheikhs had merely come to exchange pleasantries, Shapira
recalled, but, undoubtedly influenced by the merchandise in glass cases

all around them, the conversation quickly turned to the subject of ancient relics. It was foolish for the Arabs to sell antiquities to the Europeans, one of the sheikhs told him, not because they were not getting enough money, but because ancient relics were powerful charms in bringing good luck to their owner. In fact, the sheikh recalled, during the Ottoman expedition against the Bedouin of Moab in 1867, one of the men of his own clan had discovered some relics while hiding in a cave, and they had brought him great fortune. They were strange, blackened skins bearing unintelligible letters, carefully wrapped in linen. Shapira immediately sensed the importance of this find. The area that the sheikh described was in the same place as the Moabite Stone, and the prospect of ancient manuscripts excited Shapira. He therefore asked the sheikh if he would be able to contact the man mentioned in the story. The sheikh agreed to accept a small payment in exchange for arranging a meeting a few days later.

The circumstances of Shapira's meeting with the man, whom he knew only as "Salem," are shrouded in mystery. The first meeting supposedly took place under the cover of darkness on the outskirts of Jerusalem. At that time Shapira received a small piece of parchment bearing four columns of writing. Three more meetings were arranged in the subsequent weeks, and by the end of August Shapira had purchased fifteen strips of parchment from the mysterious Bedouin. At about this time, his original contact, the Bedouin sheikh, died, and Shapira lost touch completely with "Salem." Not being able to obtain any more fragments, Shapira set to work in a quiet room above his shop to decipher the strange manuscripts that had come into his possession.

The letters of the manuscript were of a form exactly like that of the Moabite Stone. Unfortunately, the strips of parchment were covered with a thick black coating that smelled like asphalt, and distinguishing the individual letters was extremely difficult. Shapira was not a trained Hebrew scholar, but as he painstakingly transcribed the text on the leather strips, and then compared it to various Biblical texts, he became more and more excited about what he found. There on the fifteen strips of smelly, blackened parchment that he had bought for only a few shillings lay an ancient copy of the Book of Deuteronomy! The forms of the letters closely resembled those of the Moabite Stone, which Shapira knew to have been dated to the ninth century B.C., thus making this by far the most ancient manuscript of the Bible ever found. If the Biblical scholars of Europe were searching for concrete proof of the antiquity and authenticity of the modern texts of the Bible, here it was.

Shapira carefully copied the wording of his "Moabite Deuteronomy" and sent it off with copies of the scrolls themselves to Professor Schlottman in Berlin. He clearly hoped that his staunchest defender in the affair of the pottery would now be sympathetic to an even greater discovery.

Schlottman, however, was enraged that Shapira should have the effrontery to call upon him again after all the ridicule he had suffered on the dealer's account. The ancient scrolls were obvious forgeries, Schlottman angrily replied. The divergences from the traditional text were so glaring as to make Shapira's claims for them ridiculous, if not blasphemous. Prussia could not allow itself to be hoodwinked again in Palestine, and Schlottman wired the German consul in Jerusalem, the ironically named Baron von Münchhausen, to prevent Shapira from exhibiting or even making public his "ancient" scrolls.

Shapira seems to have accepted the finding of Professor Schlottman, at least for the time being. He dashed off a contrite letter to Dr. Charles Rieu, keeper of oriental manuscripts at the British Museum, to whom he had previously written, saying that he had unfortunately learned that the documents were forgeries and that Rieu should no longer concern himself with the matter. But it is clear that Shapira did not abandon all hope that the scrolls might indeed be genuine. Biding his time and returning to the business of running his thriving shop on Christians' Street, he deposited the blackened strips of parchment in a vault in a Jerusalem bank. They could wait.

Repeatedly during the years since the humiliating affair of the Moabite potteries, Shapira had disappeared from Jerusalem for months at a time. Leaving his shop in the charge of his employees under the grim supervision of his Prussian wife, he would free himself from the restrictions of the civilized community that he had adopted, traveling first by steamship and then by camel and horse into the remote regions of Arabia and the Red Sea. Touring the remote, primitive Jewish communities of Yemen, Shapira would purchase discarded or disused Torah scrolls and bring them back with him to Jerusalem. Sometimes he was able to acquire manuscripts hundreds of years old, and he found a ready market for them among the scholars of medieval Hebrew in the European universities. The demand was especially high in England, for the British Museum had recently reorganized its Hebrew manuscript collection, and Shapira had sold dozens of his Yemenite Bibles to that venerable institution. Indeed, Shapira was so pleased with his connection to London that beneath the sign outside his shop, he proudly attached a small plaque that read: "Correspondent to the British Museum."

The traffic in ancient scrolls allowed Shapira to become well acquainted with the technique of manufacturing scrolls, and particularly with the changing forms of the letters over the span of centuries. Not only did the forms change, but also the text itself. If certain German scholars were correct, the present text of the Bible was actually the compilation of the earlier works of several different authors, whose contributions could be distinguished by the various names for God which they employed. Shapira's scrolls, except for the opening and closing passages, used the name Elohim exclusively. And Shapira became convinced, after reading Friedrich Bleek's *Introduction to the Old Testament,* that his scrolls were actually the work of an early "Elohistic" sect. Perhaps that might account for the strange text of the "Moabite Deuteronomy." Shapira recalled that Professor Schlottman had judged his scrolls to be forgeries on the basis of their divergences from the modern Biblical text; it was possible that the "Moabite Deuteronomy" was actually an earlier version of that book, and therefore more valuable than he had ever imagined.

By the spring of 1883, Moses Shapira was completely obsessed with the examination and retranslation of his ancient scrolls. Removing them from the safety of the bank vault, he prepared a special room above his shop where he could retreat from the bustle of the street below and absorb himself in painstaking study. As Shapira later related, he quickly began to see the errors in his earlier translation to Professor Schlottman and slowly began to make some sense of the more obscure passages. His trade in the Yemenite Torah scrolls had given him a great deal more experience in transcription, and the problems that he had faced in 1878 when he first translated the Moabite scrolls were now seen clearly.

Unfortunately, the condition of the fifteen strips had deteriorated in the intervening years. They were already covered with a thin layer of black asphalt when he had first seen them, and many of the strips had darkened even further; it was now nearly impossible to make out some of the letters. Shapira claimed that soaking the strips or dampening them in water or alcohol made the letters temporarily visible, but this process had to be repeated time and time again in order to transcribe some portions of the text. The continual dampening of the ancient parchment caused further darkening, but little by little, his reconstructed text began to fit together.

By Easter 1883, Shapira had completed his new translation. More than ever before, he was convinced that the scroll was genuine. All of the textual problems in Deuteronomy that had plagued scholars for decades were absent from this version of the book. The geographical places were not confused, the death of Moses was not mentioned, and the entire text was written in the original archaic alphabet. If not written by Moses

himself, it bore, Shapira was convinced, the authority of Mosaic composi-
tion. A new Moses from Jerusalem had unlocked the secret of the message of the ancient Moses in the Years of Wandering.

In the spring of 1883, Shapira showed his scrolls, together with his
new translation, to Professor Schröder, the German consul at Beirut who
happened to be visiting Jerusalem. This was a trial balloon, for Shapira
did not want to face another rebuke like the one he had received from
Schlottman five years before. To Shapira's delight, the consul was greatly
excited by the apparent importance of the discovery. The scrolls,
Schröder was convinced, were completely genuine. The evidence they
shed on the development of the Bible were incalculable. Schröder offered
Shapira a large sum for the purchase of the fifteen strips. He himself
wanted to present them to the scholarly world.

Shapira politely declined the consul's generous offer. He had spent
too much time and invested too much of his own reputation in the
acquisition and translation of the scrolls to sell them off like a common
antiquities dealer. Shapira had begun to think of himself as something of
a Hebrew scholar in his own right, and he would now prove to the world
that he must be treated as such. Never again would he be ridiculed as a
gullible Jewish convert who was victimized by the Bedouin of Moab in his
lust to sell "Biblical relics." Moses Shapira was determined to leave his
shop on Christians' Street and take the scrolls to Europe himself as an
actor, rather than a victim, in the great European quest to uncover the
secrets of the Bible.

During that eventful spring of 1883, once Shapira had received confirmation for the authenticity of his scrolls, great prospects began to unfold
for his future. Professor Schröder, in his rapturous discussions with
Shapira over the value of the texts, suggested that the matter be referred
directly to the Kaiser in order to ensure that sufficient funds be raised to
purchase the texts for the Imperial Museum. Shapira began to see himself
as a personage of great magnitude, anticipating the fortune that the
scrolls would bring. He purchased a huge stone mansion surrounded by
gardens outside the city walls for his family, hired a manager for the store,
and freed himself from the cares of a mere shopkeeper's life.

During the visit of the German consul, Mrs. Schröder was charmed by
Shapira's eldest daughter Elizabeth and discreetly proposed a match with
her own son back in Berlin. The idea of marrying Elizabeth into a fine
family of the Prussian intelligentsia flattered Shapira greatly, but his wife
cautioned Mrs. Schröder that at the present time the family simply did

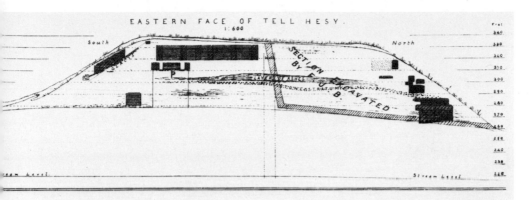

Cross-section of Tell el-Hesy, the first modern excavation in Palestine, 1890.

A sign of changing times: a western diplomatic procession through the streets of turn-of-the-century Jerusalem.

Kaiser Wilhelm and his entourage visit the Tombs of the Kings, 1898.

The American method in action: teamwork and disipline help to uncover the remains of "Ahab's Palace."

Archeology and Realpolitik: the German expedition camp on the summit of Megiddo, 1903.

Professor G. A. Reisner and an unidentified lady friend at the
Harvard excavations of Samaria, 1910.

Magazine Section
Part Five

The New York Times.

SUNDAY, MAY 7, 1911.

Magazine Section
Part Five

HAVE ENGLISHMEN FOUND THE ARK OF THE COVENANT?

A Mysterious Expedition, Apparently Not Composed of Archaeologists, Hunts Strange Treasure Under the Mosque of Omar, Sets the Moslems in a Ferment, and May Cause Diplomatic Incident.

MOSQUE of OMAR

JERUSALEM and the MOUNT of OLIVES

ARK of the COVENANT

The POOL of SILOAM outside of Jerusalem

Interior of the Mosque of Omar

The world learns of Captain Parker's improbable expedition, 1911.

An image of Ottoman rule in Palestine:
the governor of Nazareth, his staff, and
bodyguard, about 1910.

Montague Parker (at left) reluctantly
poses for a photograph.

The mayor of Jerusalem surrenders his city to two British scouts,
December 9, 1917.

The beginning of a new era: British forces enter the Holy City in triumph, December 11, 1917.

not possess a fitting dowry with which to betroth their daughter. The consul's wife, according to a later account, assured the dour Lutheran deaconess that the proceeds from the sale of the Deuteronomy manuscript to the German government would soon eliminate that problem.

In July, after dispatching Elizabeth to Berlin in the august company of her future in-laws, Shapira himself prepared to depart for Germany. He intended to have proper photographs taken of the scrolls, and also arranged, with Schröder's help, a meeting to present the ancient documents at the University of Leipzig. When he arrived in Berlin, Shapira presented the documents to a committee of experts headed by Professor Richard Lepsius, the Keeper of the Imperial Library, and the individual with power to approve the purchase of the Moabite Deuteronomy. The committee met behind closed doors on the afternoon of July 10, while Shapira himself waited patiently outside the room. After an hour and a half of deliberations, the scholars filed out of the room, grim-faced and silent, yet indicating to Shapira that the matter was still under careful consideration.

Shapira had no time to waste with the supercilious Prussians while he possessed so great a treasure. While waiting for an official reply from the Imperial Library, he took his manuscripts to the University of Leipzig and interested the famous scholar Hermann Güthe in their importance. On the basis of the study of his scroll, Güthe quickly published a pamphlet entitled *"Fragmente einer Lederhandschrift, enthaltend Moses's Letze Rede an Kinder Israel"* ("Fragments of a Leather Manuscript, Including Moses' Last Speech to the Children of Israel"). At last Shapira's great discovery had officially entered the world of academic scholarship. He wrote ecstatic letters back to Jerusalem about the reception he had received in Germany, and with excessive optimism expressed his hope that the scholars at the Imperial Library would quickly come to terms with him.

Unfortunately, no further word was forthcoming from Berlin. The professors there, apparently unimpressed by Shapira's "great discovery," had begun to drift off to their summer vacations, leaving a final decision about the scrolls to some later time. Professor Schröder was still Shapira's strongest backer, and he urged him not to tolerate such impudence. Schröder was still firmly convinced that the scrolls could bring a great fortune, and he advised Shapira to look elsewhere if the Prussian scholars were too closed-minded to acquire the great relics for the honor of the nation. Besides, the future father-in-law of his own son could command any price that he wanted for his manuscripts.

By mid-July, Shapira felt he had waited long enough for an answer from Berlin. Following the strong urging of Professor Schröder, he carefully packed up his fifteen strips of blackened parchment and headed for England, where he seemed sure that he would receive the honors and rewards properly due him.

Without warning or even introduction, Moses Shapira appeared in the offices of the Palestine Exploration Fund in London on the morning of July 20, 1883. Walter Besant, the secretary, undoubtedly absorbed in the fabrication of some new romantic novel (he wrote and published dozens), was summoned to greet the mysterious visitor. Shapira calmly announced "that he had brought to England a manuscript, which if genuine would certainly be of inestimable value, being nothing less than a text of the Book of Deuteronomy, written on sheepskin, in characters closely resembling those of the Moabite Stone, with many and most important variations." Shapira declined to show Besant the manuscripts themselves, but he arranged for a subsequent meeting at which, in the presence of Captain Conder, the former commander of the Survey of Western Palestine, he would produce them.

Conder had been one of Shapira's strongest supporters in the case of the spurious Moabite pottery, and Shapira obviously expected a sympathetic hearing from him. But when he returned with his scrolls to the P.E.F. offices at the appointed time several days later, Conder expressed dismaying doubts about the authenticity of Shapira's purported discovery; he was dubious that such ancient scrolls could survive "in a climate as damp as Palestine's" and in all his travels to Moab he had never heard any talk from the local Bedouin about the discovery of written documents. But Conder freely admitted that he was not a Hebrew scholar and he suggested that Dr. Christian David Ginsburg of the British Museum examine the documents.

Shapira waited anxiously for another two days. Understandably edgy, he returned to the P.E.F. offices on July 26. He had specifically instructed Besant and Conder to keep the word of their meetings quiet, but when he arrived for the official presentation of his "Mosaic Deuteronomy," he found much to his dismay that not only were Besant, Conder, and Ginsburg there, but also nearly the entire staff of the Manuscript Department of the British Museum.

There was no turning back now. Shapira handed over his fragments and retired to an outer office while the English scholars examined the fifteen blackened strips. The situation must have seemed ominously like that which had been played out at the Imperial Library in Berlin, but its conclusion was entirely different. The scholars were genuinely excited about Shapira's scrolls. Arrangements must be made quickly to purchase them for the British Museum, they told Shapira, and with his permission they would put them on display at once. "This is one of the few things," said one of the scholars in attendance, "that cannot be a forgery or a fraud."

On August 3, Christian David Ginsburg's letter to the *Times* officially announced the imminent acquisition of the scrolls and provided a brief translation of their contents. The story was quickly picked up by other newspapers, and soon "the World's Oldest Bible" became the talk of every stratum of London society. While the *Illustrated London News* published facsimiles of two of the strips, crowds thronged into the British Museum to see the ancient documents for themselves. The work of the P.E.F. in the Holy Land had created a great interest in the antiquities of the Bible, and during the first few weeks of August 1883 that interest reached a feverish pitch. Reports stated that Shapira had requested one million pounds for the purchase price of the scrolls and that Queen Victoria herself had agreed to guarantee that huge sum. Prime Minister Gladstone personally came to the British Museum to view the manuscripts, and in his conversations with Shapira reportedly displayed a great interest in and knowledge of Biblical antiquities.

Moses Wilhelm Shapira had suddenly become the toast of London. As reports of his great success filtered back to Jerusalem, his family assumed a position of great fame, if not actually respect, among the members of the Anglican community. The day-to-day operation of the little shop on Christians' Street became less and less important to their existence. Shapira's wife began to spend recklessly. Merchants freely offered unlimited credit to the family of the great antiquarian who would soon come into the possession of one million pounds sterling.

Charles Clermont-Ganneau had other plans for Shapira. On August 15, in the midst of the celebration and excitement over the British Museum's pending purchase of "the world's oldest Bible," he quietly arrived in London with instructions from the French minister of public instruction. He was to examine the manuscripts thoroughly and report back to Paris on his findings. Clermont-Ganneau was no longer an impetuous young man in search of a reputation; he was by this time a distinguished scholar of long standing, and he fully expected that his position in the world of Biblical archeology would afford him every courtesy in his examination of the scrolls.

Undoubtedly influenced by his previous encounter with Shapira during the affair of the Moabite potteries, Clermont-Ganneau held serious doubts as to the authenticity of Shapira's manuscripts even before arriving in London. He was not alone in this feeling, for as early as August 13, two prominent British scholars, Professors Adolf Neubauer and Archibald Henry Sayce, had condemned the scrolls as forgeries in articles in the prestigious *Academy* magazine. But the general public, roused by expansive descriptions of the value of the "Moabite Deuteronomy" and delighted that "the world's oldest Bible" would soon become the possession of the great British Empire, ignored the phlegmatic mutterings of the two stuffy scholars. Clermont-Ganneau was convinced that they were right, and he was determined to prove it.

Clermont-Ganneau lost no time in making his way to the Manuscript Department of the British Museum. There he found Ginsburg and Shapira huddled over a few of the parchment strips, deep in contemplation of the ancient text. The Frenchman's arrival filled the air with tension, for both Shapira and Ginsburg had suffered humiliation at his hands: Shapira in the case of the pottery, and Ginsburg in the case of the Moabite Stone. Ginsburg was hesitant at first to allow Clermont-Ganneau to examine the fragments at all, but Clermont-Ganneau assured him that he had no intention of publishing the text himself. Promising that he wanted to examine only the "external and material state of the fragments," he managed to look over two or three of the strips of parchment before Ginsburg announced, after a conference with Shapira, that Clermont-Ganneau would have to return in two days to continue his examination.

When Clermont-Ganneau arrived on Friday he was curtly informed by a minor museum official that he would not be permitted to examine the scrolls as promised. This was on direct instructions from Mr. Shapira, who was still the legal owner. Clermont-Ganneau refused to accept this insult to his academic reputation. Battling the weekend crowds that streamed into the exhibition hall, Clermont-Ganneau spent Friday and Saturday standing before the glass case where a few of the strips were displayed, with notebook in hand. On Saturday afternoon, Clermont-Ganneau returned to his lodgings to compile his findings, which he sent off immediately in the form of an open letter to the *Times*.

"The fragments," wrote Clermont-Ganneau, leaving no room for hesitation or discussion, "are the work of a modern forger." In the short time that he had been able to handle the strips of leather, he had come to the conclusion that they had been cut from the bottom margins of larger parchment scrolls, exactly like the Torah scrolls Shapira had acquired and sold to the British Museum. As conclusive proof of this assertion, Clermont-Ganneau described the presence of vertical incised lines near the edge of each column of the manuscript. These vertical guide lines were normal on large Bible scrolls, for they marked the vertical margins of the writing. But the compiler of the Moabite Deuteronomy completely disregarded these lines, with the letters extending beyond them on both sides. Clermont-Ganneau suggested that the authorities of the British Museum, instead of being so anxious to purchase the relics, simply lay them against the bottom margins of the scrolls that they had already purchased from Shapira. If they did so, Clermont-Ganneau assured them, "the trick would stare them in the face."

As a final jab at the credulity of the British scholars, Clermont-Ganneau cynically volunteered to carry out an experiment for the British Museum. "Let there be given me a synagogue roll, two or three centuries old," he wrote, "with permission to cut it up. I engage to procure from it strips in every respect similar to the Moabite strips, and to transcribe upon them in archaic characters the text of Leviticus, for example, or of Numbers. This would make a fitting sequel to the Deuteronomy of Mr. Shapira, but would have the slight advantage over it of not costing quite a million sterling."

Clermont-Ganneau's letter to the *Times* rudely punctured the bubble of elation surrounding "the world's oldest Bible." Many of the scholars who had initially believed Shapira's scrolls to be genuine now heaped scorn on the very idea of a "Mosaic Deuteronomy." Captain Conder rushed into print with the statement that he had always believed the manuscripts to be "deliberate forgeries." And in the subsequent uproar, the negotiations for the purchase of the strips were quietly suspended. Shapira remained in London, still hopeful that the final decision of Christian Ginsburg would turn back all the critics.

But the wave of derision was too much for Ginsburg, and in his official announcement printed in the *Times* on August 22, he contradicted his earlier statements by saying that "the manuscript of Deuteronomy which Mr. Shapira submitted to us for examination is a forgery." Proceeding along a line of argument similar to Clermont-Ganneau's, he contended that the strips were cut from larger scrolls and, going a step further, noted the similarity of the parchment to the margins of a Yemenite scroll sold to the British Museum by Shapira in 1878—the same year he had claimed that he had come into possession of the Deuteronomy manuscript. After adding the evidence of the incised vertical lines, and the apparent chemical treatment of the surface of the parchment to make it look darker, he summoned up the detective imagination of Sherlock Holmes to conclude, on the basis of the handwriting and the various misspellings of the Hebrew text, "that there were no less than four or five different persons engaged in the production of the forgery" and added, somewhat ominously, "that the compiler of the text was a Polish, Russian, or German Jew, or one who had learned Hebrew in the North of Europe."

This last implied insult hit close to home, for Christian Ginsburg was himself a Jew who had converted to Anglicanism. The British press, sensing blood, effectively used the symbol of the crafty Jewish merchant trying to cheat an unsuspecting British public. In a cartoon published in *Punch* on September 8, a scholarly Ginsburg is pictured throttling a hook-nosed, shifty-eyed Shapira before the impressive façade of the British Museum. Its caption reads: ". . . how Detective Ginsburg did Mr. Sharp-eye-ra out of his skin." As quickly as the documents had gripped the public imagination, they now became the laughingstock of Europe. Once again Charles Clermont-Ganneau had triumphed in the public press, and never before had the stakes been so high.

On the day following Ginsburg's official declaration and the sudden disappearance of the parchment strips from their glass cases in the Manuscript Department, a hastily scrawled letter arrived at the British Museum. It read:

London 23 Aug 1883

Dear Dr Ginzburg!
You have made a fool out of me by publishing and exhibiting things that you believe them to be false. I do not think that I will be able to survive this shame, although I am yet not convinced that the Ms is a forgery unless M Ganneau did it.
I will leave London in a day or two for Berlin

Yours Truly
M W Shapira

No one had been wounded more deeply than Shapira himself in the whole nasty affair. Elizabeth awaited her dowry in Germany, the family had run up huge debts back in Jerusalem, and Shapira's own dream of archeological glory had been smashed by insinuations of guilt. Yet in retrospect it seems almost inconceivable that Shapira would have tried to palm off a forgery that he had concocted himself; his reputation had already been marred by accusations of forgery, the fantastic price that he asked for the relic and the public attention that he encouraged were not the actions of a conscious con artist, and it is not likely that Shapira had the expertise to "compile" so apparently authentic a document as the Deuteronomy scroll. Still convinced that his scrolls were genuine,

Shapira set off for Europe hoping to sell them to anyone who would offer a decent price for them. His departure was hasty; he abandoned in his hotel room much of his luggage as well as the gift-wrapped boxes of expensive presents that he had apparently meant to bring back with him to Jerusalem.

But the situation was hopeless. The great publicity, both in England and on the Continent, had made all prospective purchasers wary. The scholars in Germany who had sat in judgment in July now publicly announced that they had always believed the manuscripts to be "a clever and impudent forgery" but had refrained from informing Shapira of that fact. The question naturally arose as to why the Germans had not warned the British of their findings while the scrolls were under consideration by the British Museum, but this quibble was lost in the wave of recriminations and counterrecriminations that echoed through the world press.

Shapira wandered aimlessly through Europe, his hopes and physical condition rapidly deteriorating as the long, cold winter wore on. His family in Jerusalem sank hopelessly into debt. Elizabeth had been sent home from Germany, her prospective marriage hastily canceled in light of her father's humiliation. The Moabite Deuteronomy, unsalable, now aroused only laughter and scorn. In the spring of 1884, Shapira arrived in Rotterdam. From that great European port city, steamers departed to every corner of the world. Had any hope or self-respect remained to him, Shapira might have embarked in search of new markets for his manuscripts; had he been the calculating conniver described in the press, he might have returned to Jerusalem to begin scheming once again. But the humiliation was too much to bear. On March 9, 1884, alone in a decrepit hotel, Moses Wilhelm Shapira shot himself. The affair of the Moabite Deuteronomy was over.

In 1885, Shapira's parchment scrolls were sold at auction in London for ten pounds. Two years later, they were displayed as quaint curiosities at an "Anglo-Jewish Historical Exhibition" at the Royal Albert Hall and were subsequently resold for twenty-five pounds. As the years passed, the interest of the public moved on to other concerns and curiosities. The Shapira manuscripts eventually dropped out of public view and disappeared.

In 1947, the scholarly world was jolted and amazed by the discovery of the Dead Sea Scrolls, at a site directly across the Dead Sea from the reported site of the Moabite Deuteronomy. Their authenticity and age completely disproved the contention, so stridently voiced by Conder, that ancient scrolls could not possibly survive in Palestine. Among the groups of writings included in the Dead Sea Scrolls were unusual variations of Biblical texts, several of Deuteronomy, including some documents that contained archaic Hebrew characters. Most telling of all, the larger scrolls bore incised vertical lines along their edges. Every piece of evidence used by Shapira's critics to attack the authenticity of his parchment strips was applicable to the Dead Sea Scrolls—yet they were real. But an official reopening of the case was never attempted. Shapira was long dead. His precious scrolls had mysteriously and forever vanished.

❖ 14 ❖

Coming of Age

NEW DIRECTIONS AND
INITIATIVES IN
BIBLICAL ARCHEOLOGY,
1886-1897

By the mid-eighteen-eighties, the developing techniques of modern archeology had produced some striking successes in Greece, Egypt, and Asia Minor. Heinrich Schliemann, excavating at the ancient sites of Troy and Mycenae, had shown that archeological investigation could actually supplement ancient texts and histories, as opposed to merely trying to validate or disprove them. Digging for Homeric Troy at the mound of Hissarlik in Asia Minor, Schliemann had uncovered not one but seven successive strata of occupation, and the artifacts and architectural plans that he recovered from each of them greatly added to the modern world's understanding of the civilizations that both preceded and followed the time of the Homeric epic. The implications of this new historical technique were not lost on the members of the Palestine Exploration Fund as they convened their twenty-first annual meeting in 1886. Biblical archeology, still reeling from the aftereffects of the Shapira affair, was badly in need of a bold new initiative. And it was right and inevitable, suggested the recently knighted Sir Charles Wilson, "that some of the wealthy men of England would follow Dr. Schliemann's example" and apply the most modern methods of scientific excavation to a specially selected Biblical site.

Ever since the beginning of the exploration of the Holy Land, the presence of ancient mounds all over the country had been noted but largely ignored. Only with Schliemann's pioneering work at the mound of Hissarlik did it become evident that the Palestinian mounds (called *tells* from the Arabic word meaning "hill") were actually the remains of an-

147

cient cities, whose repeated destructions and rebuildings had raised them to their characteristic shape. Many Palestinian tells bore names reminiscent of Biblical localities, and since they could be found in relatively remote areas of the country, they could offer the P.E.F. the possibility of extended excavations without the political complications faced by Warren in the crowded city of Jerusalem. More important, the careful excavation of the layers of a Palestinian tell could provide the first scientific evidence for the development of Biblical civilization.

The site selected for the renewed efforts of the P.E.F. in the Holy Land was a mound known by the name of Khirbet Ajlan, east of Gaza in an area of sparsely inhabited grazing land. Because of its general location and modern name, Ajlan was tentatively identified with the Canaanite city of Eglon, which had been conquered by Joshua and the Hebrew tribes and later incorporated into the Judean monarchy. The prospects for important discoveries there were impressive, but since the modern techniques of excavation to be utilized had never been attempted before in Palestine, the P.E.F. was obliged to look outside its own ranks for an expedition leader.

After considerable discussion and negotiation, the executive committee finally settled on William Matthew Flinders Petrie, a thirty-six-year-old British archeologist who had been working in Egypt since 1880. Petrie was skilled in the management and direction of large crews of locally recruited diggers, but what really distinguished him in the eyes of the P.E.F. was his reputation as an archeological innovator. In Egypt, Petrie had recognized the value of common pottery for dating ancient remains and he had devised a detailed chronology for the development of the most common pottery forms. The prospect of linking his Egyptian chronology with that of neighboring southern Palestine clearly intrigued Petrie and he readily agreed to undertake the P.E.F.'s first experiment in scientific excavation. With the help of the marquess of Salisbury and the British Foreign Office, the P.E.F. obtained an official firman for the expedition to Khirbet Ajlan, and Petrie set out from Egypt in the spring of 1890.

Upon his arrival in Palestine, however, Flinders Petrie was shocked to learn how little was actually known about the antiquities of the country. The dating of artifacts remained an extremely haphazard affair. The primary chronological guide was still the Bible itself, and no systematic attempt had ever been made to correlate Palestinian finds with other ancient sites in the Middle East. The proof of this sad ignorance was the very choice of Khirbet Ajlan as an excavation site. The distinctive forms of the pottery fragments scattered across its summit indicated to Petrie that far from being the Biblical town of Eglon, the site was not even occupied before the Roman period.

Fortunately, the firman giving permission to excavate included other ancient sites nearby, and Petrie immediately set off in search of more promising hunting grounds. Umm Lakis proved to be late as well, but when Petrie arrived at another mound situated near a deep ravine, called Tell el-Hesy, he realized that he had found just what both he and the P.E.F. wanted. In the succeeding six weeks of excavation, he directed scores of Arab workers from the neighboring villages in the removal of huge amounts of earth, ash, and debris, and was able to recognize the remains of eleven successive towns, each built on the the ruins of its predecessor, dating back to centuries before the Exodus.

At Tell el-Hesy, the first scientific framework for the study of ancient Palestinian civilization was established. Petrie was able to fix a chronology of pottery types found in each of the strata that corresponded to similar pottery he had excavated in Egypt. But Petrie did not disappoint the members of the P.E.F. in their search for Biblical remains; in addition to identifying "Amorite" and later "Jewish" pottery, he ventured to say that Tell el-Hesy was none other than the Biblical town of Lachish, conquered by both the Assyrians and Babylonians. This identification later proved to be incorrect, but the importance of Petrie's archeological achievement was indisputable. He had brought Palestinian archeology out of the realm of purely Biblical studies and he had begun to fit Palestinian antiquities into the cultural context of the entire ancient Middle East.

Flinders Petrie was unlike any previous P.E.F. explorer. Accustomed to the placid colonial atmosphere of occupied Egypt, he insisted that his meals in his tent at the excavation site be served on a mahogany table, his place set with sterling silverware. He lorded it over the workmen under his command, watching, directing, and controlling the buzz of activity all over the tell. But beyond the confines of his excavation camp in Palestine, Petrie was forced to confront a very different reality. After closing the first season of the excavations on June 1, 1890, he was attacked and robbed by bandits near Hebron. Although only his pride was seriously injured in the incident, he angrily pressed the acting British consul in Jerusalem to demand the arrest and imprisonment of his assailants. Then he returned to England and tendered his resignation to the P.E.F. While he was more than willing to continue to advise the fund on their projects, he wished to return to his own work in Egypt. Tell el-Hesy, and indeed all of Palestine, struck him as a singularly unpleasant place to work. In fact, it would take more than thirty years and a change of government to persuade Petrie to change his opinion and return to the tells of the Holy Land.

In the meantime, however, his decision placed the executive committee of the P.E.F. in a difficult position. With more than a year and a half remaining before the firman expired, and the excavation of Tell el-Hesy just begun, they needed the services of an experienced archeologist who could adapt quickly to the conditions of work in Palestine and who possessed the academic credentials to make that work suit the new scientific standard. By December, the committee had found its man. He was an American, Frederick Jones Bliss, the thirty-one-year-old son of the president of the American missionary college in Beirut, and his background seemed perfectly suited for the task at hand. Bliss had been born in the Levant, spoke Arabic fluently, held degrees from Amherst College and the Union Theological Seminary, and had already accomplished an independent exploration of the Holy Land in the years 1888–1890, publishing the results of his work in the *Palestine Exploration Fund Quarterly Statement.*

Officially appointed "explorer to the fund," Bliss was dispatched to Egypt, where he spent January 1891 with Petrie at the pyramid of Medum, learning the excavational techniques of his predecessor, though apparently not adopting his flamboyant personal style. Bliss remained a bachelor all his life, ingrained with a grimly conservative and practical bent of mind that undoubtedly owed its origins to his missionary upbringing. His attitude toward the inhabitants of the country, and indeed toward his own archeological career, was far different from Petrie's, and the resumption of the excavations at Tell el-Hesy under his command bore the hallmarks of patience and hard work far more than of innovation and genius.

Over the course of the next year, Bliss cleared some parts of the mound to a depth of over twenty feet, defining the outlines of large public buildings and fortifications, and unearthing huge quantities of the "Amorite" pottery that Petrie had first identified. For the most part, Bliss's work was an enlargement and confirmation of Petrie's initial findings, but twelve days before the expiration of the excavation permit, Bliss was rewarded with an important discovery of his own.

Beneath a layer of ash that marked the destruction of one of the later Canaanite cities, an Arab worker came upon a small inscribed tablet, identical, Bliss immediately recognized, to the cuneiform tablets that had been recently discovered at Tell el-Amarna in Egypt, and which dated from the fourteenth century B.C. This find provided an accurate date for the stratum in which it was discovered, thereby refining Petrie's preliminary chronology for the preceding and succeeding strata of the tell. But the more important value of the Tell el-Hesy tablet was the light that its text shed on the cultural history of the site: it was an official communication to the administrators of an Egyptian garrison in the Late Bronze Age —a clear indication of the political hegemony of Egypt over the city-states of Canaan.

Bliss's discovery caused an immediate sensation back in London. For the first time, a scientific excavation in Palestine had contributed to the enlargement of secular, not merely Biblical, history. Despite the unexpected change of expedition leaders, the new orientation of the P.E.F. had survived and even prospered. Science, not Biblical faith, it seemed, was now the key to uncovering Palestine's past.

In Jerusalem, the archeological activity of the various foreign communities still bore the hallmarks of religious and political concerns. The Russian Orthodox Palestine Society excavated on its property near the Church of the Holy Sepulcher, and additional investigations were undertaken by the French Dominicans at the site of their new church to the north of the city, by the Augustinians near their monastery on Mount Zion, by the White Friars at St. Stephen's Gate, and by the Reverend Selah Merrill, the former explorer for the ill-fated American Palestine Exploration Society, who was now serving as U.S. consul in Jerusalem, at any place he could. The passion for "Biblical antiquities" still flowed freely, and despite the considerable scientific progress being made by the P.E.F. at Tell el-Hesy, the interest of the general public in England, Europe, and America continued to be drawn to the prospect of discovering monuments with religious significance.

The motivation for much of the digging in Jerusalem was the lingering question of the authenticity of the traditional holy sites. The Russian excavations near the Church of the Holy Sepulcher, in particular, had rekindled this sensitive issue. Privately undertaken under the supervision of Conrad Schick, a Swiss-born engineer and part-time correspondent for the *Palestine Exploration Fund Quarterly Statement,* the excavations uncovered fragments of huge marble columns and a monumental stairway apparently connected with the original fourth-century Constantinian basilica at the site. More importantly, Schick believed that he had distinguished the remains of an ancient city wall to the east, which would indicate that the site had indeed been *outside* the city at the time of Jesus—a fact contested by Protestant critics since the time of Robinson.

Schick's archeological work for the Russian Orthodox Palestine Society earned him both a decoration from Tsar Alexander III and, predictably, the simmering disapproval of some Protestant scholars. The dramatic increase in Russian pilgrimage to the Holy Land, financed in large measure by the tsarist government, depended in part on an unquestioning belief in the authenticity of the Holy Sepulcher. The charge now was that archeology had been misused for political ends.

The main flaw in the Protestant argument was a failure to suggest a convincing alternative site for the Holy Sepulcher. Claude Conder had put forth some possibilities in 1873 when he excavated a few tombs to the north of the city walls, but all of the suggested sites for the true tomb of Jesus remained no more than scholarly hypotheses. This was the situation when General Charles Gordon paid a visit to Jerusalem in 1883.

Gordon was already a well-known figure in the British Empire, romanticized in the popular press for his military exploits in subduing the Taiping Rebellion in China (for which he gained his nickname, "Chinese" Gordon) and in wiping out the slave trade in the Sudan. Gordon's private interests included mystical speculation and Biblical study, and during his visit to Jerusalem, he charged into the battle over the holy places with characteristic dash. The topographical form of Jerusalem, he became convinced, was that of a woman's body. As the "head," he identified a prominent hill just to the north of the Damascus Gate. But Jerusalem's "head" soon became its "skull" as Gordon, himself wrapped up in the question of Jesus' tomb, sought to identify the hill with the actual site of Golgotha, the place of the Crucifixion, whose name in Aramaic roughly means "Place of the Skull." Near that site, Gordon located an ancient rock-cut sepulcher that fulfilled all the conditions of the Gospel description of Jesus' tomb: outside the city, near a "skull-shaped" hill, and surrounded by other tombs. Word spread of the plausibility of the general's theory, and it gained many adherents, among whom one of the most vociferous was Selah Merrill, the U.S. consul in the city.

After the fall of Khartoum in the Sudan two years later, where he was slaughtered along with his entire garrison, Charles Gordon was canonized as one of the martyrs in the British imperial cause. His theories about Jerusalem became bound up in the religio-patriotic fervor surrounding his memory. The tomb which he had suggested might be the authentic tomb of Jesus became something of a Protestant shrine. One English lady, Schick noted, personally cleaned and washed the ancient tomb and spent the night inside it. The charismatic evangelist Dwight Moody even held revival services nearby. And when the property on which the tomb stood was put up for sale by its native landlord, a committee was formed in London to purchase and preserve the site, no matter what the cost.

The appeals of the Garden Tomb Committee, as it came to be called, were published in letters to the *Times* in September 1892, and their appearance brought strong criticism from the officers and members of the Palestine Exploration Fund. Charles Wilson's attitude toward the committee was one of disdain; he personally believed that the traditional site of the Church of the Holy Sepulcher was probably the authentic one, and he ridiculed the naïveté of those supposedly enlightened Christians who felt the need to erect competing shrines of their own in Jerusalem. In any case, he suggested, the sum of money raised for the purchase of the Garden Tomb (reportedly many times greater than its actual market value) would have been far better spent in support of the excavations at Tell el-Hesy.

Yet, Wilson's criticism notwithstanding, there persisted even among Palestine Exploration Fund members a considerable interest in determining the location of religiously important monuments. For several years, a fierce controversy had been raging over the site of the original "City of David" and the royal tombs of the Hebrew kings. George St. Clair, an Anglican priest and amateur antiquarian, suggested that the earliest city of Jerusalem had been constructed on the southwest hill, the traditional "Mount Zion," and it was there that the Hebrew kings had been buried. W. R. Birch, archbishop of Manchester and local secretary of the P.E.F. chapter there, took extreme offense at St. Clair's view, which diverged widely from his own. Birch believed that the original city of King David had been built on the steep slope to the south of the Temple Mount and that the traditional site of David's Tomb on Mount Zion was, like the Church of the Holy Sepulcher, no more than a later invention.

Through the early eighteen-nineties the two men waged a protracted battle of words in the pages of the *P.E.F. Quarterly Statement,* each rebutting the other with increasingly esoteric Biblical quotations and topographical theories. Their argument once again aroused the emotional question of the authenticity of the traditional shrines. And by July 1891, the controversy had become so fierce, and St. Clair's defense of his own traditionalist views so outspoken, that he was dropped as an official lecturer of the fund.

Even after this moral victory, the Reverend Birch urged that his theories be put to the test. He seemed convinced that the remains of the city built by King David and perhaps even the royal tombs could be found on the southern slopes of the city if the course of the ancient southern wall could be located and traced. Since the proposed site was far from the religious buildings within the modern city, it seemed that no local opposition to excavations could possibly arise. And since Frederick Bliss had, in the meantime, advised the executive committee that it would not be worthwhile to conduct any further excavations at Tell el-Hesy, the road back to Jerusalem seemed clear. No more cuneiform tablets had been discovered at the tell, and the dry recitation of destruction levels and pottery forms so valuable to the development of scientific archeology failed to interest the general public any longer. The renewed interest in Jerusalem, on the other hand, with its overtones of national pride and sectarian honor, simply would not go away.

In April 1893, in officially announcing the conclusion of the excavations at Tell el-Hesy, the P.E.F. reported to its membership that it had applied to Constantinople "for a *firman* for excavating elsewhere." Less than a year later, that same membership was delighted to learn that through the intervention of the British Foreign Secretary, Lord Kimberley, a two-year firman for Jerusalem had been granted. In London, all seemed confident that, at last, with the resumption of excavations, "some of the problems having reference to Ancient Jerusalem may be set at rest."

The modern Jerusalem that the P.E.F. now planned to tackle had become by 1894 a very different city from that so familiar to Wilson, Warren, and the other early explorers of the fund nearly thirty years before. The increasing strength of the European religious and diplomatic communities and the rising volume of western tourism had bolstered the local economy and introduced many technological improvements and innovations. Besides the roads to accommodate the passage of wealthy tourists' carriages, a railroad had been constructed from Jaffa to Jerusalem, and the journey so painfully described by the early travelers had now become a routine ride of two hours. Gaslights now illuminated the main squares of the city, and the telephone and electric light would not be long in coming. Local newspapers were being published, some in the newly revived Hebrew language, and under the impetus of the early Zionist movement, Jews from the crowded Old City began to construct modern suburbs outside the city walls. The city had not been more prosperous since ancient times.

This frantic activity did not go unnoticed in Constantinople. Some years earlier, in 1888, Jerusalem had been administratively detached from the pashalic of Sidon and transferred to the direct control of the Sublime Porte. The Ottoman authorities had never paid any great attention to ancient artifacts, but since the antiquarian appetites of the western communities had created a flourishing market for them in Jerusalem, strict new laws were instituted to control and tax the sale of antiquities there. The interest of the Ottomans was not strictly economic, however. The preservation and display of archeological finds had come to symbolize the cultural appreciation of modern nations for their own history, and an Imperial Museum was founded at Constantinople and placed under the energetic supervision of its director, Hamdi Bey.

Such was the atmosphere into which Frederick Jones Bliss ventured, to initiate the scientific excavations of the P.E.F. By the agreement arrived at in Constantinople, all important finds would become the property of the Ottoman Empire and would have to be shipped to the Imperial Museum at the conclusion of the dig. And as was the case at Tell el-Hesy, the firman also called for an imperial "commissioner" to be present at the excavations to supervise the course of the work. The P.E.F. readily accepted these conditions, for they were no longer particularly interested in individual artifacts; they now came in search of historical fact.

Bliss arrived in Jerusalem in May 1894 with excavation equipment and an Arab foreman recommended by his father in Beirut, and promptly established his excavation camp on the southern slopes of the traditional Mount Zion. After the plans for the excavation were finally cleared by the local city council, Bliss began the work on the property of the Church Missionary Society, where an ancient scarp, or vertically hewn rock slope, had been discovered leading around the hill. Henry Maudsley, a British civil engineer and amateur antiquarian who had cleared the scarp in 1873, believed that this was the base of an ancient southern wall of Jerusalem. Bliss was now determined to follow its course and locate the extent of the ancient city to the south of the modern city walls.

With a crew of fifteen workers, supplemented by a foreman and a cook, Bliss was able to trace the scarp eastward for several hundred feet. Along the line of the excavations he uncovered remains of an ancient tower and gate to the city. The wall then passed beyond the boundary of the English property and ran toward land owned by the French Augustinian monks. The monks, having already conducted some trial probes of their own, willingly allowed Bliss to work there, specifying only that he provide them with complete plans of all the excavations. On the other side of the land of the Augustinians lay a patchwork of vegetable plots which proved to be Bliss's first serious obstacle.

Long, tedious negotiations had to be held with every owner, and in the end the prices demanded—for the crops that would be destroyed or not planted—proved far beyond Bliss's means. The inhabitants of modern Jerusalem no longer considered foreign archeologists a threat but an economic opportunity. Recognizing that fact, Bliss was forced to change his strategy. Rather than waste time and resources on a thorough excavation of the wall, he resolved to adopt the methods of his predecessor at Jerusalem, Charles Warren. He would trace the course of the wall by digging underground.

Bliss was not an experienced military miner, but by the fall he and his workers had traced the wall completely around Mount Zion, a distance of more than a thousand feet. On December 31, just at the time that they had come to a decisive turning point, Bliss was forced to halt the excavations because of heavy rains. Before him lay a Jewish cemetery under which he would not even be allowed to tunnel. All agreed that the city wall had turned somewhere within the area of this cemetery. St. Clair insisted that it turned to the northeast, to connect with the Temple Mount, and Birch believed just as firmly that it continued to the southeast, to surround what he considered to be the City of David. The dilemma that faced Bliss was where to continue the excavations: to search on the northern side of the cemetery, or on its southeast. His limited funds would not permit a mistake.

All through the first season of the digging, the Ottoman authorities, in both Constantinople and Jerusalem, had taken an active interest in Bliss's excavation, as reported to them by Ibrahim Effendi, the imperial commissioner. Bliss proved himself to be a cooperative and sometimes accommodating excavator, of great help in stemming the tide of archeological vandalism in Jerusalem. Before the first season of the digging was even finished, Bliss had been requested by the local authorities to supervise the clearance of some Byzantine remains recently discovered on the Mount of Olives. After a short excursion to Egypt in January 1895 during which he spent some time with his old mentor Flinders Petrie, Bliss was presented by Hamdi Bey with a still more ambitious project: to inspect the state of the antiquities of Moab for the imperial Ottoman museum.

Bliss was always anxious to maintain good relations with the Ottoman authorities and felt that he could hardly refuse such an important mission, despite the time and expenditure of energy. In any case, digging in Jerusalem had to be suspended until the end of the winter rains. In the company of Ibrahim Effendi he spent the month of March traveling through the region to the east of the Dead Sea where the Moabite Stone had been discovered nearly thirty years before. Never before had any of the foreign archeologists working in Palestine cooperated so willingly with the Turks. But times were changing; archeology was coming of age.

Bliss returned to Jerusalem to resume his excavations in April. Before him still lay the choice between the two alternative theories about the course of the wall, and bound up in that choice was the fate of the ongoing controversy over the traditional shrines. The logic of topography now far outweighed the piety of centuries, and Bliss, the modern archeologist, decided to follow the suggestion of the Reverend Birch and dig at the spot where the wall would run if it continued in a southeasterly direction—*away* from the traditional Mount Zion.

The presumption was correct; the ancient city did extend far to the southeast. Bliss was now aided by an experienced English architect named Archibald Dickie whom the P.E.F. had sent out to draw the plans of the excavations. Taking up the work at the eastern edge of the Jewish cemetery, they were able to follow the course of the wall toward the foot of the slope on which Birch had predicted the original City of David lay.

The continuous exertions of the excavations and the fatigue from the trip to Moab, however, soon took their toll on Bliss's habitually weak constitution. On May 29, he collapsed at the site of the digging and was carried inside the city to the Grand New Hotel. His condition was serious, and on the recommendation of a doctor from the Church Missionary Society, it was decided that as soon as he was well enough to travel, he should return to his father's home in Beirut for recuperation. This unexpected setback placed Archibald Dickie, the architect, in de facto control of the mission, and through the summer he continued to trace the course of the wall, sending detailed reports of the progress of the work back to London.

At length, Bliss was well enough to resume command, but what he found upon his return was not the simple outline of a single, Davidic city, but rather a labyrinth of ancient structures, whose relative dates and relative positions were not easy to disentangle. Dickie's conscientious excavation reports were filled with a wealth of valuable archeological information, but Bliss could clearly see that the original argument over the site of the City of David could never be settled on the terms originally proposed. Since the system of tunnels, as opposed to the stratigraphic method employed at Tell el-Hesy, could provide few reliable dates, the proponents of St. Clair's Jerusalem theories could claim that portions of the southern wall that Bliss and Dickie had traced were much later than the time of David, and therefore irrelevant to the matter at hand.

Later excavations at the site would prove that the original city of

Jerusalem was indeed founded on the southern slope, but that determination was still more than a decade away. For the time being at least, all that Bliss and Dickie could do was continue their investigations, bringing to light much new and interesting archeological data, but simply not being able to answer conclusively the questions that the P.E.F. had so confidently hoped to "set at rest."

By the summer of 1897, after an extension of the original firman, Bliss and Dickie had traced the southern perimeter of the ancient city and had made many trial probes within it, uncovering fortification walls, paved streets, water installations, and even the ruins of a fifth-century church. But more important than any of their individual discoveries, they had demonstrated for the first time the full complexity of Jerusalem's archeological deposits. The southern slope of the city, though now outside the walls, had been an integral part of the city from the Bronze Age to the Byzantine period, and that continuous occupation had resulted in an apparent confusion of overlapping constructions, quarrying pits, rubbish heaps, and erosion debris. The idea of searching there for a specific monument mentioned in the Scripture was clearly impractical. The far more important task was first to spell out the historical development of the city, to gain a more comprehensive understanding of its various periods and the character of their remains. Exploration in Jerusalem would henceforth require not merely money, enthusiasm, or imperial firmans, but generations of intensive and cumulative archeological work. In that sense, science had triumphed. Biblical archeology was moving toward a new and more modern stage.

On June 20, 1897, the Jerusalem excavations were closed for the last time. Dickie traveled alone to Damascus to map and study the great Umayyad Mosque there, and Bliss returned to London to assemble and publish the results of the work and to address the annual meeting of the fund in July. It was at that meeting that the chairman, the aged James Glaisher, active in the fund for thirty years, confessed his own disappointment at the failure of the mission to solve any of the religiously oriented questions about the location of the Biblical sites. "I wanted to know," he frankly admitted, "more about Jerusalem's revelations than it is likely that I, at my age, shall ever know. . . ."

Glaisher's generation had witnessed a profound change in the attitude of the P.E.F. toward Biblical exploration. No longer would the pursuit of Palestinian antiquities be the work of amateur scholars, daring adventurers, or military expeditions in search of "Biblical illustration." Professional archeologists, architects, and pottery specialists would now take their place. The excavations at Tell el-Hesy had opened up a new era in the history of Biblical archeology, and the excavations at Jerusalem had demonstrated that the scientific era had come to stay.

Throughout the more than three decades of its existence, the Palestine Exploration Fund had been an essentially foreign element in Jerusalem society. While the Catholic and Orthodox churches and even the various Protestant missionary societies possessed permanent headquarters in the city and conducted their activities on a continuing basis, the P.E.F. had contented itself with sporadic expeditions and temporary headquarters. Yet just as its work had deeply affected the modern understanding of Biblical history, the P.E.F.'s excavations and surveys had affected the evolution of the modern city as well. For centuries, the pilgrim trade had been an important component of Jerusalem's economy, and generations of local guides had willingly offered their fabulous descriptions and unchanging itineraries to foreign visitors to the city. The activities of the P.E.F., however, had rendered those traditional descriptions and tours obsolete. The modern tourist now came in search of facts, not legends.

To serve this need, a "local association" of the Palestine Exploration Fund was founded in Jerusalem itself in 1892, under the direction of its honorary secretary, the Reverend T. E. Dowling of the Church Missionary Society. Its first action was to open a shop inside the Jaffa Gate where tourists to the city might purchase the various publications of the fund and attend lectures by its resident explorers. This effort proved so successful that the Jerusalem association of the P.E.F. soon began to train tourist guides of its own, and the booming business that they did eventually convinced the municipal council of Jerusalem that the standard of all tourist guides in the city should be upgraded. A scientific consciousness had begun to replace the time-honored historical legends about the city, and from 1895, all prospective guides were required to pass an examination on the history of Jerusalem, which was based largely on the findings of the P.E.F. excavations.

Biblical archeology was no longer a foreign obsession or alien presence; by the eighteen-nineties, the P.E.F. could count among its subscribers residents of Palestine itself, including, significantly, members of the recently founded Jewish settlement of Zikhron Ya'acov, one of the first of the Zionist agricultural colonies. Archeological activity in Palestine was becoming a part of its cultural landscape, and as the turn-of-the-century visitor to the Holy City wandered past the forbidding entrance of the Turkish garrison, he or she could plainly see evidence of that permanent change. Slightly to the left of the huge sign of the "Mission to the Jews" stood the squat stone building whose own boldly lettered sign identified it as the local headquarters of the Palestine Exploration Fund. Archeology in the Holy Land had come of age. And its continuing influence would eventually prove more powerful than the efforts of any of the missionaries.

❖ 15 ❖

The Kaiser and the Sultan

GERMANY ENTERS
THE RACE FOR ANTIQUITIES,
1898-1909

In the unusually hot summer of 1898, at a time when life in Palestine would ordinarily have come to a near-standstill, frenzied activity suddenly sprang up all over the country. At the port of Haifa in the north, Turkish engineers supervised the hurried construction of modern dock facilities. Along the coast to Jaffa and up through the hills to Jerusalem, scores of forced labor gangs toiled day and night to level and pave new carriage roads. From Jerusalem down to the Jordan River at Jericho, a new telegraph line was strung, and at Jerusalem itself, workers began to tear away a section of the ancient city wall to permit the entrance of European-style carriages. Under direct orders from Sultan Abdul Hamid in Constantinople, Palestine was to be tidied up and made presentable, no matter what the cost. Kaiser Wilhelm II, the sultan's newfound ally in an increasingly hostile western world, was coming on an official pilgrimage to the Holy Land.

The Ottoman Empire's disastrous defeat by the Russians in 1877 had cost the sultan the last shreds of his self-esteem, and had at the same time provided a convenient opening for the international strategies of the German Reich. While England, France, and Russia bickered over plans for an eventual partition of the sultan's empire, Germany alone extended a hand of friendship to Abdul Hamid. With the tacit consent of the Austrian Emperor, Wilhelm II dispatched a number of German military and economic missions to Constantinople during the eighteen-eighties. In 1889, the young Kaiser had traveled to Constantinople to consecrate his friendship with the sultan, and in 1895, Wilhelm had thwarted the designs of the British and the French to divide the Ottoman Empire, thereby further ingratiating himself with the Sublime Porte. Loudly demanding a "place in the sun" for his empire, Wilhelm II had staked a German claim in the Middle East.

The official announcement of the Kaiser's imperial visit to the Holy Land came as a shock to the other European powers, which had carefully increased their influence in Palestine during the previous half century. The British community had long feared the expansion of independent German interests, while the French, still hungering for revenge for the debacle of 1870, were openly hostile. But never before had the Ottoman authorities made such an effort to woo a European ruler, and, considering the growing ties between the Kaiser and the sultan, there were fears that the German ruler might actually gain unprecedented privileges, establishing a recognized German protectorate over the Holy Land.

Assuming the identity of a "new Crusader," Wilhelm II and his lavish entourage traveled first to Constantinople, where they were welcomed personally by the sultan and rewarded with the long-coveted concession for the construction of a railroad from Berlin to Baghdad. Then the imperial party proceeded to Palestine aboard a private yacht. Disembarking at the new dock at Haifa to the martial sounds of a Turkish military band, Wilhelm was greeted by a welcoming delegation of German colonists, headed by Gottlieb Schumacher, one of the leaders of the Templar community in Haifa and a part-time explorer for the P.E.F. From Haifa, the huge imperial caravan moved southwards toward Jaffa, stopping briefly at the Templar colony of Sarona, its prosperous houses and barns festooned with banners and German flags. At Jerusalem, a special "imperial campground" awaited the royal visitors, its perimeter guarded by hundreds of Turkish soldiers and its tents furnished with oriental carpets, ivory inlaid beds, tables, and chairs. Flags and lanterns were hung throughout the city. Beggars and stray dogs were rounded up and kept out of sight. Even the Dome of the Rock was cleaned and refurbished for the occasion.

On October 29, 1898, the Kaiser entered the Holy City as a conquering hero, riding on a white stallion, his spiked helmet glistening in the sun, accompanied by dozens of Prussian and Turkish cavalrymen. That night, fireworks filled the sky over Jerusalem. During the following two days of their visit, Kaiser Wilhelm and the Kaiserin Augusta Victoria visited the holy shrines and ancient sites of the city, dedicated an orphanage in Bethlehem and a magnificent Protestant church near the Holy Sepulcher, and presented a plot of ground on Mount Zion to the German Catholics for the erection of a new church of their own. "From Jerusalem a light has arisen upon the world," announced the Kaiser, "the blessed light in whose splendor our German people have become great and glorious." Never again would the German presence in Jerusalem take second place to anyone; it seemed that the visit of the Kaiser had brought a new age to the Holy Land.

New age or not, the British had only contempt for Kaiser Wilhelm's dreams. The imperial visit had in fact been arranged by a British tourist firm, Thomas Cook & Son, and the London newspapers gleefully jumped on this intelligence, ridiculing Wilhelm as "Cook's Crusader." The Palestine Exploration Fund was itself equally unabashed. Barely a year after the completion of the excavations at Jerusalem, Frederick Bliss returned to Palestine armed with a new firman and new plans. The P.E.F. had resolved to abandon the theological thicket of exploration in Jerusalem and to resume its excavation of Palestinian tells. The target this time was not a single ancient mound, however, but four of them, all situated close together in an area southwest of Jerusalem. One of them, Tell es-Safi, had been tentatively identified as the Philistine city of Gath. The others, though less clearly identified, seemed likely to provide additional information on the development of Biblical civilization, and more importantly, a wealth of new finds.

On his arrival in early autumn 1898, Bliss noted in a report that "the chief subject of interest at present is, of course, the coming visit of the German Emperor." Yet despite the excitement, the official excavation permits were delivered to Bliss by the British consul, and the renewed P.E.F. excavations quietly began in the countryside while the attention of the rest of the country was thoroughly occupied with the imperial visitors.

Archibald Dickie, Bliss's faithful colleague in Jerusalem, had resigned his official connection with the P.E.F., and a replacement had to be found for the renewed excavations. Several members of the executive committee recommended Robert Alexander Stewart Macalister, the twenty-one-year-old son of Professor John Macalister of the University of Dublin, who had, by assisting at the excavations of his archeologist father, gained considerable experience in the techniques of modern archeology. Intrigued by the prospects of scientific excavation in the Holy Land and anxious to add professional credentials to his own budding career, R. A. S. Macalister accepted the assignment to Palestine and joined Frederick Bliss in Jerusalem. Unfortunately, their personalities proved to be ill matched, and to compound the problem, unexpected labor difficulties also arose. The Ottoman commissioner assigned to the excavations demanded a substantial increase in pay, and the friendliness of the local inhabitants toward the excavators could no longer be assured.

In the course of nearly two years of steady excavation, however, the Bliss-Macalister mission accomplished an unprecedented amount of work. Turning the energies of the endeavor from personal and financial concerns to the process of digging, Bliss and Macalister moved quickly from one tell to another within the area outlined by the firman, eventually uncovering the basic plans of four distinct ancient Palestinian cities. At Tell Zakariyah, they uncovered remains of an Israelite fortress which had guarded the vital trade route from Egypt in the time of the Hebrew kings. The numerous small articles discovered beneath it—scarabs, beads, implements of flint, bronze, iron, and pottery—confirmed in the minds of the excavators the "intimate connection with Egypt prior to the Israelite invasion of Palestine." Moving to Tell es-Safi, the P.E.F. excavators were unable to distinguish the expected Philistine remains, but they did identify the line of an Israelite city wall and, on the summit of the mound, uncovered the Crusader castle of Blanche-Garde. At Tell el-Judeideh, they concentrated on the remains of a Roman city, and at Tell Sandahannah, the last of the sites in the area outlined by the firman, Bliss and Macalister filled out their historical sequence by stripping away the entire upper layer of the tell, laying bare, for the first time, the complete plan of a Hellenistic city in Palestine.

In the fall of 1900, the excavations at Tell Sandahannah had to be suspended when the firman expired. The shafts and trenches were filled in and the land returned to its native proprietors. Yet never before had any expedition to Palestine worked so long without interruption or uncovered so much raw archeological data. The excavations at Tell el-Hesy had been, by comparison, just an experiment in technique, the excavations in Jerusalem a theological disappointment. But the excavation of the Judean tells now showed clearly where the future of Palestinian exploration lay. Not only had the P.E.F. succeeded in excavating a continuous series of archeological remains that spanned the millennia from the Bronze Age to the age of the Crusaders, but it had also carved out for itself a geographical sphere of influence: Jerusalem and the tells to the south had become its exclusive archeological domain.

The only dim spot on the otherwise bright horizon was the still unresolved personal differences between Bliss and Macalister. The executive committee of the P.E.F. had long been unsatisfied with Bliss's failure to lead and his constant bending to pressure from the Ottoman authorities. In the fall of 1900, Frederick Bliss returned to his boyhood home at the American mission in Beirut, severing his official connection with the P.E.F. "for reasons of ill-health." Macalister, in the meantime, returned to London to complete the work on the excavation reports and prepare them for publication. It would be Macalister who would now carry the archeological banner onward for the British in Palestine, and he would do it alone.

In the wake of the Kaiser's triumphant visit to the Holy Land, the political status of the German consulate in Jerusalem rose considerably. A new consul, Dr. Friedrich Rosen, son of the Prussian consul at the time of Wilson and Warren, assumed his post there, and being himself both an Oriental scholar and practically a native of the country, he was in a position to promote German archeological activity. German academic circles had always been wary of participation in the efforts of the British Palestine Exploration Fund, and in 1877 they established a society of their own, commonly called the Deutscher Palästina Verein—the German Palestine Society. The German society produced numerous publications, sponsored geographical investigations, and gained a respected place for itself in the world of Biblical archeology. But up to the time of the Kaiser's visit, it did not conduct any excavations.

Among the many favors bestowed upon the Kaiser by Abdul Hamid was permission to excavate the magnificent Roman temples at Baalbek in Lebanon. A large staff of German archeologists, under the authority of the "Imperial Oriental Society," was dispatched to the site and cleared the huge sacred areas, shipping the most valuable pieces of ancient sculpture to the Berlin Museum. The *Palestine Exploration Fund Quarterly Statement* reacted to the German excavations at Baalbek by protesting what it characterized as a large-scale spoliation of the ancient site; but for the time being at least, the Kaiser's archeological encroachment approached no closer than Lebanon to the P.E.F.'s sphere of influence.

That breathing space, however, was soon to disappear. In January 1901, the P.E.F. received reports that the Deutscher Palästina Verein had obtained a firman through the intervention of the German embassy in Constantinople to survey the lands lying to the east of the Jordan, where Captain Conder's work had been halted in 1882. The idea of the Germans completing the most difficult part of the mapping of the country must have been especially galling to the P.E.F., but more upsetting still was the fact that the fund's longtime contributor, Gottlieb Schumacher of Haifa, had acceded to the demands of his country, accepting the appointment to direct the project. "We congratulate the German Society on their good fortune," announced the P.E.F. executive committee, "and we wish Dr. Schumacher every success in carrying out this important work." Unlike the P.E.F. itself, which from a financial standpoint had just experienced the worst year in its existence, the Deutscher Palästina Verein boasted a healthy treasury. The German Eastern Palestine Survey was allotted the equivalent of £1250, more than double the entire budget of the P.E.F. for the preceding three years.

But the most serious threat to the British supremacy in Biblical archeology was to come a year later in the person of Professor Ernst Sellin, an obscure Austrian theologian who traveled to Palestine for the first time in the spring of 1899. An Austrian expedition to the Greek island of Samothrace in the eighteen-seventies had pioneered the art of scientific excavation, and Sellin sought to bring the new Austrian techniques to the Holy Land as well. Visiting many tells in the northern part of the country with an eye toward selecting the most promising remains, Sellin finally chose the towering mound of Tell Ta'annek, whose modern Arabic name clearly preserved the name of the Canaanite city of Taanach.

Sellin returned to Palestine in the spring of 1902, armed with an imperial firman and the financial support of the Vienna Academy of Sciences, the Austrian Ministry of Education, and a large number of wealthy private contributors. Accompanying him was a classical archeologist and an epigrapher, but since none of them had any experience in the particular problems of excavation in Palestine, they acquired the services of Schumacher, who had completed his survey work in eastern Palestine. Together the Austrians and the German established an excavation camp on the summit of the tell, hired work gangs of nearly 150 Arab laborers from the surrounding villages, and officially began their first excavations in the Holy Land.

The results of those excavations were impressive for a first effort. Sellin and Schumacher were able to trace the course of a massive system of ancient fortifications, and discovered a Canaanite temple, child burials, and cultic objects. They also unearthed an archive of forty cuneiform tablets, a collection of even greater significance than the spot find at Tell el-Hesy more than ten years before. By the middle of July 1902, the first season of the Austrian excavations was completed, but its results would have a continuing effect. The Middle Eastern interests of Kaiser Wilhelm had been turned toward the excavation of additional sites within the Holy Land. The Deutscher Palästina Verein, gaining a promise of generous funding from the German government, sent out some representatives of its own "to travel through the country and select the most favorable sites for excavation." The German archeological effort in Palestine was growing apace.

·   ·   ·

The significance of the large-scale Austrian excavations at Ta'annek did not escape the executive committee of the Palestine Exploration Fund; their next mission would also concentrate on the detailed investigation of a single site. After completing the reports on his previous work, R. A. S. Macalister returned to the Holy Land in 1902 and set up an expedition camp on the mound of Abu Shusheh, situated about halfway between Jaffa and Jerusalem along the newly constructed railroad line. The identification of the site as the ancient city of Gezer, one of the royal fortresses of King Solomon, had been conclusively established with the discovery of a bilingual boundary inscription by Charles Clermont-Ganneau in 1873. The conditions for extended excavations seemed ideal; the whole area of the mound was located on the private estate of a wealthy local merchant, and for the proper consideration, he was more than willing to offer it for any use that the P.E.F. might see fit.

On June 14, 1902, R. A. S. Macalister officially began the excavation of Gezer. Although his restricted budget did not allow for the hiring of more than seventy-five workers at a time (only half the work force that was employed at Ta'annek), Macalister was able to lay bare extensive areas of the tell in a relatively short time. Supervising the Arab workers single-handed, sketching and mapping the remains himself, Macalister identified successive occupations at the site, including ancient burial caves, a Canaanite temple and high place, and the perimeter of the ancient fortifications.

The excavation of Gezer was planned as a long-term venture, and Macalister remained at the site through the summer and fall of 1902. The archeological value of many of his undated finds would later be called into question by more advanced archeological investigations at the site. But there was no denying the force of his personality. In an age when excavations succeeded or failed on the strength of their director, the continuing P.E.F. effort in Palestine was clearly in very good hands.

During the year 1902, Kaiser Wilhelm had contributed the equivalent of more than twelve thousand pounds to the excavations of his Oriental Society in Egypt and Mesopotamia. The success of the Austrian excavations at Ta'annek proved that German scholarship was equally well equipped to tackle the remains of Palestine. What was more important, however, was the fact that Sellin had been the first to excavate a northern tell; since the P.E.F. had restricted its operations to Jerusalem and the south, the time had come for the Germans to establish their own sphere of archeological influence. The representatives sent out by the Deutscher

Palästina Verein were favorably impressed by the possibilities of Tell el-Mutasellim, "the mound of the governor," situated to the northwest of Tell Ta'annek. This site was believed by many to be the remains of the Biblical city of Megiddo, the Armageddon of the New Testament, where the final battle at the end of days would be fought. Like Gezer, the city had been a royal fortress of Solomon, and it undoubtedly held many equally valuable ancient remains.

By the beginning of 1903, the Deutscher Palästina Verein had raised forty thousand marks—the equivalent of two thousand pounds—for the excavation of Megiddo, a sum unheard of in the annals of Palestinian exploration. Of that amount the Kaiser had contributed twenty-six thousand marks from government funds. The national interest of the Second Reich would be furthered by official sponsorship of the ambitious undertaking, which like Ta'annek was situated close to a railroad line under construction by German engineers for the Ottoman government.

Gottlieb Schumacher was appointed to lead the expedition. After leaving Sellin's excavations, he had returned to the Templar colony at Haifa, and it was there, at the beginning of February 1903, that he received the official firman for the work at Tell el-Mutasellim. The document itself was forwarded by Consul Schröder, still at his post in Beirut despite his unfortunate involvement with Moses Shapira twenty years before. Schumacher quickly recruited a small staff of German architects from the colony in Haifa and set up headquarters on the tell at the end of March. Wooden barracks for the staff and storehouses for the finds were built, the Turkish commissioner arrived at the site to supervise the work, and the red, black, and gold German flag was proudly unfurled over the hill of Armageddon.

Excavation began with a force of local laborers, following lengthy negotiations with the village dignitaries who held title to the land. Wide trenches were opened on the surface of the tell, and Schumacher had to devise a complicated system for maximizing efficiency. About one-third of the workers that Schumacher had hired were men; the other two-thirds were women and children. The men were divided into work parties of five men each. Two of them would actually dig with pick and shovel, while the other three would place the loosened earth into straw baskets. Attached to each of these "digging parties" was a group of about fifteen women who would lift the filled baskets to their heads and carry them to the steep sides of the tell for dumping. A few native overseers wandered from group to group making sure that the work was proceeding at full speed. Bonuses were paid to any workers who uncovered interesting or unique finds. Payday came every two weeks. The average workday was ten hours.

Under the Germans, Biblical archeology was quickly becoming a carefully regulated industry.

After a temporary halt through the summer, the second season of excavations at Megiddo began on September 20, under the direction of Dr. Immanuel Benziger of the Deutscher Palästina Verein, as Gottlieb Schumacher had been called away on a special assignment. The nature of that assignment was yet another indication of the determination of the Kaiser to stake a German claim on the antiquities of the Holy Land. As the *Palestine Exploration Fund Quarterly Statement* noted with dismay, unusual activity on the part of the Germans had been observed in the preceding months at Khan Mashetta in Transjordan. The extensive Umayyad remains there had been presented as a gift by the sultan to the Kaiser, and Gottlieb Schumacher's new job was to see to the stripping of the marble sculpture of Khan Mashetta for shipment to the Imperial Museum at Berlin. "It is understood that, in ordering the practical destruction of this unique and remarkable monument," reported the executive committee of the P.E.F., "the Emperor acted upon the advice of several eminent German Orientalists and archeologists." The wholesale removal of antiquities injected a new element into the struggle for Biblical relics, but in the light of the developing political and economic ties between Germany and the Ottoman Empire, there was little that the British could do but protest.

In the spring of 1904, Schumacher returned to take command of the excavations at Megiddo, and the renewed effort now put forward by the German government made all previous British efforts in Palestine suddenly seem humble. Schumacher raised the number of his daily workers to nearly two hundred and, during a season that lasted from the first of April to the end of May, uncovered a huge city wall, a Canaanite altar, and sacrificial remains which shed fresh light on the civilization of the pre-Israelite period. Even more important was the discovery of a beautifully carved jasper seal bearing the ancient Hebrew inscription "To Shema', Servant of Jeroboam." This official seal was oval and bore the image of a roaring lion. Its discovery marked the first time that the name of King Jeroboam, one of the monarchs of the Northern Kingdom of Israel in the eighth century B.C., had been found in any source other than the Bible itself.

The continuing success of the Germans at Megiddo caused a certain nervousness among the membership of the Palestine Exploration Fund, and in 1906 they applied for a continuation of the firman for Gezer. Macalister was ordered to return to London to help raise the funds needed for the renewed dig by lecturing the local associations of the

P.E.F. on his finds at Gezer and about the dangerous threat to British superiority in Biblical archeology. "While welcoming kindred societies," he noted in one of his lectures, "let us not drop behind them."

Unfortunately for the P.E.F., the renewal of the firman for the dig at Gezer did little to stem the tide of German archeological activity in the Holy Land. In 1905, while the excavations at Megiddo were still going at full speed, the Kaiser's own Oriental Society sent two archeologists, Heinrich Kohl and Carl Watzinger, to carry out excavations in the ruins of the ancient synagogues of the Galilee. Up to this time, little had been discovered of the New Testament period; the German excavations at Tell Hum uncovered what were said to be remains of the synagogue at Capernaum, where Jesus had preached. By 1907, Ernst Sellin began excavations under the sponsorship of the Vienna Academy of Science at the site of the ancient city of Jericho, the famous Canaanite town destroyed by Joshua and the Israelite tribes. Schumacher traveled to Jericho to assist him. The "imperial campground" of the Kaiser's visit to the Holy Land in 1898 had been purchased by the German government, and the large building constructed on the site became the headquarters for the German Archeological Institute for the Exploration of Palestine. In sheer activity, at least, there was no question that the British were falling far behind.

On the political front, the Kaiser's cooperation with the sultan continued. Work began on a new railroad line from Damascus to Mecca, supervised by German engineers and equipped with the latest German military locomotives and troop carriers. The Deutsche Palästina Bank, with the benefit of the huge assets of its parent institution in Germany, funneled large amounts of ready capital into the awakening Palestinian economy. The new German ascendancy in Biblical archeology was in fact merely a symptom of the overall penetration by Germany into the Middle East. But the effect of that ascendancy was to change the balance of archeological power in the Holy Land. The British had lost their advantage; now money and political influence were the primary requirements for success.

❖ 16 ❖

The American Method

FALSE STARTS AND
SUCCESS AT SAMARIA,
1905–1910

Turn-of-the-century America, with its bursting cities, bustling factories, and well-endowed universities, was at last ready to resume its place in the exploration of Palestine. The pioneering work of Robinson and Lynch had played a decisive role in the establishment of the science of Biblical archeology, and although the participation of Americans had lagged since the demise of the Palestine Exploration Society of New York in the eighteen-seventies, the time and funds were at last available for a reentry. In 1895, a great "corporation" of American universities was gathered together by the Society of Biblical Literature and Exegesis for the purpose of establishing a permanent American School of Oriental Research in Jerusalem. With an annual contribution of a hundred dollars from each member institution and a large private endowment, a spacious stone villa in Jerusalem was purchased and in 1900 Professor Charles C. Torrey of Yale journeyed to Palestine to take up residence as the first annual professor of the American School.

The new American institution took its place with the other foreign archeological establishments in the city, and throughout the first decade of the twentieth century, a significant number of American scholars were offered the opportunity to spend a year in Palestine and deepen their understanding of the archeology and culture of the country as an aid to serious Biblical research. But the establishment of the American School was only a beginning, for the unassuming academic presence of the Americans in Palestine contrasted sharply with their intensive archeological activities in other parts of the Middle East.

As early as 1889, the University of Pennsylvania had dispatched an expedition to Mesopotamia, and its results compared favorably with excavations conducted by the British, Germans, and French. The result of that first reconnaissance was a flood of contributions from wealthy patrons of the university and the beginning of extensive American excavations at the site of the ancient city of Nippur. In Egypt, at the opposite end of the Fertile Crescent, the newly founded University of California entered the field with a well-equipped excavation of its own under the lavish patronage of Mrs. Phoebe Apperson Hearst. The rich harvest of ancient Egyptian artifacts reaped by these American excavations prompted Harvard University, in cooperation with the Boston Museum of Fine Arts, to sponsor further excavations in Egypt, in search of both art treasures and scientific fact.

The leader of the American excavations in Egypt was George Andrew Reisner, and he stands alongside W. M. F. Petrie as one of the most influential forces in the development of archeological technique. Reisner worked at a far slower pace than the British or the Germans, who employed huge armies of untrained workers to move vast amounts of ancient debris. His object was not volume but scientific detail, and he attempted to wrest every particle of relevant data from the limited areas he chose to excavate. While other archeologists paid workers bounties for artifacts, Reisner recognized that mere possession of the objects was not enough; it was equally important to determine their position in a stratum of deposits. Reisner selected his workers carefully, paid them well, and trained them to understand that their work was not mere ditchdigging. His goal was the creation of "a working organization carrying out, as a matter of habit, the principles laid down for efficient work."

Many of the finds unearthed by Reisner and his well-regulated work crews eventually made their way into the collections of the Harvard Semitic Museum, which had been set up in 1889 as an adjunct to the university's new Semitic Department. Among the founders of that museum was a wealthy New York banker and philanthropist named Jacob Henry Schiff, whose support of American archeological research was but one of his many charitable endeavors. Schiff, as one of the leaders of the American Jewish Reform movement, took particular interest in the excavation of Biblical cities then going on in Palestine, and by 1905 the time had come, he felt, for the Harvard Semitic Museum to have some Biblical antiquities of its own. Schiff believed that any American excavations in Palestine should be conducted on a scale at least equal to those of the British and the Germans, and to ensure an even higher scientific standard, he contributed the enormous sum of fifty thousand dollars—five times more than the initial budget of the large-scale German excavations at Megiddo. President Charles Eliot of Harvard, moved to action by this generous gift, assembled a "committee on exploration in the Orient," composed of some of the most distinguished Biblical scholars, historians, and archeologists on the faculty.

Their unanimous choice for an excavation site was the hill of Sebastiyeh, located approximately thirty-five miles north of Jerusalem. Its modern Arabic name was an obvious survival of the Greek name Sebaste, which Herod the Great had given to the city in the first century B.C. Herod's city was built upon the ruins of Samaria, capital city of the ancient northern kingdom of Israel, and this twofold appeal made the site especially attractive. Biblical references to Samaria were plentiful, for it had been a rival to Jerusalem until its destruction by the Assyrians in 722 B.C. Samaria's lavish palaces and public buildings, built by King Omri and his son Ahab, promised some of the most exciting discoveries in Palestine, a prospect clearly demonstrated by the fact that the P.E.F., the Deutsche Orient-Gesellschaft, and even the Spanish consul at Jerusalem had all at various times expressed interest in working there.

But the Americans were determined to forestall any rival claims. In the summer of 1905, the Harvard committee forwarded an official application for an excavation permit to Hamdi Bey at the Imperial Museum in Constantinople, then proceeded with the selection of an archeological director. This proved to be an unexpectedly difficult task, for the few Americans with practical experience in Palestinian archeology, with the notable exception of Frederick Bliss, were either clerics or amateurs in search of historical confirmation of the Bible. The Harvard excavations at Samaria would be a scientific endeavor, not a theological one, so in the end the committee turned to an American with no previous experience in the Holy Land, the noted Egyptologist George Andrew Reisner.

Reisner, like Petrie before him, was anxious to extend his Egyptian researches into Palestine, and he accepted the assignment. In November he traveled to Constantinople to meet with Hamdi Bey and obtain the necessary firman. Reisner took with him an additional five thousand dollars that had been supplied by Schiff for the customary expenses involved in negotiation with the Ottoman authorities, and, to emphasize the importance with which the work was viewed in America, he was also armed with a personal letter of recommendation from President Theodore Roosevelt.

At the Ottoman capital, Reisner met with great cordiality and a private assurance by Hamdi Bey that the excavation permit would be approved quickly. But weeks of waiting eventually accumulated into months. Accepting a three-year contract with the Egyptian government to supervise the excavation of some ancient Nubian cemeteries expected to be inundated by the new dam at Aswan, Reisner left Constantinople in disgust. Nothing more was heard about the firman for Samaria. Neither American money nor American political influence seemed able to bring Jacob Schiff's dream of Palestinian excavation to life.

When the permit for the excavation of Samaria unexpectedly arrived at Harvard in November 1907, all of those who had been involved in the original plan were taken completely by surprise. No one had realized that the long silence from Constantinople might be merely a symptom of bureaucratic inefficiency rather than an outright refusal. But they pulled themselves together quickly. Jacob Schiff offered the fifty thousand dollars again, and Reisner, contacted by telegraph in Nubia, agreed to take a leave of absence from his Egyptian work. But Reisner's commitments would not allow him to be present in Samaria for much more than the very start of the excavations, so a competent successor was needed to follow through. The Harvard committee offered the job to the most experienced Palestinian excavator they could find, and the offer was accepted: the American dig would be headed by none other than the former correspondent for the P.E.F. and director of the massive German excavations at Megiddo, Dr. Gottlieb Schumacher.

At the end of April 1908, George Reisner left his work in Nubia to travel to Palestine and meet Gottlieb Schumacher on the hill of Samaria. Physically the two men resembled each other: portly, determined, and confident, each was accustomed to a position of authority in the search for ancient remains. To Reisner, however, Schumacher was merely an agent, hired to carry out specifically outlined plans. Reisner closely examined the features of the site and determined what he believed to be the most promising areas for excavation. He carefully supervised the hiring of the labor force and ordered them to open the first trenches on the summit of the hill so that Schumacher, under his guidance, would become familiar with the desired archeological technique. By early June, George Reisner felt confident that the proper scientific framework for the continuation of the excavations had been established. Schumacher apparently agreed. The Harvard professor quickly packed up his bags and departed from Samaria, leaving his German agent in complete control.

Gottlieb Schumacher was, above all, a practical man, and he had been able to direct the excavation of Megiddo by the force of his own personality. He registered finds, sketched plans for all the remains, prepared his own maps of the excavations, and even supervised the disbursements of money on paydays. As was the case with Macalister at Gezer, the success of archeological excavations was measured, to a great extent, by the strength of their director. That strength was largely a function of the funding that backed him, and Schumacher had more funds at his disposal than any previous excavator in Palestine.

The workers soon uncovered a wide marble stairway near the summit of the mound, which Schumacher ordered them to clear completely. Revealed were the remains of a massive building, undoubtedly the temple to Augustus that Herod the Great had built on the site. Schumacher had sought monumental architecture at Megiddo, but had found little. Here he had been rewarded in his first attempt. Despite Dr. Reisner's orders to restrict the work to carefully defined trenches, Schumacher ordered the excavation of the entire temple. In the weeks that followed, workers found a mosaic floor, a votive altar of the Roman period, a vaulted storeroom, and a large imperial statue. This archeological richness was unprecedented—and Schumacher had not even begun to probe the remains of the Israelite period that lay farther down.

Through the blistering hot month of August, Schumacher increased the pace of work at the site, intent on uncovering the entire summit of the hill. He raised the work force to more than four hundred—double the number of workers he had employed at Megiddo—and ordered that huge masses of earth and debris be stripped away from the area around the temple. On August 21, he brought the first season of digging to an end and dismissed the workers. Schumacher himself spent several days at the site alone completing the photography, measurements, lists of finds, and accounts, and ordered the marble statue to be "boxed in heavy boards" and stored on the site.

Proud of the quantities of ancient remains that he had laid bare in the first season of digging, Schumacher spent the autumn of 1908 preparing his report. Having excavated at Taanach, Megiddo, and now Samaria, he could undoubtedly be considered the most experienced archeologist in Palestine. Experience, however, was not enough to satisfy his American employers. After reviewing the material that Schumacher had dispatched, George Reisner coldly advised the Harvard committee that for all the money and effort that had been expended on the Samaria excavations, "the desired result did not seem to have been fully attained." Schumacher, carried away by the lavish funds at his disposal, had turned the American effort into little more than a treasure hunt. "From an examination of Dr. Schumacher's notes and plan and of the trenches themselves," wrote Reisner, "I could learn little more than that a temple stood on the summit, and that the debris deepened towards the western bluff. . . . In short, the whole problem of the history of the site remained to be worked out."

Isolated artifacts were of only secondary interest to the Americans. Yet the main results of the Samaria excavations were a catalogue of undated finds, tangled stubs of walls, and a crated statue. The Harvard committee, concurring in Reisner's recommendation, did not deem it wise to publish the report, and quietly demanded the resignation of its author. Whereupon Schumacher quickly took up new employment at the new Austrian excavations being conducted at Jericho. The Americans were left with his half-dug site and the problem of what to do with it. In order to salvage the remaining year-and-a-half on the firman, it was agreed that Reisner must take complete control. His contract with the Egyptian government would expire the following spring, and he would return to the hill of Samaria, beginning from scratch if he must, in order to investigate carefully the remains of the royal city of Omri and Ahab.

Arriving at the site in May 1909, Reisner began by cutting down the size of the work force drastically, rehiring only 62 of Schumacher's 450. The haphazard trenches on the summit of the hill cut through the precious debris like open wounds and the huge dumps piled beside them obscured the probable continuations of ancient walls. If Schumacher's results were to be checked, the dumps would have to be moved, and Reisner was forced to devote the opening week of the excavation to this unpleasant task. Dividing the site into equal strips, he ordered the workers to excavate one strip at a time, filling in the already excavated strips with the dumps of the succeeding ones. This was the method that had been employed by Macalister at Gezer, and it enabled Reisner to map the entire framework of the ancient city plan, while at the same time returning the land to its previous condition as required by the firman.

But Reisner's original plan—to dig up the successive ancient strata separately—proved to be impossible. In theory, the idea that ancient Palestinian cities were built on top of one another was correct, but in reality those successive strata were often intermixed and hard to distinguish. Since the builders in every period of Samaria's history had reused stones from the structures of the previous stratum, or, as in the case of the Roman period, sunk their foundations down to the surface of the bedrock, the remains of various periods were often found side by side rather than layered. Hitherto, because this phenomenon was not understood, all of the excavations in Palestine had grossly erred in their historical conclusions. This would soon change, however, for Reisner attacked the problem of stratigraphy with his characteristic genius and discovered the secret that would be the guiding principle of all future excavations in the Holy Land: the layers of debris at ancient sites were as important as the remains that they covered.

By studying the sharply cut sides of the excavation trenches with the analytical eye of a geologist, Reisner was able to distinguish the characteristic hallmarks of lapses in occupation, destruction, and rebuilding. The construction of every large wall required a foundation trench to be dug into the remains of the previous stratum, and by carefully tracing the outline of the ancient trench, Reisner was able to find the dividing line between the two periods. Although the study of pottery forms had progressed little since the time of Petrie, Reisner was able to determine the relative dates of the pottery discovered in each of the carefully defined strata.

Never before had a Palestinian site been subject to such careful scrutiny, and the new methods introduced at Samaria required far greater skills on the part of the local work force. No longer could the excavator contentedly watch the work gangs tear away at the earth from the comfortable shade of his tent. "It must be remembered," noted Reisner, "that the workmen are merely the excavator's hands, and the closer [the] connection between the actual diggers and the directing intelligence, the more satisfactory the result." In order to improve this connection, Reisner brought with him a small corps of highly trained Egyptian foremen who had worked with him on the Hearst and Harvard expeditions and who had great experience in overseeing the work of excavation. Standing atop the piles of freshly dug debris, the white-robed Egyptians proved efficient taskmasters.

In order to control the pace and quality of the work, Reisner drafted a long list of regulations which the diggers would have to obey: all workers must come every day without fail; they must obey all commands of the Egyptians; work must be steady and all baskets must be completely filled. Quarreling and fighting were strictly prohibited, as were obscene conversation and songs. "But ordinary worksongs were encouraged," noted Reisner, "as they helped to pass away the tedium of the day's task." Owing to the strict conditions and high pay that Reisner's workers received for their efforts, entire families would often share a single wage in order to split up the tremendous workload it represented for any individual laborer. The careful division of labor produced the results that Reisner had hoped. Like the proud manager of a booming American factory, the Harvard professor had accomplished nothing less than a technological revolution in Biblical archeology. "Long before the end of the first year," Reisner proudly reported to his superiors back in the United States, "we had a body of well disciplined people, gaining in skill and endurance with every day they were employed."

In stark contrast to virtually all of the earlier Palestinian archeologists, Reisner understood that the act of excavation was, in fact, the act of destruction, and that only complete records of every part of the work would save it for future generations. In addition to his own general diary of the work and the normal plans and maps that all excavators were accustomed to draw, Reisner insisted on complete vertical sections and continuous photography, with the negatives being brought to him for inspection every morning. Every find unearthed in the course of the work was recorded on a catalogue card bearing complete information on the place it was found, along with a photograph. Several copies were made of each card so that they could be arranged either by type or by location. Even discarded fragments were recorded by this system. Reisner was confident that by the end of the excavations the entire nature of the debris would be carefully recorded. Future archeologists might be able to argue with his conclusions, but there would be no question about what he had found—or where he had found it.

The first season of the Harvard excavations at Samaria under the direction of George Reisner ended early in November after more than six months of almost continual digging. Reisner spent the rainy winter months in the comparatively dry climate of Egypt, and returned to Samaria early the following June to resume work. The same methods were applied in the second season of digging, and Reisner was gratified to see that a layoff of seven months had not adversely affected the disipline of his workers. "Everyone fell into line," Reisner was proud to note, "and the work began without a hitch, as if we left off yesterday."

Once again the work continued through the summer into the fall. In addition to redefining the stratigraphy of the Roman temple and tracing the limits of Herod's city, Reisner and his staff uncovered extensive remains of the Israelite capital beneath it. Meticulously analyzing the debris deposits, he was able to distinguish a series of successive Israelite fortification walls and begin a scientific reconstruction of the development of the city in Biblical times. Although many of his findings would be revised in the course of later excavations in the nineteen-thirties, the value of the historical and archeological information he assembled remained unchallenged.

Undoubtedly the most sensational finds of the Samaria excavations

were a group of more than sixty *ostraca*—inscribed pottery fragments—
discovered on the floor of one of the Israelite buildings. Written in black
ink in a cursive Hebrew script of the eighth century B.C., the Samaria
Ostraca shed dramatic new light on the daily life of the later Biblical
periods. The inscriptions that they bore were records of tax payments on
wine and oil produced in the vicinity of the Israelite capital, and many of
the personal names which they mentioned showed close similarity to
common names used in the Bible.

Because the American team had excavated with such thoroughness,
a new standard had been established for all future archeological work in
Palestine. With increased specialization and systemization, Biblical ar
cheology was quickly losing its sacred associations. Instead of the odd
artifact and yet another identified place-name, there was now a blizzard
of highly technical reports and cross-cultural conclusions. The pious aims
of the pioneer explorers had become irrelevant to the scientists and
specialists of the early twentieth century. The act of digging itself had
become the modern art.

Secrets of the Temple Mount

AMBITION, GREED, AND
A SEARCH FOR TREASURE
IN JERUSALEM,

1909-1911

The personal origins of Valter H. Juvelius are shrouded in mystery. A Finn by nationality, apparently wealthy, he seems to have been obsessed by two subjects: spiritualism and Biblical archeology. He was first heard of in 1906, when he presented a paper before a Swedish university audience on the subject of the destruction of Solomon's Temple by the Babylonian king Nebuchadnezzar in 586 B.C. His unorthodox theories received little attention from the academic world. But he was undaunted. He believed that he had discovered great mystical and symbolic meaning in the destruction of Solomon's Temple, and in 1908, seeking to further his research on the subject in the ancient libraries of Constantinople, he accidentally stumbled upon a truly incredible manuscript.

Juvelius never revealed either the circumstances or the location of his discovery, but among the dusty books and scrolls of some unnamed library, he claimed to have uncovered a "coded" passage in an ancient text of the Book of Ezekiel that disclosed the hiding place of the Temple treasure in Jerusalem. This fabulous treasure, supposedly buried by Hebrew priests at the time of Nebuchadnezzar's conquest, was said to be located in a cave beneath the Temple Mount that was connected to the city by a secret underground passage.

The precise contents of this ancient depository remained Juvelius's closely guarded secret. By all accounts, however, it was of spectacular value, far beyond that of any archeological discovery made in Palestine —and probably anywhere else. By some later reports, based largely on hearsay or speculation, Juvelius's treasure was "the gold-encrusted Ark of the Covenant, brought by the Children of Israel out of Egypt." In other versions, it was "the treasure of the Jewish kings, and ancient tablets which will set to rest all doubts concerning the resurrection of Christ." Whatever its exact nature, Juvelius was convinced that the ancient treasure of Solomon's Temple was real and that he had almost in his grasp the means of recovering it for himself.

Careful study of the reports of the Palestine Exploration Fund excavations in Jerusalem gave Juvelius striking confirmation for the geographical details of his mysterious "coded" text. Charles Warren had explored a complex of subterranean tunnels and shafts to the south of the Haram ash-Sharif, on a steep ridge of land known as the Ophel. Bliss and Dickie had discovered additional underground channels in roughly the same area. Juvelius felt sure that the secret passage mentioned in his ancient document was among these. If a new expedition to Jerusalem could locate the correct passage and clear it, the fantastic treasure was as good as found.

In order to organize such an expedition, Juvelius traveled through the centers of European wealth and influence hoping to attract financial backers with promises of a share in the $200 million that he estimated the recovered relics would bring on the open market. But lacking the proper connections and introductions, the Finnish scholar could find no investors. Those few who took him seriously enough to discuss the plan repeatedly warned that the political implications were too dangerous, the goal too improbable, and the amount of capital needed too great to warrant the risk of failure. Yet Juvelius refused to abandon his quest. All he needed, he was sure, was someone possessing the social connections that he himself lacked, someone with enough influence in aristocratic circles to raise the necessary funds. Eventually, he found him.

Montague Brownslow Parker, the thirty-year-old son of the Earl of Morley, had never been quite satisfied with the quiet life of the English gentry. At an early age, while most of his peers were safely tucked away at Oxford and Cambridge, Parker undertook a military career, serving with distinction in the Boer War and rising to the rank of captain in the Grenadier Guards. Back in London after the war, Parker left the army and plunged into the social whirl of the capital, but his desire to return to a life of adventure never left him. The circumstances of Parker's meeting with Juvelius are uncertain, but when the Finn revealed to him the object of his proposed excavations and explained his desperate need for someone to raise the necessary funds, Parker jumped at the chance to join in the enterprise.

Parker succeeded where Juvelius had failed. Over the course of several months, he raised more than $125,000 from such diverse sources as the Duchess of Marlborough and Chicago's meat-packing Armour family. Once Parker had the money in hand, however, he ceased to be interested in a partnership with Juvelius. While the Finn busied himself in feverish consultations with an Irish clairvoyant about the location of the secret passage, Captain Parker (as he now preferred to be called) traveled to Constantinople to obtain the cooperation of the Turkish authorities personally.

At the time of Parker's arrival, the Ottoman capital was buzzing with rumors and uncertainty in the wake of intense civil and political unrest during the previous summer and fall. In April, a group of young officers, supported by large segments of the army and a rebellious populace, forced the abdication of Sultan Abdul Hamid in favor of his ineffectual brother Mehmet V, and it seemed certain that the centuries-old power of the sultan had finally been broken. No one knew what the future would hold for the Ottoman Empire, and for the time being the normal processes of law and administration ground to a halt. Officially, at least, the old antiquities policy of the sultan remained in force. The British, American, and German archeological excavations in Palestine were still required to have an Ottoman commissioner supervise their work, and all finds that they unearthed were still regarded as state property. But even in the uncertain atmosphere of revolutionary Constantinople, Parker was able to engage in his own brand of personal politics and circumvent the law. Secretly making contact with two high-ranking members of the Young Turk government, Parker offered them 50 percent of any treasure he might find in Jerusalem, in return for their official confidence and support. Accepting the offer and agreeing to come to Jerusalem themselves as the "official" commissioners, the two Turks promptly dispatched a messenger to the governor of Jerusalem with instructions to purchase all available land on the southern slopes of the Temple Mount.

Parker returned to London, apparently satisfied with the arrangements he had made. During the spring he assembled an "excavation staff," consisting of his good friends Clarence Wilson, R. G. Duff, and a certain Major Foley who had taken part in the ill-fated Jameson Raid into the Transvaal before the Boer War. The mission to Jerusalem would be no less daring and dangerous an operation. Out of the large amount of capital that he had raised, Parker purchased expensive excavation equipment and fitted out Clarence Wilson's yacht for the long voyage to Pales-

tine. Parker was determined to lead the expedition himself. The super-
seded Juvelius would remain in Europe, faithfully transmitting the telepathic instructions of the Irish clairvoyant to Jerusalem by telegraph.

In August 1909, the Parker expedition landed at Jaffa and traveled
overland to Jerusalem. During the previous several months, the country
had been plagued by unrest and occasional outbreaks of violence in
reaction to the events in Constantinople. The British excavations at
Gezer and the Austrian-German excavations at Jericho had both been
suspended, and many of the foreign residents in Palestine feared that the
current disorders were merely the prelude to even greater political
upheavals in the immediate future. Montague Parker had no such fears.
With complete confidence in the arrangement he had concluded in Constantinople, he was determined to make his stay in Jerusalem as enjoyable
as possible.

Moving into the spacious Augusta Victoria Hospice on the Mount of
Olives, Parker spared no expense in the purchase of tents, rifles, camp
furniture, and imported provisions. He also hired a small army of cooks,
guides, bodyguards, housemaids, and workers. His efforts to create a
respectable image for his expedition were apparently rewarded, for the
governor of the city, Azmey Bey Pasha, proudly introduced him to the
local dignitaries and lavishly entertained the entire expedition staff at a
banquet in the official residence.

When the two "commissioners" arrived from Constantinople to supervise the search for the treasure, Parker officially began the excavations
on the Ophel slope. Closely following the instructions of the Irish clairvoyant, Parker ordered the workers to reopen one of the shafts dug by
Charles Warren in 1867. Large detachments of bodyguards and soldiers
were placed around the opening of the shaft to keep away unauthorized
onlookers, but as might have been expected, these highly public security
measures only intensified the curiosity of the local inhabitants.

In the meantime, the possessive scholars of the American and European archeological institutions in Jerusalem had grown highly suspicious.
Excavations on a site as important as the Ophel required highly skilled
excavators, but the young Englishmen surrounded by Ottoman guards
seemed to possess absolutely no technical training. Parker's staff did not
maintain accurate records of the digging, nor did they classify the finds;
in fact, the object of the mission itself remained a puzzling secret. The
distressed archeologists quickly dispatched letters of protest to col-
leagues in London and New York, and sent off frantic inquiries to Con-

stantinople in an effort to find out more about Captain Parker's intentions. No one seemed to know who he was or what he was up to, but as rumors spread of "hidden treasure" and "telepathic guidance," the foreign archeologists loudly registered their outrage with the pasha of the city.

Although Parker was admittedly no archeologist, he was more sensitive than most to the power of public opinion, and sought to refurbish his mission's image by inviting Père Hughes Vincent of the Ecole Biblique to serve as "archeological adviser." Vincent, a longtime resident of Jerusalem, was acknowledged to be one of the most prominent authorities on the city's antiquities. Suspicious of Parker, yet realizing that his excavations provided a unique opportunity to gain further information on the ancient water supply system and early development of the city, Vincent accepted the invitation to participate in the work.

With Père Vincent overseeing the progress of the digging, the criticism of the archeological community was gradually dying down, when new objections were voiced by the Jews of the city. Accusing the excavators of defiling sacred ground, they demanded that the governor intervene to stop the work. But Parker, protected by his Turkish patrons, was able to pull rank and the excavation continued, with the workers clearing out and investigating an underground tunnel known as Warren's Shaft, in search of the secret passage.

Then the weather turned against them. The rains of the winter of 1909–1910 came early, transforming clouds of dust to oceans of thick mud. Parker had expected to find the passage to the treasure quickly; when he looked up, three fruitless months had passed. In November he called a temporary halt and returned with his men to England to await the following summer.

Back in England, with much of the expedition funding still at his disposal, Parker totally reorganized his procedures, hiring several civil engineers who had worked on the recently completed London subway. At their suggestion, he purchased "expensive and perfected machinery" for the next season of tunneling. The setbacks, he was sure, were merely temporary; the power of technology, harnessed to his clairvoyant's psychic abilities, would enable him to retrieve the treasure at last.

In August 1910, Parker and his reinforced staff of subway engineers returned to Jerusalem, but it soon became clear that his cozy relationship with the Turks was over: the two commissioners had returned to Constantinople in obvious disgust at the failure of the Englishmen to find anything resembling the treasure they had promised. The Jewish protest was vigorous as ever, and had now found a powerful patron in the person of Baron Edmond de Rothschild.

Rothschild, scion of the French branch of the international banking family, was an active supporter of the ideal of Jewish restoration in Palestine. Over the course of the previous three decades he had purchased agricultural land and provided professional guidance to many of the early Zionist settlements. Hearing of the suspicious activity around one of the holiest and most historic sites of Jerusalem, Rothschild was determined to stop it if he could. He arranged for the purchase of a piece of land adjoining Parker's, and applied for permission for his own archeologist to excavate there.

Rothschild's political influence at Constantinople was considerable, and the Ottoman authorities accordingly informed Parker of the competing claim and announced that he must complete his work in Jerusalem by the end of the summer of 1911, only eleven months away. Time had never been much of a factor for Parker, but now he saw that it was running out. Leaving his comfortable accommodations on the Mount of Olives and renting a house close to the site of the digging, he set the excavation gangs to work day and night, clearing out the entire length of Warren's tunnels by torchlight in a desperate push to find the opening to the secret passage that would lead him to the Temple Mount— and to the treasure.

In the succeeding months of grueling work, while Parker and his men searched for their secret passage, Père Vincent carefully recorded and analyzed the many structures and objects that they uncovered. Noting the presence of Bronze Age burial caves dug into the bedrock and meticulously mapping the extensive subterranean water system and traces of ancient fortifications, Vincent was able to piece together evidence that Bliss and Dickie had overlooked, concluding with near-certainty that the pre-Davidic city had been located on the Ophel.

The rains came early again in 1910, yet Parker had no choice but to continue. Taking even greater risks in the narrow shafts deep beneath the surface of the now-wet ground, Parker's men worked steadily all through the winter.

Spring came, but still no secret passage. Until then, Parker had been keeping in close touch with his backers in the United States and England, faithfully sending them optimistic reports on his progress. But now Parker himself sensed possible failure: only four months remained before the permit to excavate would expire and he knew that even if his men were able to find the secret passage in time, they would be unable to clear it all the way to the Temple Mount. His communications with the outside world suddenly stopped. Desperation now guided his actions.

Since the departure of the commissioners, Parker had developed close contacts with the local officials and had gained their confidence. Closest of all was the governor, Azmey Bey Pasha, who came down to the excavation site every day. Parker believed he had read Azmey's character correctly. He now offered him a bribe of twenty-five thousand dollars to arrange for the expedition to excavate within the Haram ash-Sharif itself —an opportunity that had been denied all previous western explorers. Azmey Bey accepted Parker's bribe and arranged that Sheikh Khalil, the hereditary guardian of the Dome of the Rock, would also be bribed handsomely and included in the secret scheme.

During the following week, Parker and a small group of excavators disguised in Arab dress were secretly admitted to the Temple Mount under the cover of darkness. Every night for more than a week, they stealthily excavated in the southeast corner of the Haram platform, where Juvelius's clairvoyant had assured them that the treasure lay. After seven nights of digging, however, they still had found no treasure.

The time of the year was especially dangerous for risking offense to religious sensibilities. In April 1911, Passover, Easter, and the Muslim feast of Nebi Musa all coincided, and the city was mobbed with religious pilgrims from all over the world. At such times of festival, Jerusalem was always an explosive place, but that was of little concern to Parker. Far more pressing was his desperate search. Time was slipping away.

On the night of April 17–18, 1911, Parker and his men entered the sanctuary of the Dome of the Rock. Juvelius's clairvoyant, consulted yet again, had now directed them to concentrate their efforts in a natural cavern beneath the surface of the sacred stone. Islamic legend associated this cavern with a passage to the bowels of the earth—a passage filled with spirits and demons and leading to a fantastic treasure. They lowered themselves by ropes into the cavern and began to excavate, breaking apart the pavement to open an ancient shaft below. At last, it seemed, their treasure was near.

That same night, a mosque attendant, his own home overflowing with out-of-town guests in Jerusalem for the festival season, decided that he would sleep on the Temple Mount. Unfortunately for Parker, he had not been paid off. Arriving after midnight, he heard strange noises inside the Dome of the Rock and came upon the strangely attired Englishmen hacking away at the holy shrine. Shocked and horrified by the sacrilege, he bolted from the mosque and ran shrieking into the darkened streets of the city. Parker and his panic-stricken men quickly gathered up their tools and escaped. But they knew that they had played their final hand and lost.

By the time they reached the port of Jaffa, the first telegraphed dispatches had already arrived from Jerusalem. The Holy City was in an uproar. Azmey Bey had reportedly ordered the immediate closing of the Haram ash-Sharif, but before his soldiers had a chance to take up positions there, a raging mob had carried off Sheikh Khalil. Azmey Bey himself was said to have been confronted by an angry crowd who spat upon him and called him a pig for his suspected complicity in the sacrilege. The disturbances grew more violent as wild rumors spread that the Englishmen had discovered and stolen the Crown and Ring of Solomon, the Ark of the Covenant, and the Sword of Muhammad.

Customs authorities in Jaffa, alerted by these frantic reports, immediately impounded the personal baggage of Parker and his men for a thorough search. The officials found nothing, but nonetheless decided to detain Parker and his men until further instructions arrived from Constantinople. But Parker knew that he must make his escape at once. Calmly denying all accusations, he invited the customs officials to discuss the matter in the more comfortable surroundings of Clarence Wilson's yacht, which lay at anchor in the harbor. Things would be quickly sorted out, he assured them. Besides, he had nothing to hide.

The authorities grudgingly accepted the arrangement. Parker and his men were permitted to row out into the harbor to illuminate the yacht and prepare to receive their official guests. Long before the guests had a chance to arrive, however, the yacht was under way, steaming for the open sea. Parker and the others could point, after all those months of labor, to only one success: they had escaped with their lives.

The rioting and disturbances in Jerusalem continued unabated for several days, and it was not long before newspapers and magazines all over the world were filled with the strange story of the Parker expedition and its aftermath. Publicity was the last thing that Parker needed at this time, for the exposure of the names of some of his backers and the public ridicule of his project put him into a very awkward position. Almost all of his investors' capital had been expended in the preceding three years, and there was pressure on Parker to recoup at least part of it.

Safely back in London, he refused all comment on the events of the preceding weeks. Instead, he announced that he would be returning to

Jerusalem the following summer. In an effort to publicize the concrete archeological achievements of his mission, he arranged for Père Vincent to publish the results of the first two seasons in a volume entitled *Underground Jerusalem*. But even the important finds of Early Bronze Age pottery and the final resolution of the question of ancient Jerusalem's topography did little to restore confidence in the aims or motives of the Parker expedition.

An Ottoman commission of inquiry ordered the appointment of a new sheikh for the Dome of the Rock, the recall of Azmey Bey Pasha, and the official censure of the two "commissioners" who had dealt with Parker. The entire affair created unpleasant political tensions between Great Britain and the Ottoman Empire, and the position of all foreign archeologists in Palestine was badly jeopardized. The Palestine Exploration Fund was reduced to steadfast denials of any knowledge of the activities of Parker and his men, while Sir Charles Warren, the aging pioneer of Jerusalem exploration, issued a scathing condemnation of the treasure hunt.

Montague Parker's wealthy investors, however, still sought satisfaction. Parker himself, uncontrite, announced in September to a correspondent of the London *Times* that he was about to return to Palestine —to continue the important scientific work that he had left unfinished. On September 30, he once again boarded Clarence Wilson's yacht, arriving at the port of Jaffa on October 26. But, as the *Times* reported, "The explorers were advised by friends that it would be unwise to land." The yacht immediately sailed off for Port Said.

Captain Montague Brownslow Parker wisely abandoned further dreams of ancient treasure. Valter H. Juvelius, the displaced instigator of the plan, receded into the mists of obscurity, the Irish clairvoyant was never heard from again, and the investors' $125,000 had quite thoroughly vanished. It was clear now, if it had not been before, that the days of lavishly funded private archeological investigations were over. International tensions in Palestine were rapidly rising toward a flash point. The real battle for the Holy Land was about to begin.

✤ 18 ✤

The Last Crusade

THE P.E.F. AND
THE BRITISH CONQUEST
OF PALESTINE,
1913-1917

By the end of 1913, the world was preparing for war. Constant crises in the Balkans and continuing tensions in Europe gave rise to an arms race unprecedented in the history of the world. Two irreconcilably hostile power blocs—Britain, France, and Russia on the one hand, and Germany and Austria on the other—readied themselves for the coming confrontation and drew much of the world into their respective camps. At Constantinople, the Young Turks were firmly in power, and in an effort to prepare their armed forces for the possible outbreak of hostilities in the Middle East, they agreed to accept the assistance of German military advisers. The implications of that tacit alliance were far-reaching. The coming war would clearly settle the "Eastern Question" once and for all.

In Palestine, the effects of the Turkish military build-up were frighteningly evident. Djemal Pasha, a member of the ruling Young Turk triumvirate, established a military command center in Jerusalem, initiated a program of general conscription, and ordered the summary arrest and exile of potentially dangerous Jewish and Arab nationalists. The Ottoman troops stationed in Palestine requisitioned foodstuffs and draft animals in growing quantities, and an air of grim uncertainty gripped residents as the tensions of the world began to affect their daily lives.

For the foreign archeologists in Palestine, the political and military developments brought excavation to a near-standstill, and with the completion of the latest P.E.F. excavations in 1912, only the Germans continued active digging. In light of the alliance between the Turks and the Germans, future plans for British exploration in Palestine became in-

189

creasingly uncertain, and the executive committee of the P.E.F. resolved to mount one final expedition before world events brought everything to a stop.

Only one region of the Land of the Bible remained uncharted by the great Survey of Western Palestine, and the successful mapping of that area would provide the Palestine Exploration Fund with a fitting culmination to the exploration begun by Clarke, Seetzen, and Burckhardt more than a hundred years before. This region was known to Biblical scholars as the Wilderness of Zin, or more generally as the Negev, and it stretched southward from Beersheva to the Gulf of Aqaba. Crisscrossed by twisting canyons, rugged mountains, and desolate plateaus, this region guarded the entrance to Palestine from the Sinai and the south.

Only a few western explorers had ever devoted much attention to the topography and ancient remains of the Negev, but not because it lacked for Biblical associations. The Children of Israel had passed through the Wilderness of Zin on their way to the Promised Land, and during later Biblical times, the Hebrew kings had constructed a string of fortresses there to guard the important caravan routes that led from Egypt into Judea. Those routes and fortresses remained lost, and in light of the growing threat of war, an opportunity to locate them might not come again for many years.

On December 13, 1913, two young British archeologists set out from the site of their excavations at Carchemish in Syria to travel southward to Palestine and participate in the upcoming survey of the Wilderness of Zin. Arriving at Gaza, they were received by the British vice-consul and the head of the Church Missionary Society station, who provided them with their first detailed instructions. The two archeologists were to make contact with several parties of Royal Engineers already proceeding across the Sinai to Beersheva; while accompanying the surveyors, they were to study the "character" of the country, trace the ancient caravan routes of the region, and pay particular attention to the oasis of Ain Kadeis, thought by many Biblical scholars to be the site of the spring of Kadesh-barnea, from which Moses dispatched spies into the Land of Canaan.

Both of the young archeologists hired by the Palestine Exploration Fund for this mission possessed impressive credentials and bright futures. One of them, Leonard Woolley, would gain international prominence later in his career as the excavator of the Mesopotamian city of Ur. His colleague would find fame in less scholarly pursuits. His name was T. E. Lawrence.

Lawrence had traveled through Palestine before. In 1909, at the age of twenty-one, he had spent a summer exploring ruined Crusader fortresses and strategic outposts in the north of the country, and his thesis at Oxford, "The Influence of the Crusades on European Military Architecture," was the product of his love for archeology and fascination with military strategy. He privately hoped that the survey of the Wilderness of Zin would provide him with an additional opportunity to combine those two interests, for the area to be surveyed had become of increasing military importance in recent years.

At the time of Edward Robinson's visit to Beersheva in 1838, the "town" had consisted of little more than a group of wells on the fringe of the desert. By the early years of the twentieth century, however, the Turks had constructed a provincial administrative center there to govern the newly created subprovince of the Negev. As the British tightened their control over Egypt and the Sinai, the Turks likewise built up the defenses of southern Palestine, constructing a line of military camps and fortresses across the area. Because of the obvious importance of this region should hostilities ever break out between Britain and the Ottoman Empire, Lawrence suspected from the start that his appointment was merely intended to provide an archeological cover for a military reconnaissance. Yet the prospect of participating in a secret mission clearly excited him.

Lawrence and Woolley traveled from Gaza to Beersheva, where they made contact with Captain Stewart Newcombe of the Royal Engineers and made a respectful courtesy call on the Turkish governor. Securing camels and the promise of protection from several Bedouin sheikhs in the area, Lawrence and Woolley moved southward in search of ruins, while Newcombe directed the work of the surveying parties. Although there were few tells in the area, Lawrence and Woolley thoroughly explored the imposing remains of several ancient caravan cities built during the Roman period by the Nabateans. They carefully photographed and sketched those remains, noting the traces of water-supply installations, agricultural fields, public buildings, and monumental churches—all evidence of the rich culture that had once flourished in the now largely uninhabited desert.

Atop the towering site of the Nabatean city of Nitzana, beneath which the Turks had constructed a fortress and military camp, Lawrence also had the opportunity to examine the Ottoman line of desert defense at close range. From his observations he concluded that the Turks' preparations were basically fruitless. The extent and complexity of the desert paths and passages mapped for the first time by the Royal Engineers

indicated to Lawrence that "fortresses are of little avail against a mobile
enemy in a desert country where roads run everywhither. . . ." An understanding of how to fight a guerrilla war in the desert against strongly
entrenched Turkish fortifications would later win T. E. Lawrence immor-
tality at the head of the Arab Revolt.

Lawrence and Newcombe separated from the others after completing
the survey of the Nabatean cities and the topography of the region and
traveled south to investigate the area around Aqaba and its outlet to the
Red Sea. The exploration of this region was not included in the original
permission granted to the P.E.F. and the Turkish garrison commander
at Aqaba became suspicious, prohibiting Lawrence and Newcombe from
conducting any reconnaissances within the area of his authority. Lawrence pretended to accede to the commander's demands, but nevertheless carried out a risky nighttime exploration in the vicinity of the
ruined Crusader fortress of Ile de Graye, a few miles to the south of Aqaba.
This was his only such venture. The plan to locate previously unknown
valleys leading down to the Gulf of Aqaba had to be canceled as, in Lawrence's cool assessment, "the state of the country was unfavorable for
exploration."

The archeological and strategic components of the Palestine Exploration Fund survey were becoming increasingly blurred, but its general
success was obvious. By June 1914, both the War Office and the Palestine
Exploration Fund were pleased to hear from Captain Newcombe that "all
roads have been marked on a new map, and some interesting information
has been obtained." The Survey of Western Palestine was complete. The
entire extent of Palestine from the upper Galilee in the north to the approaches to Aqaba in the south had been carefully mapped by the surveyors and explorers of the Palestine Exploration Fund. With the latest
expedition, the last piece had been finally fitted into the puzzle.

Less than a month after the announcement of the completion of the
survey of the Wilderness of Zin, the world slid into the war that had been
threatening for decades. Within five weeks of the assassination of Austrian Archduke Franz Ferdinand at Sarajevo, Austria had declared war on
Serbia, German troops had invaded Belgium, and all of Europe was
engaged in conflict.

Assuming that war would soon spread to the Middle East, the Ottoman Empire began a secret mobilization of its troops and concluded a
private agreement with Germany, its long-standing ally. The choice was
clear. The Turks knew that if Germany were to win the war, the Ottoman

Empire would become little more than a German satellite, but even that prospect was to be preferred to dismemberment at the hands of Britain, France, and Russia. More immediately, the Germans had promised them the return of the province of Egypt, which had been cut off from the empire since the time of Napoleon. So the Turks allowed German warships to pass through the Dardanelles and thus openly entered the war in November 1914.

In Palestine, the Turks severed all communications with the West as they prepared to strike a blow at the British in Egypt. During the fall and winter of 1914–1915, Turkish troops moved into positions along the Sinai border as streams of reinforcements began to flow into Palestine itself. The headquarters of the Turkish VIII Corps were established in Jerusalem, and a joint German-Turkish High Command formulated the plan of battle. The commanders at Jerusalem correctly realized that the Suez Canal was the heart of British imperial war strategy, and they prepared their forces to attack the waterway and put it out of use.

In mid-January 1915, approximately one hundred thousand Turkish troops massed around Beersheva struck into the Sinai. That the attack was unsuccessful did not diminish its strategic importance in the mind of the German general Kress von Kressenstein, who ordered another, more powerful attack on the canal in the summer of 1916. This time, fifty thousand Turkish shock troops, reinforced by German machine gunners, heavy artillery, and airplanes, were beaten back after two desperate attempts to pierce the British defenses around the Suez Canal. But the long-term strategic dilemma of the eastern front was clear: as long as hostile forces remained in Palestine, additional attempts would undoubtedly be made on the lifeline of the British Empire.

Field Marshal Horatio Kitchener, former explorer for the Palestine Exploration Fund, now Secretary of State for War, saw that some bold action was required. He had long recognized the military significance of the P.E.F.'s mapping program. (As, in fact, did the P.E.F. itself: as early as 1915, the *Quarterly Statement* had noted that "surveying, map-making, and all that contributes to a better knowledge of a country, its resources, and its people are, as we plainly see, of enormous practical importance and what has been achieved by the P.E.F. has been helpful in many ways to causes which we value, and which need not be particularly enumerated. . . .") Newcombe, Lawrence, and Woolley had all been called into the intelligence service of the British forces in Egypt at the outbreak of the war, and the final drawing and completion of the maps of the Wilderness of Zin were given the highest priority. Subscribers of the P.E.F. received copies of the archeological report of that survey, "in which the

Turks will not find much help," but the rest of the material remained a military secret. "We do not want the Turks to get maps which they might find rather useful in their feeble attempts to get to Egypt," noted Charles Watson, the new honorary secretary. Yet the long-term prospects for the fund were anything but dim. "It is almost impossible to conceive," remarked the archbishop of Canterbury at a P.E.F. fiftieth-anniversary meeting, "that there will not be hereafter a better opportunity to investigate the things that we have hitherto found it difficult to investigate." For the time being, however, the efforts of the Palestine Exploration Fund would be put at the disposal of the British war effort. In January 1916, the War Office officially requested that the P.E.F. suspend the sale of all its maps and geographical publications, and the leaders of the fund readily acceded to this request. In doing so, they expressed their long-standing gratitude to the Royal Engineers who had accomplished so much of their work and looked forward to the time when the British exploration of the Holy Land might resume "without long official delays."

The summer of 1916 saw the death of Lord Kitchener aboard H.M.S. *Hampshire* on a mission to Russia, and a decided turn for the worse in the tide of the war in Europe. But with the fall of the conservative Asquith government and the accession of David Lloyd George as prime minister, support grew for Kitchener's idea that the stalemate in the trenches of France could be broken by a stunning victory in the Middle East. Prospects seemed promising for an Arab revolt against the Turks in the Arabian peninsula, and the potential weakness of the Ottomans in Palestine convinced the British government that the time had come to accept Kitchener's advice posthumously and permanently eliminate the threat to the Suez Canal.

Armed with the full backing of the Lloyd George government, the Egyptian Expeditionary Force of the British army moved out from their bases in the Sinai at the end of December 1916. They followed the same route taken by Napoleon Bonaparte in 1799, capturing al-Arish and Rafah with little opposition. The entire Sinai peninsula now lay firmly within British military control, but that conquest was worthless unless the southern part of Palestine could be taken as well.

The British invasion force met its first determined resistance at Gaza. Heavily fortified trenches ringed the ancient port city, and the first British attack was repulsed with heavy losses. The dry season was rapidly approaching and the military objectives of the campaign would have to be gained quickly, before heat and thirst became the most dangerous enemies of the British. In order to hasten things, Sir Archibald Murray, commander of the Egyptian Expeditionary Force, ordered that fresh supplies and reinforcements be brought up to the front along a railway that had been built across the Sinai. Another assault on Gaza was ordered in April, but the enemy positions were also stronger now. They had been reinforced by troops of the German Asienkorps and proved to be too much for the British in the second attack. British losses were again heavy; as in the case of Napoleon, the invasion's momentum had been lost in a costly siege.

The unexpected defeat at the second battle of Gaza shocked and infuriated the British government, which became more determined than ever to achieve a victory in Palestine. General Murray was relieved of command of the Egyptian Expeditionary Force and replaced by General Edmund Allenby, an unrelenting leader who had gained the nickname "the Bull" in the trenches and gore of the Western Front. From the time of Allenby's appointment, all historical similarities to the Napoleonic invasion of Palestine ceased. Everything necessary to achieve victory would be supplied. Prime Minister Lloyd George, meeting with Allenby shortly before his departure from England, made the intentions of the British government clear. The Bull must devote all his energy in the next several months to preparing a "Christmas gift" for the British people. The city of Jerusalem, Lloyd George insisted, must be taken by the end of the year.

Allenby arrived in Egypt in June 1917 and transferred the headquarters of the E.E.F. from the comforts of Cairo to the dusty harshness of the Sinai front. He quickly saw that another headlong attack on the trenches surrounding Gaza was doomed to fail, but noted a possible point of Turkish vulnerability at the eastern end of the Turkish line, where it terminated at Beersheva in territory that had been explored by the survey of the Wilderness of Zin less than four years before. In August, word reached the British command that T. E. Lawrence at the head of a band of Bedouin irregulars had taken the port of Aqaba and captured its Turkish defenders. Lawrence had been in Aqaba before, and his brief exploration of the region undoubtedly provided one of the keys to his victory. Allenby himself began to study the publications of the Palestine Exploration Fund as well as an extensive library of Biblical and Crusader history, and by the autumn he was ready to execute a daring plan.

On October 31, the Turkish defenses around Gaza received an intensive bombardment from the British fleet, in apparent preparation for a renewed offensive. On the same day, far to the east on the outskirts of Beersheva, Turkish sentries discovered a document pouch dropped by a fleeing British scout. Among the papers it contained was a British war plan, apparently secret, detailing massive troop movements for an imminent attack on Gaza. In response to this intelligence, Turkish forces from Beersheva immediately moved westward to strengthen the trenches at Gaza, leaving Beersheva itself virtually unprotected.

A large body of British troops, secretly brought up through the desert, received the signal to attack. Guided by precise topographical maps, they captured the vital wells of the town in a lightning-fast movement, cleared a nest of German machine gunners from Tell esh-Sheba to the north of the city, and forced the remaining Turkish troops to beat a disorganized retreat.

With the Ottoman line of defense broken in the east, Allenby now initiated an attack on Gaza itself. The Egyptian Expeditionary Force was for the first time equipped with airplanes for support and reconnaissance, while armor-plated tanks—never used before in the Holy Land—proved effective in storming heavily fortified trenches and overcoming the resistance of German and Austrian machine gunners. In little more than a week, the entire Turkish line of defense had given way, and Allenby ordered his forces to pursue the enemy at full speed northward along the coast.

To the readers of the papers and reports of the Palestine Exploration Fund, many of the place-names mentioned in the excited war dispatches from the East were familiar. On November 11, 1917, Tell el-Hesy was captured by British troops, and less than a week later another contingent of Allenby's forces cleared Tell Gezer of the German positions that had been set up in the remains of Macalister's archeological trenches. As the Germans and Turks continued their retreat, the British gained ground throughout southern Palestine, conquering the territory that had been so thoroughly explored by the archeologists. Turning eastward from Jaffa and proceeding up into the Judean hills, Allenby directed his forces to concentrate on their primary objective—Jerusalem.

Following the battle of Beersheva and the conquest of Gaza, an air of near-panic gripped the Turkish-German High Command at Jerusalem. The city was crowded with prisoners of war and wounded troops of both sides, and much of the local population was near starvation. British forces were advancing from the west, south, and north when Djemal Pasha, faced with the prospect of imminent defeat, ordered the Turkish evacuation of the city. German and Turkish headquarters staff officers requisitioned automobiles, primitive carts, and even camels, loading them with furniture, oriental rugs, official records, and gold bullion for the frantic retreat to Damascus. Anything of value that they could not take with them was hidden or destroyed. The once lavish Augusta Victoria Hospice on the Mount of Olives, which had been equipped for the Germans with a searchlight and antiaircraft guns, was now left empty and deserted, except for the few Lutheran deaconesses who had served the German High Command. Near the Jaffa Gate, the barracks of the Turkish garrison, which had served as the center of Ottoman power in Jerusalem since 1516, lay unattended. It was as if every trace of Turkish rule over Jerusalem had suddenly been swept away.

By December 9, the last of the Turkish troops had evacuated Jerusalem, and the residents were left to themselves briefly, awaiting the final British attack. The civilian mayor, Haj Amin Nashashibi, remained the only official source of authority. With British forces ringing the city and the last Turkish snipers going into hiding, he borrowed a bedsheet from an American missionary and walked out of the city through the Jaffa Gate, followed by a small entourage of local boys. On a barren, rocky ridge on the outskirts of the city, the humble delegation came upon two startled British scouts. A few words of broken English were exchanged, and the mayor's intentions were made clear: he had come to surrender Jerusalem.

Within a few hours, large contingents of British troops marched into the city to the cheers and prayers of thanksgiving of all the religious communities. British officers toured the city and made preliminary arrangements for a military occupation. Native Jerusalemites greeted the arriving British soldiers with all the enthusiasm they could muster. Each community looked forward to an imminent fulfillment of its national hopes. The Muslims, buoyed by the success and British support of the Arab Revolt against the Turks, saw the arriving British forces as the protectors of an independent Arab state. The Zionist majority of the Jewish population greeted the British conquest as a major step toward the "National Home" promised by Lord Balfour, the foreign secretary, less than a month before. The Christian community, long held hostage to Islamic rule, offered up its own prayers of relief that the holy sites would no longer be under infidel domination.

On December 11, 1917, General Edmund Allenby arrived at the Jaffa Gate in a symbolic victory procession. Dismounting from his horse and taking the military cap from his head, he strode through the Jaffa Gate as the clock tower and church steeples of the city rang in the beginning of a new era. On the steps of the Turkish citadel, he read out a proclamation addressed to the inhabitants of "Jerusalem the Blessed" that assured them of the intention of the occupation force to uphold the freedom of all the religious communities and to protect scrupulously the holy shrines of each. Then, in the open courtyard of the Turkish garrison where the Ottoman militia had for so long lorded it over the people of the city, he formally extended his greeting to the chief rabbis, the mufti, the Latin and Orthodox patriarchs, and the leaders of every other religious denomination in the city.

By the following September, with British victory at the battle of Megiddo—site of the German excavations and of Armageddon of Revelation—the conquest of the Holy Land was complete. The age-old quest of the Christian world to control the holy places had been crowned with success. The Crusades, it seemed, were finally over.

❖ EPILOGUE ❖

The Future of the Past

THE TRANSFORMATION OF
BIBLICAL ARCHEOLOGY

One hundred and twenty wooden packing cases, hidden in basements and storerooms all over Jerusalem, were all that remained of the once bitter struggle for the antiquities of the Holy Land as the year 1917 came to an end. Inside those crates were the hundreds of ancient artifacts that the Ottoman authorities had received from western archeologists during the previous fifty years, sometimes by confiscation, sometimes by formal agreement, objects which had seemed valueless or simply too awkward to be carried away at the time of the fall of Jerusalem. The British conquerors understood the value of this booty; the London *Times*, in its extensive coverage of the occupation of the city, reported on the discovery and reclamation of the artifacts and put forth the suggestion that they become the nucleus of a national museum.

The defeat of the Turks and the establishment of British civil rule in the summer of 1920 laid the foundations for the incorporation of the principles of scientific archeology into the law of the land. Under the terms of the League of Nations Mandate for Palestine, ratified in the fall of 1923, the guidelines for the excavation and preservation of the country's archeological remains were explicitly outlined. Henceforth all member nations of the League would enjoy equality of excavation rights; an efficient and scientific Department of Antiquities would be established; and its British-appointed director would have the power to expropriate land for excavations, deny permits to the unqualified, and punish looters or destroyers of archeological remains. The science of Biblical archeology, so long hindered by recalcitrant pashas, feuding consuls, "imperial commissioners," and foreign treasure hunters, could now enter a new and in many ways more promising age.

·   ·   ·

In the summer of 1920, during the course of leveling operations for the construction of a new road along the western shore of the Sea of Galilee, some Jewish workmen uncovered traces of ancient walls and columns at a site to the south of the town of Tiberias. In accordance with the newly instituted British civil law, the work was halted and officials of the Department of Antiquities were summoned to the site. Since the nearby town was largely Jewish and the remains did not appear to be of any particular significance, the British director of antiquities, John McKay, decided to allow a new group to enter the field of Biblical archeology. The Jewish Palestine Exploration Society, founded in Jerusalem shortly before the war, would be permitted to conduct its first excavations.

Digging through the winter of 1920–1921 at the site, which was identified with the ancient town of Hammath-Tiberias, the Jewish excavators uncovered the ruins of a Byzantine structure which proved to be a synagogue, mapped its ground plan through the various stages of its existence, and discovered a large stone menorah lying on the floor, where it had been toppled centuries before. The humble results of this first excavation of the Jewish Palestine Exploration Society aroused little scholarly attention at the time, but its significance was to be long-lasting. The Jewish scholars of Palestine had gotten their first taste of archeological discovery, and promptly presented their plans for further excavations to the British authorities.

Throughout the troubled decades of British rule that followed, as growing Arab-Jewish violence flared across the country, the Jewish Palestine Exploration Society quietly continued its work at various sites of Jewish antiquity. Archeology had not been among the most important priorities of the founders of the Zionist movement, but the scientific discovery of remains of the Biblical and post-Biblical periods now offered a potent rallying point for Jewish nationalism at a time when that nationalism was moving toward statehood. The individual efforts of Jewish scholars were now united in a common cause. The nineteenth-century western competition for Biblical antiquities was over, but its political implications had survived. Biblical archeology was to become a persuasive weapon in a new struggle for possession of the land.

Throughout the centuries of pilgrimage to the Holy Land, an area of ash heaps to the north of Jerusalem's city walls had attracted the interest of Christian and Jewish travelers alike. These ash heaps, according to rabbinic and medieval legends, were the remains of the burnt sacrifices offered by Hebrew priests in the Temple of the Lord. And according to a prophecy of Jeremiah, they would be included in the rebuilt city at the end of times. Thus, what might have been considered in any other city in the world just an old dumping ground became, in Jerusalem, a religious shrine.

But unlike the other sacred shrines in the Holy City, the ash heaps offered the pious visitors a tangible link between the present and the past. Without hovering ecclesiastical custodians, chancel screens, or guides, they could kneel down humbly and run their own hands through the ash, feeling for themselves the leavings of the Biblical past. Handfuls, pocketfuls, boxes, and phials of the holy ash were taken away by the steady stream of pilgrims over the course of centuries. Scattered all over the world, the small samples of ash spread the lure of Jerusalem's antiquity to those who had not been adventurous enough, wealthy enough, or pious enough to brave the dangers of a journey to Palestine themselves.

In time, however, the ash heaps began to shrink. During the nineteenth century, as the city of Jerusalem expanded and new buildings began to spring up outside the city walls, the ash heaps were no longer so remote, and local builders found their material useful for making cement. New Arab and Jewish neighborhoods grew up around them, mortared and bonded by the expropriated ash. By the year 1900, the historical erosion was complete. The city, as Jeremiah had prophesied, had incorporated the ash heaps—but the ash heaps themselves had disappeared without a trace.

The era in which the ash heaps vanished was the era of archeological science, and it was that science that finally destroyed their myth. A laboratory test performed on a small sample effectively severed any Biblical link. Far from being sacred, or even ancient, they were apparently rubbish from some long-forgotten soap factory. Few modern inhabitants mourned them; new relics and shrines had already taken their place. Ancient pottery, inscriptions, and buried cities had become the new objects of veneration. Scientific archeology had become the new system of belief.

Yet despite this transformation, the past has lost none of its power to inspire. Today, one need only mention the words "Masada" and "Dead Sea Scrolls" to understand the political and emotional force that it still commands. The excavated remains of antiquity have become Israel's most visible symbols—a means to national identity and a tangible link with the land. The political struggles of the nineteenth century have given way to new conflicts, but the fascination of Biblical archeology endures. To possess the Land of the Bible is to interpret its history. This fact has remained constant. Only the interpreters have changed.

Bibliography

GENERAL WORKS

Archeology

William F. Albright, *The Archaeology of Palestine and the Bible* (New York, 1931).

Yehoshua Ben-Arieh, "The Geographical Exploration of the Holy Land," *Palestine Exploration Quarterly* (1972), pp. 81–92.

———, *The Rediscovery of the Holy Land in the Nineteenth Century* (Jerusalem, 1979).

Walter Besant, *Thirty Years' Work in the Holy Land* (London, 1895).

———, *Twenty-One Years' Work in the Holy Land* (London, 1886).

Frederick J. Bliss, *The Development of Palestine Exploration* (New York, 1906).

H. V. Hilprecht, *Explorations in Bible Lands During the 19th Century* (Philadelphia, 1903).

R. A. S. Macalister, *A Century of Excavation in Palestine* (London, 1925).

Palestine Exploration Fund (Walter Besant), *Our Work in Palestine* (New York, 1873).

Keith N. Schoville, *Biblical Archeology in Focus* (Grand Rapids, 1978).

Charles M. Watson, *Fifty Years' Work in the Holy Land* (London, 1915).

Social Conditions

Shmuel Avitsur, *Daily Life in Eretz Israel in the XIXth Century* (Jerusalem, 1975), Hebrew.

Yehoshua Ben-Arieh, *A City Reflected in Its Times: Jerusalem in the Nineteenth Century*, Vol. 1, *The Old City* (Jerusalem, 1977); Vol. 2, *New Jerusalem* (Jerusalem, 1979), Hebrew.

Arnold Blumberg, *A View from Jerusalem, 1849–1858: The Consular Diary of James and Elizabeth Anne Finn* (Rutherford, N.J., 1980).

Alex Carmel, *Palästina-Chronik 1853 bis 1882* (Bonn, 1978).

Elizabeth Ann Finn, *Home in the Holy Land* (London, 1866).

Ben-Zion Gat, *The Jewish Community in Eretz Israel 1840–1881* (Jerusalem, 1974), Hebrew.

Jacob M. Landau, *Abdul Hamid's Palestine* (London, 1979).

Laurence Oliphant, *Haifa or Life in Modern Palestine* (London, 1887).

Sarah Searight, *The British in the Middle East* (London, 1969).

Bertha Spafford Vester, *Our Jerusalem* (Garden City, N.Y., 1950).

Charles W. Wilson (ed.), *Picturesque Palestine, Sinai, and Egypt* (New York, 1881–1884).

Diplomatic, Economic, and Political History

James A. Field, *America and the Mediterranean World 1776–1882* (Princeton, 1969).

James Finn, *Stirring Times, or, Records from Jerusalem Consular Chronicles of 1853 to 1856* (London, 1878).

Derek Hopwood, *The Russian Presence in Syria and Palestine 1843–1914* (Oxford, 1969).

J. C. Hurewitz, *Diplomacy in the Near and Middle East* (Princeton, 1956).

A. M. Hyamson, *The British Consulate in Jerusalem in Relation to the Jews of Palestine* (London, 1939–1941).

C. Issawi, *The Economic History of the Middle East 1800–1914* (Chicago, 1966).

Lord Kinross, *The Ottoman Centuries* (New York, 1977).

Bernard Lewis, *The Emergence of Modern Turkey* (London, 1968).

Frank E. Manuel, *The Realities of American-Palestine Relations* (Washington, 1949).

Moshe Ma'oz (ed.), *Studies on Palestine During the Ottoman Period* (Jerusalem, 1975).

William Miller, *The Ottoman Empire and Its Successors 1801–1927* (Cambridge, 1927).

Vernon J. Puryear, *France and the Levant* (Los Angeles, 1941).

———, *International Economics and Diplomacy in the Near East* (Stanford, 1969).

H. Temperly, *England and the Near East: The Crimea* (London, 1936).

A. L. Tibawi, *American Interests in Syria 1800–1901* (Oxford, 1966).

———, *British Interests in Palestine 1800–1901* (Oxford, 1961).

———, *A Modern History of Syria* (Edinburgh, 1969).

Barbara Tuchman, *The Bible and the Sword* (New York, 1956).

Jehuda L. Wallach (ed.), *Germany and the Middle East 1835–1939* (Tel Aviv, 1975).

CHAPTER SOURCES

CHAPTER 1

The Lure of the Holy Land

The opening quotation is taken from the end of chapter LVI of *The Innocents Abroad*. For additional background on western travel and tourism to Palestine, see David Finnie, *Pioneers East* (Cambridge, Mass., 1967), and Franklin D. Walker, *Irreverent Pilgrims* (Seattle, Wash., 1974)

Jonathan Sumption, *Pilgrimage: An Image of Medieval Religion* (London, 1975), and John Wilkinson, "Christian Pilgrims in Jerusalem During the Byzantine Period," *Palestine Exploration Quarterly* (1977), 75–101, provided material for the account of the establishment of the Christian pilgrimage tradition. Michael Avi-Yonah, *The Holy Land, from the Persian to the Arab Conquests 536 B.C.–A.D. 640* (Grand Rapids, 1966), includes a comprehensive history of the country in the Roman and Byzantine periods.

For Islamic rule, shrines, and traditions in Palestine, see Guy Le Strange, *Palestine Under the Moslems* (London, 1890).

The historical literature of the Crusades is voluminous. See especially Steven Runciman, *A History of the Crusades* (Cambridge, 1951–1954), and Joshua Prawer, *The Crusaders' Kingdom* (New York, 1972)

On the partition of the Christian shrines by the Ottoman authorities, James Finn, *Stirring Times* (London, 1878), provides the most detailed account and description.

The Protestant idealization of the Holy Land is discussed in Howard M. Jones, "The Land of Israel in the Anglo-Saxon Tradition," in Moshe Davis (ed.), *Israel: Its Role in Civilization* (New York, 1956), pp. 229–250. For another survey of the English tradition, see Barbara Tuchman, *The Bible and the Sword* (New York, 1956).

CHAPTER 2

Rumblings in the East

The account of the Napoleonic invasion of Egypt and Palestine is based primarily on J. Christopher Herold, *Bonaparte in Egypt* (New York, 1962), which includes an extensive bibliography of primary sources. A detailed, if opinionated, discussion of the Franco-British rivalry over the Suez caravan route can be found in John Marlowe, *Perfidious Albion* (London, 1971).

For the selection and activities of Napoleon's corps of savants, see F. Charles-Roux, *Bonaparte Governor of Egypt* (London, 1937). Their massive scientific report is Commission des sciences et arts d'Egypte, *Description de l'Egypte* (Paris, 1809–1828).

The first modern topographical map of Palestine was published by Colonel Pierre Jacotin as an appendix to *Carte Topographique de l'Egypte* (Paris, 1828). For additional background, see Y. Karmon, "An Analysis of Jacotin's Map of Palestine," *Israel Exploration Journal* 10 (1960), 157–173, 241–254.

The tradition of Napoleon's public proclamations in Palestine is traced in Franz Kobler, *Napoleon and the Jews* (New York, 1976).

Two articles by Mordechai Gihon provide details of the military progress and strategy of the battle of Acre: "Napoleon in Western Galilee in the Spring of 1799" and "Napoleon's Siege of Accho," in *Western Galilee and the Coast of Galilee* (Jerusalem, 1965) (Hebrew).

Sir Sidney Smith's march to Jerusalem is recounted in Edward Daniel Clarke, *Travels in Various Countries of Europe, Asia, and Africa*, Vol. 4 (London, 1817), p. 292.

CHAPTER 3

The Land of the Butcher

Among the earliest travel accounts of the Holy Land in the wake of Napoleon's invasion are those of William Wittman, *Travels in Turkey, Asia Minor, and Across the Desert into Egypt, During the Years 1799, 1800, and 1801* (London, 1803); and J. B. Spilsbury, *Picturesque Scenery in the Holy Land and Syria Delineated During the Campaigns of 1799 and 1800* (London, 1803). Both authors were officers with the British forces.

The account of Edward Daniel Clarke's journey is based on his own narrative in *Travels in Various Countries of Europe, Asia, and Africa* (London, 1810–1823). The section devoted to Palestine appears in Vols. 4 and 5 (both published in 1817).

For the background to Ulrich Seetzen's travels, see Robin Hallett, *The Penetration of Africa* (New York, 1965). Seetzen's own journal was published long after his death: *Reisen Durch Syrien, Palästina, Phönicien* (Berlin, 1854–1859). The excerpt translated by the Palestine Association was *A Brief Account of the Countries Adjoining the Lake of Tiberias, the Jordan, and the Dead Sea* (London, 1810).

On the establishment of the Palestine Association, see *Palestine Exploration Fund Quarterly Statement* (1876), 154–155.

The career of John Lewis Burckhardt is detailed in Katherine Sim, *Desert Traveller* (London, 1969). Additional information was provided by Burckhardt's personal letters to Dr. Edward Clarke published in William Otter, *The Life and Remains of Edward Daniel Clarke* (New York, 1827), and by his own journal, *Travels in Syria and the Holy Land* (London, 1822).

James Silk Buckingham's expansive description of his own achievements in the Holy Land can be found in his *Travels in Palestine through the Countries of Bashan and Gilead, East of the River Jordan* (London, 1822) and his *Travels Among the Arab Tribes* (London, 1825).

Lady Hester Stanhope's colorful experiences in the Middle East are related in her authorized biography, *The Travels of Lady Hester Stanhope in Three Vols. Narrated by Her Physician* (London, 1846). Other sources are Joan Haslip, *Lady Hester Stanhope* (London, 1934), and Frank Hamel, *Lady Hester Lucy Stanhope* (London, 1913). The account of her treasure hunt at Ashkelon is based on these sources, as well as on a contemporary handwritten report, signed by Lady Hester and dated April 1815, in the collection of the Beinecke Library of Yale University.

CHAPTER 4

Visions of the End of the World

For the general background to the nineteenth-century millennialist movement, see Ira V. Brown, "Watchers for the Second Coming," *Mississippi Valley Historical Review* 39 (1952–1953), 441–458; David E. Smith, "Millennarian Scholarship in America," *American Quarterly* 17 (1965) 535–549; and with regard to the Jews and their millennial return to Palestine, Meir Verete, "The Idea of the Restoration of the Jews in Protestant Thought in England 1790–1840," *Zion* 23 (1968) 145–179 (Hebrew), which includes extensive bibliographical references.

The special emotional and religious connection between New England and the Holy Land is surveyed in Moshe Davis, "The Holy Land Idea in American Spiritual History," in Moshe Davis (ed.), *With Eyes Towards Zion: Scholars' Colloquium on America-Holy Land Studies* (New York, 1977), pp. 3–33; the same volume includes seven pages of Biblical place-names used in America. Other sources include Samuel H. Levine, "Palestine in the Literature of the United States to 1867," *Early History of Zionism in America* (New York, 1958), pp. 21–38; and Robert T. Handy, "Zion in American Christian Movements," in Moshe Davis (ed.), *Israel: Its Role in Civilization* (New York, 1956), pp. 284–297.

For the establishment of the American Board of Commissioners for Foreign Missions, see Oliver W. Elsbree, "The Rise of the Missionary Spirit in New England 1790–1815," *The New England Quarterly* I (1928) 295–322; A. L. Tibawi, *American Interests in Syria 1800–1901* (Oxford, 1966); and James A. Field, *America and the Mediterranean World 1776–1882* (Princeton, 1969).

The account of the organization and departure of the mission to Jerusalem is based on Daniel O. Morton, *Memoir of Rev. Levi Parsons* (Burlington, Vt., 1830); Alvan Bond, *Memoir of the Rev. Pliny Fisk* (Edinburgh, 1829); and on a monograph of the farewell service in the Old South Church entitled *Instructions from the Prudential Committee of the American Board of Commissioners for Foreign Missions to the Rev. Levi Parsons and to the Rev. Pliny Fisk* (Boston, 1819), which also includes the texts of their sermons.

The difficulties of the American missionaries and their subsequent evacuation from Beirut is described by William Goodell in his *Forty Years in the Turkish Empire* (Boston, 1891).

The dispatch of Eli Smith and his special assignment is recorded in the A.B.C.F.M. Annual Report for the year 1833, p. 44.

CHAPTER 5

The Evolution of a Dream

The only biography of Edward Robinson was written by the president of the Union Theological Seminary shortly after Robinson's death: Roswell D. Hitchcock, *The Life, Writings, and Character of Edward Robinson* (New York, 1863).

For the theological climate faced by Robinson upon his arrival at Andover, see

Jerry W. Brown, *The Rise of Biblical Criticism in America 1800–1870* (Middletown, Conn., 1969). And for the broader trends of European scholarship on which it was based, see Emil G. Kraeling, *The Old Testament Since the Reformation* (New York, 1955).

The account of Robinson's first visit to the Holy Land is based on his own *Biblical Researches in Palestine, Mount Sinai, and Arabia Petraea* (Boston, 1841), which is also the source for the quotes and identifications used in this chapter.

The political changes occasioned by the resumption of Ottoman rule are fully analyzed by Moshe Ma'oz, *Ottoman Reform in Syria and Palestine* (Oxford, 1968). On the establishment of western consulates in Jerusalem, see James Finn, *Stirring Times* (London, 1878); A. L. Tibawi, *British Interests in Palestine* (Oxford, 1961); and Yehoshua Ben-Arieh, *A City Reflected in Its Times* (Jerusalem, 1977), Hebrew.

The quote ascribing divine intervention to the modern exploration of Palestine comes from James A. Wylie, *The Modern Judea, Ammon, Moab, and Edom, Compared with Ancient Prophecy* (Glasgow, 1841).

CHAPTER 6

Conquering the Wilderness

For the background to the western strategic interest in the Ottoman Empire in general, and in Palestine in particular, see Halford L. Hoskins, *British Routes to India* (Philadelphia, 1928), and James A. Field, *America and the Mediterranean World* (Princeton, 1969).

On the beginnings of Dead Sea exploration, see John Lloyd Stephens, *Incidents of Travel in Egypt, Arabia, and the Holy Land* (New York, 1837), and E. W. G. Masterman, "Three Early Explorers in the Dead Sea Valley," *Palestine Exploration Fund Quarterly Statement* (1911) 12–27.

The account of the Lynch mission is based largely on Lynch's *Narrative of the United States Expedition to the River Jordan and the Dead Sea* (Philadelphia, 1849). Additional background material was provided by Yehoshua Ben-Arieh, "William F. Lynch's Expedition to the Dead Sea, 1847–8," *Prologue: The Journal of the National Archives* 5 (spring 1973) 15–21; and James A. Field, *America and the Mediterranean World*.

For additional details of the life and reputation of Aqil Agha, see Walter P. Zenner, "Aqiili Agha: The Strongman in the Ethnic Relations of the Ottoman Galilee," *Comparative Studies of Social History* 14 (1972), 169–188.

The rival (and unauthorized) memoir of the mission was published by Edward P. Montague (ed.), *Narrative of the Late Expedition to the Dead Sea* (Philadelphia, 1849).

A guide to the Georama "moving painting" exhibition, written by the artist John Banvard, entitled *Description of Banvard's 'Pilgrimage to Jerusalem and the Holy Land'* (New York, 1853), is in the collection of the Sterling Memorial Library at Yale University.

CHAPTER 7

For the Glory of France

The account of the disturbance in the Church of the Nativity is based on the details provided in James Finn, *Stirring Times* (London, 1878), which also documents the subsequent political maneuvering by the various western consuls in Jerusalem.

On the establishment of the Jerusalem Literary Society, see Finn, *Stirring Times;* and for excerpts from its proceedings, see R. A. S. Macalister, "Gleanings from the Minute-Books of the Jerusalem Literary Society," *Palestine Exploration Fund Quarterly Statement* (1908–1910).

For additional background on the western archeological activity in the Middle East, see Brian M. Fagan, *The Rape of the Nile* (New York, 1975) for Egypt, and *Return to Babylon* (Boston, 1979) for Mesopotamia.

The details of de Saulcy's early career and travels come from his *Carnets de Voyage en Orient, 1845–1869* (Paris, 1955), edited by Fernande Bassan, which include supplementary biographical data. De Saulcy's account of his first journey to Palestine, *Voyage autour de la Mer Morte* (Paris, 1853), was also published in an English translation: *Narrative of a Journey Round the Dead Sea and in the Bible Lands* (Philadelphia, 1854).

For the causes and aftermath of the Crimean War, see H. Temperly, *England and the Near East: The Crimea* (London, 1936).

The final report of Ernest Renan's expedition was published under the title *Mission de Phénicie* (Paris, 1864). Additional details on his excavations and subsequent travels in Palestine can be found in Lorenzo O'Rourke (trans.), *Renan's Letters from the Holy Land* (New York, 1904).

The quotation concerning the nature of de Saulcy's government service comes from *Grand Dictionnaire Universel du XIXe Siècle* (Paris, 1875), Vol. 14, p. 261.

De Saulcy's second trip to Palestine was documented in his *Voyage en Terre Sainte* (Paris, 1865). The condemnation by the Jerusalem Jewish community appeared in the Hebrew newspaper *HaMelitz* and was quoted in Shlomo Shva and Dan Ben Amotz, *Eretz Zion Yerushalayim* (Jerusalem, 1973), p. 47, Hebrew. The subsequent condemnation in the London *Times* appeared on February 1 and 3, 1864. A further critical notice appeared in *The Journal of Sacred Literature and Biblical Record* IX (1864) 75.

CHAPTER 8

A Matter of Honor

Information concerning Pierotti's archeological activities in Jerusalem and the chronology of the later controversy over his conclusions were provided by a pamphlet written by George Williams, *Dr. Pierotti and His Assailants, or A Defence of Jerusalem Explored* (London, 1864), in the collection of the Beinecke Library of Yale University.

James Fergusson's works on the subject of Jerusalem are *An Essay on the Ancient*

Topography of Jerusalem (London, 1847), *The Holy Sepulchre and the Temple at Jerusalem* (London, 1865), and the later *The Temples of the Jews and Other Buildings in the Haram Area at Jerusalem* (London, 1878).

George Williams' traditionalist view was expressed in his *The Holy City* (London, 1845).

For the origins of George Grove's interest in Biblical archeology, see Charles Graves, *The Life and Letters of Sir George Grove* (London, 1903).

The court-martial document and a notarized translation can be found in the archives of the Palestine Exploration Fund in London (PEF/JLS/8/1–3).

CHAPTER 9

Building the New Jerusalem

For the background of the Evangelical movement and its philanthropic societies, see Ian Bradley, *The Call to Seriousness: The Evangelical Impact on the Victorians* (London, 1976), especially chapters 4 and 7.

For a detailed account of the British missionary effort in Jerusalem, see A. L. Tibawi, *British Interests in Palestine* (Oxford, 1961), and for the origin of the idea for the new water supply system, see John Irvine Whitty, "The Water Supply of Jerusalem—Ancient and Modern," *Journal of Sacred Literature and Biblical Record* IX (1864) 133–157.

A copy of the prospectus for the Jerusalem Water Relief Society can be found in the archives of the Palestine Exploration Fund (PEF/JER/9/1–2).

The account of Wilson's appointment and subsequent work in Palestine is based on Charles M. Watson, *The Life of Maj. Gen. Charles William Wilson* (London, 1909), and Wilson's own report, published in *The Recovery of Jerusalem* (London, 1871).

Reference to George Grove's participation in the preparations for the Survey of Jerusalem is made in Charles Graves, *The Life and Letters of Sir George Grove* (London, 1903).

The establishment of the Palestine Exploration Fund is related in Charles Watson, *Fifty Years' Work in the Holy Land* (London, 1915), and the quotations of the opening speeches come from the *Palestine Exploration Fund Proceedings and Notes* (London, 1865–1869).

Wilson's work was officially published under the title *The Ordnance Survey of Jerusalem* (Southampton, 1866).

CHAPTER 10

The Pastimes of an Empire

The main sources used for the narrative of the Jerusalem excavations are Charles Wilson and Charles Warren, *The Recovery of Jerusalem* (London, 1871), and Warren's independent (and far more candid) account, *Underground Jerusalem* (London, 1875).

Additional biographical information on Warren can be found in Watkin W. Williams, *The Life of General Sir Charles Warren* (Oxford, 1941).

For the political and religious repercussions of Abdul Azziz's accession and provincial reorganization, see Bernard Lewis, *The Emergence of Modern Turkey* (London, 1968).

The description of the long, acrimonious correspondence between Warren and Grove is based on Warren's account in *Underground Jerusalem;* their original letters and dispatches are missing from the Palestine Exploration Fund Archives.

For a representative selection of the popularized accounts of the Jerusalem excavations, see *The Illustrated London News,* April 24, 1869; John Macgregor, *Rob Roy on the Jordan* (New York, 1870); and Robert Morris, *Freemasonry in the Holy Land* (New York, 1872).

CHAPTER 11

Race for a Relic

The main sources for this chapter are: Charles Warren's account of the affair in *Underground Jerusalem,* pp. 523–550; F. A. Klein, "The Original Discovery of the Moabite Stone," *Palestine Exploration Fund Quarterly Statement* (1870), 281–283; H. Petermann, "The Moabite Stone," *Palestine Exploration Fund Quarterly Statement* (1871), 135–139; and Richard F. Burton and Charles F. Tyrwhitt-Drake, *Unexplored Syria* (London, 1872), Vol. II, pp. 317–345, which includes an extensive bibliography.

Background for the organization of the Bedouin of Transjordan comes from Claude R. Conder, *The Survey of Eastern Palestine* (London, 1889), and from an article published by "A Palestine Explorer" (probably Conder himself) entitled "The Belka Arabs," in *Blackwood's Magazine,* August 1883, pp. 171–189.

Of the many popular articles that appeared in the western press, G. Rawlinson, "The Moabite Stone," *The Contemporary Review* XV (August 1870) 97–112, is representative, and it is the source of the quotation about the stone's sudden popularity.

The quotation at the end of the chapter comes from Edward H. Palmer, "The Desert of Tih and the Country of Moab," *Palestine Exploration Fund Quarterly Statement* (1871), 65.

CHAPTER 12

Spying Out the Land

For the debate and decision to undertake the complete survey of the Holy Land, see the reports of the P.E.F.'s annual meetings of 1870 and 1871 in the *Palestine Exploration Fund Quarterly Statements* for those years.

The results of Wilson's expedition to Sinai were published as *The Ordnance Survey of the Peninsula of Sinai* (Southampton, 1869–1872).

The organization and early history of the American Palestine Exploration

Society are documented by its briefly published *Bulletin* and *Statements* (New York, 1871–1877). Additional information comes from Warren J. Moulton, "The American Palestine Exploration Society," *Annual of the American Schools of Oriental Research* VIII (1926–1927) 55–78.

The Reverend Selah Merrill's popular account of his travels is *East of the Jordan* (New York, 1881). Charles Clermont-Ganneau also participated in the survey of the P.E.F., undertaking a special assignment in Jerusalem. The result of his work is *Archaeological Researches in Palestine During the Years 1873–1874* (London, 1899).

For Horatio Kitchener's early experiences with the Palestine Exploration Fund, see Sir George Arthur, *Life of Lord Kitchener* (London, 1920) and Dr. Samuel Daiches, *Lord Kitchener and His Work in Palestine* (London, 1915). Kitchener's own publication from this period was his *Book of Photographs of Biblical Sites* (London, 1876).

Details concerning the violent interruption of the Palestine Survey come from H. H. Kitchener, "The Safed Attack," *Palestine Exploration Fund Quarterly Statement* (1875), 195–199; "The Trial at Acre," *Palestine Exploration Fund Quarterly Statement* (1876), 7–8; and Claude Conder, *Tent Work in Palestine* (New York, 1878), which provides a detailed narrative of the progress of the entire survey.

The official publication of the mapping project is C. R. Conder and H. H. Kitchener, *Memoirs of the Survey of Western Palestine* (London, 1881–1888). Conder's subsequent work in the territory abandoned by the Americans was published by him in *The Survey of Eastern Palestine* (London, 1889) and in his *Heth and Moab* (London, 1883).

For Professor Palmer's experiences among the Bedouin, see Edward H. Palmer and Charles F. Tyrwhitt-Drake, *The Desert of the Exodus* (New York, 1872), and for a full account of his secret mission, see Walter Besant, *The Life and Achievements of Edward Henry Palmer* (London, 1883).

CHAPTER 13

One Million Pounds Sterling

Reliable biographical details on Moses Shapira are, at best, sketchy. Much information can be gleaned from the fictionalized autobiography of his daughter: Myriam Harry, *La Petite Fille de Jérusalem* (Paris, 1914); from the biographical supplement appended to the Hebrew translation of the same by Ya'acov Assia, *Bat Yerushalayim HaKatana* (Tel Aviv, 1975); and from John Allegro, *The Shapira Affair* (Garden City, N.Y., 1965).

For the events surrounding the Moabite pottery affair, see the correspondence published in *The Athenaeum*, January 24 and March 7, 1874, reprinted in the *Palestine Exploration Fund Quarterly Statement* (1874), 114–124. Clermont-Ganneau's final word on the matter is his *Les Fraudes Archéologiques en Palestine* (Paris, 1885), which also includes his account of the Moabite Deuteronomy.

A list of the most valuable Torah scrolls obtained by Shapira in his various

Egyptian and Arabian travels is contained in Reinhart Hoerning, *British Museum Karaite Mss.* (London, 1889).

Shapira repeated his story of the discovery of the manuscripts many times with virtually no variation in detail. His most complete account is contained in a personal letter to Professor Hermann L. Strack of Berlin, dated May 9, 1883, preserved in dossier Additional 41294 of the Department of Manuscripts of the British Library in London. Other similar accounts were published in the *Times* of London and reprinted in the *Palestine Exploration Fund Quarterly Statement* (1883), pp. 195–209, which contains a chronology of Shapira's activities in London.

Shapira's letter to Ginsburg is reproduced in Allegro, *The Shapira Affair,* p. 15 and Pl. 3.

The cartoon in *Punch* appeared in the issue of September 8, 1883.

Sir Walter Besant, in his *Autobiography* (London, 1902), provides some unflattering reminiscences of Shapira which seem strongly colored by hindsight.

In the nineteen-fifties, the discovery of the Dead Sea Scrolls sparked renewed scholarly interest with regard to the possible authenticity of the Shapira manuscripts. Cf. a monograph by Menahem Mansoor, *The Case of Shapira's Dead Sea (Deuteronomy) Scroll of 1883* (New York, 1956).

For the ultimate fate of the manuscripts themselves, see A. D. Crown, "The Fate of the Shapira Scroll," *Revue de Qumrân* 27 (1971) 421, which theorizes that they were destroyed by a fire in the private library of an amateur Biblical scholar and rare book collector.

CHAPTER 14

Coming of Age

For the advancement of archeological technique in the eighteen-seventies and -eighties, see Glyn Daniel, *A Hundred and Fifty Years of Archaeology* (Cambridge, Mass. 1976).

Sir Charles Wilson's suggestion is recorded in the report of the twenty-first annual meeting, *Palestine Exploration Fund Quarterly Statement* (1887), 5.

For more on Petrie's background and archeological technique, see his *Seventy Years in Archaeology* (London, 1931). The fullest accounts of the excavation of Tell el-Hesy (in addition to the ongoing progress reports published in the *Palestine Exploration Fund Quarterly Statement*) are: W. M. F. Petrie, *Tell el-Hesy (Lachish)* (London, 1891), and Frederick J. Bliss, *A Mound of Many Cities; or Tell el-Hesy Excavated* (New York, 1894).

The social and political background to the Russian excavations near the Church of the Holy Sepulcher is provided by Derek Hopwood, *The Russian Presence in Syria and Palestine 1843–1914* (Oxford, 1969).

The persistence and disruptiveness of Consul Merrill's excavations in Jerusalem were almost legendary; see, for example, Bertha Spafford Vester, *Our Jerusalem* (Garden City, N.Y., 1950); and Alexander Hume Ford, "Our American Colony at Jerusalem," *Appleton's Magazine* VII (December 1906), 643–655. Merrill's own definitive account of his Biblical theories is contained in his *Ancient Jerusalem* (New York, 1908).

A report on Schick's excavations near the Church of the Holy Sepulcher can be found in the *Palestine Exploration Fund Quarterly Statement* (1886), 135.

On General Charles Gordon, his visit to Jerusalem, and his theories, see Laurence Oliphant, *Haifa* (New York, 1887), pp. 276–279, and Conrad Schick, "Gordon's Tomb," *Palestine Exploration Fund Quarterly Statement* (1892), 120.

George St. Clair's views on Jerusalem can be found in his book *Buried Cities and Bible Countries* (London, 1891).

On the administrative and physical changes in the city of Jerusalem in the last two decades of the nineteenth century, see Yehoshua Ben-Arieh, *A City Reflected in Its Times* (Jerusalem, 1977–1979), Hebrew.

The account of the Jerusalem excavations of the P.E.F. is based largely on Frederick J. Bliss and Archibald C. Dickie, *Excavations at Jerusalem 1894–1897* (London, 1898), and from the progress reports in the *Palestine Exploration Fund Quarterly Statement.*

On the establishment of the "Jerusalem association" of the P.E.F., see *Palestine Exploration Fund Quarterly Statement* (1892), 86, 178.

A photograph which shows the two characteristic signs inside the Jaffa Gate is published in Jacob Landau, *Abdul Hamid's Palestine* (London, 1979), p. 41 bottom.

CHAPTER 15

The Kaiser and the Sultan

For the extensive public works projects undertaken in Palestine in the summer and fall of 1898, see Conrad Schick, "Preparations Made for the Visit of the German Emperor," *Palestine Exploration Fund Quarterly Statement* (1899), 116–117; and Bertha Spafford Vester, *Our Jerusalem* (Garden City, N.Y., 1950).

The political background and progress of Kaiser Wilhelm's Middle Eastern policy is surveyed in Jehuda L. Wallach (ed.), *Germany and the Middle East 1835–1939* (Tel Aviv, 1975).

Wilhelm's "pilgrimage" to the Holy Land was followed closely in the western press. See, for example, *The Illustrated London News,* November 19, 1898; Samuel Ives Curtis, "The Emperor William in the Holy Land," *The Cosmopolitan,* February 1899, pp. 363–378; and for more politically oriented commentaries, "The German Emperor and Palestine," *Fortnightly Review* 70 (1898) 548–555; "Germany's Influence at Constantinople," *Blackwood's Edinburgh Magazine,* May 1899, pp. 921–924; and Frederick Greenwood, "The Kaiser in Palestine," *The Pall Mall Magazine* 17 (1899) 382–388.

The P.E.F. expedition to the Judean tells is fully documented in Frederick J. Bliss and R. A. S. Macalister, *Excavations in Palestine During the Years 1898–1900* (London, 1902). Additional personal details come from Olga Tufnell, "Excavator's Progress: Letters of F. J. Bliss, 1889–1900," *Palestine Exploration Quarterly* (1965), 112–127.

For the history of the German consulate in Jerusalem see Mordechai Eliav, "German Interests and the Jewish Community in 19th Century Palestine," in Moshe Ma'oz (ed.), *Studies on Palestine During the Ottoman Period* (Jerusalem, 1975), pp. 423–441. Additional information is provided in the autobiography of the German consul appointed immediately after the Kaiser's visit: Friedrich Rosen, *Oriental Memoirs of a German Diplomat* (London, 1930).

Gottlieb Schumacher's eastern Palestine explorations were published by him in *Across the Jordan* (London, 1886); *The Jaulan* (London, 1888); *Abila of the Decapolis* (London, 1889); *Pella* (London, 1888); and *The Northern Ajlun* (London, 1890).

For the Austrian excavations at Tell Ta'annek, see Professor Sellin's preliminary reports in *Anzeiger der kaiserlischen Akademie der Wissenschaften, Phil.-Hist. Klasse* 39 (1902) 94–97, 120–123; and his final reports in *Tell Ta'annek* (Vienna, 1904) and *Eine Nachlese auf dem Tell Ta'annek in Palästina* (Vienna, 1905).

R. A. S. Macalister published the results of the renewed P.E.F. activity in *The Excavation of Gezer 1902–1905 and 1907–1909* (London, 1912) and in his earlier work, *Bible Sidelights from the Mound of Gezer* (New York, 1906).

On the organization and progress of the German expedition to Megiddo, see Gottlieb Schumacher, *Tell el-Mutasellim* (Leipzig, 1908), and his several preliminary reports published in *Mitteilungen und Nachrichten des Deutsche Palästina-Vereins*.

The survey of the ruins of ancient Palestinian synagogues was published in Heinrich Kohl and Carl Watzinger, *Antike Synagogen in Galilea* (Leipzig, 1916). The Austrian-German excavations at Jericho were published by Sellin and Watzinger in *Jericho* (Leipzig, 1913).

For a general review of German archeological activity and the impression it made on the other archeological powers, see Ira Maurice Price, "The German Oriental Society," *Biblical World* 23 (1904) 64–65, and "German Activity in Oriental Exploration," *Biblical World* 24 (1904) 304–310.

CHAPTER 16

The American Method

For the early history of American archeological involvement in the Middle East and the establishment of the American School of Oriental Research, see G. Ernest Wright, "The Phenomenon of American Archaeology in the Near East," in James A. Sanders (ed.), *Near Eastern Archaeology in the Twentieth Century* (Garden City, N.Y., 1970).

The philanthropic activities of Jacob Henry Schiff are described at length in Cyrus Adler, *Jacob H. Schiff: His Life and Letters* (New York, 1928).

The account of the American expedition is based for the most part on George A. Reisner, Clarence S. Fisher, and David G. Lyons, *Harvard Excavations at Samaria 1908–1910* (Cambridge, Mass., 1924).

CHAPTER 17

Secrets of the Temple Mount

For an example of Valter H. Juvelius's unique brand of Biblical speculation, see his *Judarnes Tideräkning i ny belysning* (Kuopio, 1906).

The narrative of the Parker affair is based largely on contemporary press accounts at the time of the exposure of the true aims of the expedition in April and May 1911. Additional information comes from Bertha Spafford Vester, *Our Jerusalem* (Garden City, N.Y., 1950).

The only archeological record of the "excavations" was compiled by Père Hughes Vincent in *Underground Jerusalem* (London, 1911), also published in a French version, *Jérusalem Sous Terre.* Vincent includes a discreetly brief account of the circumstances which led him to join the expedition.

The result of Baron Edmond de Rothschild's purchase of an adjoining strip of land on the Ophel was a later excavation led by a French archeologist named Raymond Weill. Weill worked at the site in 1913–1914 and again in 1923–1924, clearing a wide area and uncovering two badly damaged rock-hewn cavities, which he identified as the remains of the long-sought royal tombs. See Raymond Weill, *La Cité de David* (Paris, 1920). For an opposing view of this identification, see Kathleen Kenyon, *Digging Up Jerusalem* (London, 1974), pp. 31–32.

For the traditions associated with the "Well of the Spirits" on the Temple Mount, see Zev Vilnay, *Legends of Jerusalem* (Philadelphia, 1973), pp. 26–27.

A battle raged in the pages of the *Palestine Exploration Fund Quarterly Statement* in the months that followed Parker's escape from Jerusalem; cf. *Palestine Exploration Fund Quarterly Statement* (1912): Gustav Dalman, "The Search for the Temple Treasure at Jerusalem," 35–39; Charles Warren, "Recent Excavations on the Hill of Ophel," 68–74; and a defense by Père Vincent himself, 131–134.

The quotation about the failure of the "renewed" Parker expedition can be found in the London *Times,* October 30, 1911.

CHAPTER 18

The Last Crusade

The account of the survey of the Negev is based on T. E. Lawrence and C. Leonard Woolley, *The Wilderness of Zin,* published first in the *Annual of the Palestine Exploration Fund,* Vol. 3 (1914–1915), and later as an independent volume (New York, 1936). Additional information and personal details were provided by John E. Mack, *A Prince of Our Disorder* (Boston, 1975); *The Home Letters of T. E. Lawrence and His Brothers* (New York, 1954); and by David Garnett (ed.), *The Letters of T. E. Lawrence* (London, 1938).

Lord Kitchener's continuing strategic interest in Palestine for the defense of the Suez Canal is discussed in Uri Ra'anan, *The Frontiers of a Nation* (Westport, Conn., 1976), which also provides an interesting examination of the contribution of the P.E.F. surveys to the ultimate political boundaries of the Palestine Mandate.

For the course of the early military operations along the Suez Canal and the first British counteroffensive, see Colonel A. P. Wavell, *The Palestine Campaigns* (London, 1928); Alexander Aaronsohn, *With the Turks in Palestine* (New York, 1916); and General Friedrich Freiherr Kress von Kressenstein, *Mit dem Türken zum Suezkanal* (Berlin, 1938).

General Allenby's appointment and strategic successes are detailed by W. T. Massey in *How Jerusalem Was Won* (London, 1919) and *Allenby's Final Triumph* (London, 1920).

The account of the surrender of Jerusalem and the subsequent British entry into the city is based on details from Bertha Spafford Vester, *Our Jerusalem* (Garden City, N.Y., 1950), and from a pamphlet written by E. W. G. Masterman, honorary secretary of the Jerusalem association of the P.E.F., *The Deliverance of Jerusalem* (New York, 1918).

EPILOGUE

The Future of the Past

For the recovery of the confiscated artifacts, see the London *Times*, June 1, 1921, "Archaeology in Palestine—Local Interests to Be Preserved."

The guidelines for the archeological future of Palestine were enumerated in Article 21 of the League of Nations Mandate.

On the establishment of the Jewish Palestine Exploration Society, see A. J. Braver, "From the Early Days of the Israel Exploration Society," in *Western Galilee and the Coast of Galilee* (Jerusalem, 1965), pp. 228–236 (Hebrew). A preliminary report of the Hammath-Tiberias excavation appeared in the *Palestine Exploration Fund Quarterly Statement* (1921), 183–184, and in the journal of the J.P.E.S., *Qovets*, Vol. 1, No. 1, 35–37; Vol. 1, No. 2, 49–52 (Hebrew).

For the tradition of the Jerusalem ash heaps, see Jeremiah 31:38–40, and Zev Vilnay, *Legends of Jerusalem* (Philadelphia, 1973), p. 226. For their location and travelers' descriptions, see Yehoshua Ben-Arieh, *A City Reflected in Its Times* (Jerusalem, 1977–1979), Vol. I, pp. 54–55; Vol. II, p. 89, Hebrew. The disappearance of the ash heaps was reported by Conrad Schick in the *Palestine Exploration Fund Quarterly Statement* (1900), 194.

Index

A Note About the Author

Neil Asher Silberman was born in Boston and educated at Wesleyan University. He did his post-graduate studies at the Institute of Archaeology, Hebrew University, Jerusalem. He has worked as a field archeologist for Israel's Department of Antiquities and Museums, and as a staff archeologist for the University of Haifa's Akko excavation project. He lives in Connecticut with his wife, Ellen Glassburn Silberman.

A Note on the Type

This book was set via computer-driven cathode-ray tube, in a typeface called Baskerville. The face is a facsimile reproduction of types cast from molds made for John Baskerville (1706–1775) from his designs. The punches for the revived Linotype Baskerville were cut under the supervision of the English printer George W. Jones.

John Baskerville's original face was one of the forerunners of the type style known as "modern face" to printers—a "modern" of the period A.D. 1800.

Composed, printed, and bound by
The Haddon Craftsmen, Inc., Scranton, Pennsylvania

Typography by Joe Marc Freedman